AF867430

# Bridging Research and Practice in Counseling

# DEMYSTIFYING RESEARCH METHODS


Daniel Bates

*Truman State University*



innovativeink PUBLISHING
A Division of Kendall Hunt

innovativeink
PUBLISHING
A Division of Kendall Hunt

www.innovativeinkpublishing.com
*Send all inquiries to*:
4050 Westmark Drive
Dubuque, IA 52004-1840



Print ISBN: 979-8-3851-5950-5
Ebook ISBN: 979-8-3851-5951-2



Published in the United States of America

# CONTENTS

# PREFACE

Research plays a really important role in the counseling profession and improving client outcomes. As counselors, we have an ethical obligation to base our practice on rigorous evidence and to contribute to the knowledge base of our field. However, developing research competency can be challenging for many counseling students and professionals. This book aims to provide a comprehensive examination of research competencies in counseling—what they entail, how they can be developed, and why they are so important. Drawing on both theoretical frameworks and empirical studies, each chapter will explore various aspects of research competency and literacy, with an emphasis on starting with a conceptual understanding of research that connects to practical applications in a clinical setting. However, for most counseling students, research feels disconnected from their interests and their professional goals. The intention behind this book is to bridge the gap between research and counselors' professional goals by revealing the invaluable role research plays in clinical practice. I hope readers will find this book informative and useful as they seek to enhance their own research competencies and positively impact clients in their clinical work.

Daniel Bates, PhD
Truman State University, United States

# INTRODUCTION
## Starting With the Why

Let's face it: You didn't become a counselor to wade through the complexities of research methodology and design. You chose this path because you're passionate about helping people. That doesn't mean you're uninterested in research—in fact, you might remember a time when a particularly intriguing study caught your attention. Perhaps it sparked a deep curiosity, leading you to explore the research regarding a theory, unique intervention, or a significant problem faced by a population you care about.

But that initial curiosity may have quickly turned to frustration when you encountered the methods section of a study. The abstract was clear, the introduction was compelling, but then you hit a wall of technical jargon—discussions of instruments, complex statistical analyses, and mixed findings that only partially supported the hypotheses. It was like trying to decode an ancient, unfamiliar language.

So, like many counselors before you, you might find yourself concluding that research isn't for you and that it has little relevance to your clinical work with clients. It's easy to start forming arguments in your mind about why research isn't just unhelpful but an obstacle—something you need to get through in your education, but not something that will actually serve you in the therapy room.

Let's break down some of the common reasons counselors in training often cite for why they believe research is unnecessary. First, there is the perception that the abstract nature of research doesn't directly apply to day-to-day interactions with clients. This leads many to see it as irrelevant. Research can seem too theoretical and too detached from the practical realities of counseling sessions, making its utility in clinical work appear questionable at best.

Additionally, the complexity and inaccessibility of research are often stumbling blocks. Research articles can be dense, packed with technical language and terms of art, and nearly impossible to decipher without a solid grounding in research methodology and statistical analysis. For many, this feels like a steep, uninviting hill to climb—requiring more training, more time, more money, and more effort. And what do you get for all that trouble? A mountain of information that often seems difficult, if not impossible, to translate into practical strategies for the therapy room (Wester et al., 2018).

After all, counseling is about a relationship. It is about intuitively understanding and supporting a person, a real, live person. In order to do this work, you must possess skill, connecting with clients and providing effective interventions. It is more an art than a science, right?!

Even more, you may have a legitimate concern for client care that leads some to view adherence to research-based protocols as a potential threat to their professional judgment. You may feel that being told to follow "what the research says" undermines your ability to make personalized, intuitive decisions about client care. After all, you're the one in the room with the client, not the researcher. Counseling is about the unique individual sitting across from you, not about some generalized findings based on a sample that might not even remotely resemble your client's experience or context (Boisvert & Faust, 2006).

Some students go even further, questioning the entire enterprise of research. They may believe that science is the product of biased scientists, wrapped up in the illusion of scientific authority. From this perspective, trusting your gut and listening to the client's own narrative might seem like a more authentic, trustworthy approach than relying on research that feels distant and impersonal (Lilienfeld et al., 2013).

My response to these arguments is: "YES! AND!"

**Yes, And!**

The reason I agree (partially) is because the very concerns that counselors in training express can be addressed not by tossing research out the window, but by developing a better understanding of research methodology and design. In fact, gaining this knowledge places them in a stronger position to tackle their legitimate worries head-on. For example, a deeper understanding of research enhances a counselor's ability to use clinical interventions that are evidence-based and tailored to individual client needs (Levitt et al., 2020).

Yates (2013) discussed the importance of integrating evidence-based practices (EBPs) in clinical work. Using EBPs is directly related to quality clinical work (see Yates, 2013 for a review of the literature), yet how many counselors can define and articulate the importance of EBPs? Who are aware of the research that went into developing EBPs like cognitive behavioral therapy (CBT) or dialectical behavior therapy?

Sackett et al. (2000) defined EBPs as the "evidence-based practice is the integration of the best research evidence with clinical expertise and patient values" (p. 147). Yates outlined the benefits EBPs include: promoting effective and ethical treatments, cost-effectiveness, and facilitating informed clinical decision-making. But EBPs are not without their downsides. There are barriers to learning of, being trained in, and knowing the science behind EBPs: time demands, training costs, and potential overreliance on manualized treatments can be prohibitive. So, why invest the time?

Let's take a moment to look at how other fields think about EBPs. Burke et al. (2005) discussed the importance of developing research competence among nursing professionals to support EBP. Burke et al. (2005) placed a high degree of importance on nurses acquiring skills in research methodology to effectively evaluate and apply research findings in clinical practice. Amirova et al. (2020) made a similar case for teachers developing research competencies as a key component of professional training for future teachers, specifically arguing that the competencies are essential for effective teaching. The teaching and nursing fields recognize that knowledge of research (i.e., research competence) is highly important for practitioners. EBP is recognized as a standard practice across many disciplines including clinical psychology, medicine, social work, and so on.

Moreover, the American Counseling Association (ACA) Code of Ethics (American Counseling Association, 2014) states that "counselors have a responsibility to the public to engage in counseling practices that are based on rigorous research methodologies" (Section C). The 2024 Council for Accreditation of Counseling and Related Educational Programs (CACREP) states that "graduates demonstrate both knowledge and skill across the curriculum as well as professional dispositions ... including the ability to critique and utilize research to inform counseling practice and engage in evidence-based counseling practices" (CACREP, 2024, p. 13). However, a survey conducted by (Mobley & Wester, 2007) revealed that nearly half (45%) of the counselors who participated admitted that they did not use data collection to assess their effectiveness with clients. Furthermore, almost a third (30%) of the respondents stated that they neither kept up with current research nor incorporated research findings into their clinical practice. Jensen-Doss et al. (2018) found that out of a sample of 504 mental health professionals, only 13.9% reported the use of standardized progress measures on a monthly basis. Their survey results also revealed varied practices and preferences regarding the use of certain tools or assessments among the participants. The majority (61.5%) reported never using them consistently or using them only as needed. About a quarter (24.6%) used them regularly but less frequently than once a month, such as every 90 days or at the beginning and end of treatment. A small portion (8.7%) reported monthly use, while only 5.2% used them every one to two sessions. When asked about their preferred frequency of administration, the responses differed somewhat from actual practice. Nearly half (45.0%) preferred never to use them, while 29.5% favored some regular interval, less frequent than monthly. Monthly administration was preferred by 17.5% of participants, and 6.8% would choose to use them every one to two sessions. A small percentage (1.2%) were unsure of their preference. These data suggest a discrepancy between current practices and preferences, with a general tendency toward less frequent use or nonuse of these tools or assessments. To state the obvious, in order to use assessments, counselors need to understand the research that supports the reliability and validity of the assessments. In order to practice EBPs, I need basic knowledge of research to know the strengths and limitations of the model I'm practicing.

There is an alarming disconnect between professional standards and actual practice among counselors, which highlights a critical need in our field. It's not enough to acknowledge the importance of research at a theoretical level; we must bridge the divide between research and practice in meaningful ways (Wester et al., 2020). In ways that are demonstrable, that can be observed in our education, professional training, and clinical outcomes.

Wester and Borders (2014) argued that knowledge and competence in research are very important for effective counseling and supervision. They open their article with "Research is imperative for advancing a profession" (p. 447). Wester and Borders affirmed the importance of research in advancing the field but highlighted concerns about the quality of research being conducted. The quality of counseling research, compared with other fields, is lacking, leaving counselors to rely on the research produced by other fields (Yates, 2013). Ray et al. (2011) analyzed research articles from ACA's division journals published over a decade, from 1998 to 2007. Their findings revealed that out of the total articles examined, 31% (1,382 articles) were research-oriented. Subsequent analysis revealed that only 6% (83 articles) of these research-oriented papers specifically investigated the efficacy of counseling interventions, and only 1.9% was outcome research. Additionally, 10% (134 articles) of the research articles focused on clinical populations. Now compare that to the finding that only 47% of counselors indicate that they regularly use EBPs in their clinical work with clients (Cook et al., 2017). This analysis highlights the abysmally small proportion of counseling research dedicated to intervention effectiveness and clinical populations during that period.

If our field is producing poor research, and thereby being consumed by counselors who do not possess the research literacy to critically evaluate it, the quality of clinical practice will decline, and clients will be negatively affected. In the least-worst case scenario, our field is not producing and utilizing the best possible science and we run the risk of our profession losing credibility. In the worst-worst case scenario, our field is not meeting our ethical obligations of protecting client welfare by delivering counseling informed by fallacious research, which harms clients or doesn't produce optimal outcomes for them. Wester and Borders cited issues with sampling, statistical analyses, and the lack of clear research questions as their concerns with the quality of research coming out of the counseling field. They go on to suggest that the quality of research directly impacts clinical practice, and thus, improving research competencies is imperative.

Understanding and applying research isn't just about professional development—it is an ethical imperative. As the ACA Code of Ethics states, we have a responsibility to our clients and to the public to base our practice on rigorous research. This ethical obligation underscores the critical need for counselors to develop research competence (Kaplan et al., 2014).

In the following chapters, we'll explore how to develop the research competencies that will not only meet our ethical obligations but also enhance our clinical effectiveness. We'll learn how to critically evaluate research, apply findings to our practice, and even contribute to the body of knowledge in our field. By the end of this book, you'll see research not as a burden or as a hurdle, but as a tool in your counseling tool kit—one that will help you provide the best possible care for your clients (Bager-Charleson, 2014).

## PRACTITIONERS AND CRITICAL CONSUMERS OF RESEARCH

It is standard in the counseling field that counselors in training should be trained in EBPs, which have been shown to significantly enhance counselor skills and improve client outcomes (Martino, 2010). Moreover, a comprehensive understanding of research can help bridge the gap between theory and practice, making interventions not only more relevant but also more tailored to individual clients, thereby increasing treatment efficacy (Kazdin, 2008). However, it is not enough to be a skilled practitioner of an evidence-based treatment. You must also be knowledgeable of the philosophical and evidential underpinnings of the model you practice.

But, you may be skeptical about the claim that skill is not enough; you also need knowledge as it relates to research. I want you to consider that clients come to counseling with complex, multifaceted issues, and no amount of gut instinct alone can fully prepare you to navigate these situations in an ethical and evidence-based manner. This is where a strong foundation in the literature on specific populations or mental health conditions can significantly enhance your decision-making, especially when you're feeling uncertain or lost. Familiarity with the counseling literature can lead to better outcomes for your clients, helping you provide the most effective care possible. To see an example of this, please see the case example below in Table 1.

**TABLE 1** Case Example: Navigating Complexity Beyond the Model

| |
|---|
| Imagine a counselor working with Sarah, a client presenting with persistent anxiety, depression, and relationship issues. The counselor initially uses CBT, a well-established model, but finds that Sarah's progress is minimal. Sarah's complex trauma history and cultural background seem to influence her symptoms in ways the standard CBT protocol doesn't fully address.<br><br>Realizing the limits of her current approach, the counselor seeks additional research on treating complex trauma, particularly in clients from Sarah's cultural group. She finds literature on trauma-informed care and culturally responsive interventions, which highlight the need for integrating somatic therapies and narrative approaches alongside CBT. To further support her work, she consults her supervisor, who offers guidance on how to approach the case effectively, leaning on her own knowledge of the research and identifying specific strategies from recent studies that could be adapted to Sarah's case.<br><br>Equipped with this new knowledge, the counselor adjusts her treatment plan, incorporating techniques like mindfulness-based stress reduction and culturally tailored psychoeducation. As a result, Sarah begins to show significant improvement, demonstrating that the counselor's ability to seek out and apply research-based knowledge was crucial in providing effective care. |

The case example illustrates that relying solely on clinical skills, without a solid foundation in research, can be insufficient when addressing complex client issues. In Sarah's case, the counselor recognized the limitations of CBT and sought out additional research to enhance her approach, leading to significant improvements. Research knowledge and the cognitive skills necessary to evaluate and apply it effectively work hand in hand. As we move forward, we'll get into the specific aspects of research competence so that you are well equipped to provide evidence-based care.

## RESEARCH COMPETENCE FOR COUNSELORS: A CORNERSTONE OF EFFECTIVE PRACTICE

Practicing EBPs, using assessments in counseling, and critically reading the research literature all require research competence, which are directly connected to provide effective therapeutic interventions and upholding ethical standards in counseling (Wester & Borders, 2014). Research competence is a skill set that involves handling several tools, often simultaneously. In the hands of a capable counselor, the tools enable you to critically analyze existing research, integrate findings into practice, and contribute new insights through original research (Gelso, 2006). But most importantly, they allow you to digest new knowledge and apply that knowledge in your work with clients.

# KEY COMPONENTS OF RESEARCH COMPETENCE

## CRITICAL APPRAISAL

Comprehending what you are reading is an excellent starting point, but you can't stay there. You have to move onto reading and critically assessing what you are reading. This is also known as *critical appraisal*, which is the foundation of research competence. It involves the ability to critically and thoroughly examine research for its validity, results, and relevance to clinical practice (Meltzoff & Cooper, 2018). Counselors must develop a discerning eye toward the reliability and methodology of research findings, cultivating skepticism that enables them to evaluate the quality and merit of a finding and new research, rather than passively consuming them.

For instance, when evaluating a study on a new therapeutic intervention, counselors should be able to assess the appropriateness of the research design, the quality of the methodology, the legitimacy of the statistical analytic approach, and the generalizability of the results to the population of interest. Developing these skills allows counselors to differentiate between high-quality, impactful research and studies that may not meet rigorous standards (Heppner et al., 2015). Studies that do not meet rigorous standards may produce dubious findings. Studies that have novel findings, but little to no replication, also warrant caution. It is easy to be duped by an eye-catching research finding that may be due to error, systematic or random. Counselors are well within their rights to be skeptical of such study results and should be cautious about integrating them in their work with clients.

## STATISTICAL LITERACY

While counselors are not expected to be statisticians, a fundamental grasp of statistical concepts is crucial for interpreting research findings (Trusty et al., 2019). Statistical literacy enables counselors to navigate the "results" section of research papers, assessing the reliability and validity of the presented findings. Key statistical concepts that counselors should understand include measures of central tendency (such as mean, median, and mode) and measures of variability (like standard deviation and range).

Additionally, counselors should be familiar with the concept of statistical significance and *p-values*, which help determine whether observed effects are likely to be genuine or due to chance. Understanding *effect sizes* is equally important, as it allows counselors to gauge the practical significance of results beyond mere statistical significance. Knowledge of *confidence intervals* is also valuable, as it helps in evaluating the precision of estimated effects.

By developing this statistical literacy, counselors can more critically engage with research, discerning between studies with robust statistical foundations and those with potential weaknesses. You can then make informed decisions about incorporating research findings into their clinical practice if you find the results to be solid. This allows us to based our interventions on well-supported evidence rather than on potentially misleading or imprecise results (Kline, 2019).

## METHODOLOGICAL AWARENESS

Different research questions necessitate distinct methodological approaches. Counselors need a comprehensive understanding of various research methodologies to evaluate whether a study's design addresses its stated questions and objectives (Hays & Singh, 2012). Key methodological approaches in counseling research include quantitative methods (such as randomized controlled trials and correlational studies), qualitative methods (like phenomenology and grounded theory), and mixed-methods designs. Familiarity with these approaches enables counselors to evaluate research findings and choose appropriate methodologies for their own research endeavors (Creswell & Creswell, 2018). Understanding the strengths and limitations of each method allows counselors to assess whether the chosen methodology aligns with the research question and whether the conclusions drawn are justified based on the study design.

## ETHICAL CONSIDERATIONS IN RESEARCH

*How* researchers conduct research is just as important as *what* researchers discover. A critical ethical evaluation of research is just as important as understanding statistical evidence, or methodological approaches. Critical ethical appraisal includes a deep understanding of issues such as informed consent, confidentiality, and the principle of nonmaleficence (American Counseling Association, 2014). Counselors must safeguard the welfare of research participants, maintain confidentiality and data security, navigate potential conflicts of interest, and address ethical dilemmas that may arise during the research process. By applying ethical standards systematically, counselors enhance the integrity of their research and build trust with participants and the broader community (Levitt et al., 2018). Our commitment and consistent application of ethical principles in research are essential not only for protecting research subjects but also for maintaining trust with the general public.

## EBP INTEGRATION

So, we've established that it is important to learn how to read research (comprehension), with a critical lens (evaluation), being knowledgeable of the statistics (knowledge), being aware of the methodological approaches and how they need to match research questions and data analytic approaches (awareness), and, most importantly, understanding the ethical considerations informing the research and findings (ethical appraisal), but what does any of that matter if it is for your own personal benefit? What does it matter to have these skills, but not the motivation or ability to effectively translate your new knowledge into new or enhanced clinical practice? The ability to translate research findings into clinical practice is not just a bonus, or icing on the cake. It is not a decorative garnish to the meat of your clinical work. It is, in fact, a buttress of evidence-based counseling (Norcross & Wampold, 2011). This skill involves staying current with the latest research developments, critically evaluating how new evidence aligns with existing treatment modalities, adapting therapeutic approaches based on empirical evidence, and balancing research findings with clinical expertise and client preferences.

By infusing research into clinical practice, counselors enhance their therapeutic work by adding new interventions that are appropriate to the clients' needs and are grounded in the latest scientific evidence (APA Presidential Task Force on Evidence-Based Practice, 2006). Counseling practices need to keep pace with counseling research. Sadly, the trend is typically that research is way out ahead of practice, and practice is always trailing behind.

## RESEARCH CONTRIBUTION AND DISSEMINATION

Yes, reading, evaluating, and translating research into effective practice are all great, but what if we all decided to be merely consumers and not producers? Where does that leave the field, primarily composed of practitioners, when the good research dries up? Or, that it is strictly produced by non-counselors? Beyond consuming existing research, counselors are increasingly encouraged, rightly so, to contribute to the body of knowledge within their field (Wester et al., 2018). This involves designing and conducting original research studies, securing ethical approval for research projects, collecting and analyzing data effectively, and disseminating findings through peer-reviewed journals, conferences, or digital platforms.

Actively participating in research, counselors not only bolster their own understanding and skills but also contribute to the advancement of the counseling profession as a whole. So, we have to think on three separate, but interconnected levels: your personal development, the enhancement of your clinical work, and the needs of the field as a whole. Research affects each level. Engagement with research creation and dissemination cultivates a practice of continual learning and deliberate improvement within the field, benefiting both practitioners and clients.

This will be explored in greater detail in Chapter 1, but in short, counselors have something really powerful to offer the world of research. Our values, professional identity, and philosophical approach to the work of helping individuals, families, couples, and communities are special and unique. Counselors contribute to the advancement of their field, leading to improved outcomes for clients and a more scientifically grounded practice (Lenz, 2020).

### CONTINUAL PROCESS

Developing research competence is a continuous process that requires an ongoing effort that extends beyond graduate school. Graduate school only provides students the briefest of exposures to research. We already have a 60-credit hour master's degree. You are welcome to take more elective classes (and I personally think you should in research methods), but who has the time and money? So, that means it is on you to continually seek out and refine your knowledge and skills of research. The master's degree is the beginning, not the end. By keeping up with the latest research, your practice will be informed by the most current and rigorous evidence available, enabling your treatment to be effective and upholding the ethical integrity of their practice since we have an obligation to our clients to provide best practice (Trusty et al., 2019).

## CONSEQUENCES OF LOW RESEARCH COMPETENCY

If you are not convinced of the benefits of research competence, I believe, an awareness of the consequences of inadequate research skills will. I say that because low research literacy and competence can have significant and far-reaching effects, impacting not only individual counselors but also their clients and the broader field of mental health care.

### WHAT ARE THE CONSEQUENCES?

Let's start by answering the question: What are the consequences of a counselor possessing low research literacy and competency? For starters, low research literacy and competency can lead to compromised client care. When counselors lack research competency, they may rely on outdated or ineffective practices, leading to suboptimal client outcomes. Lilienfeld et al. (2013) argued that failure to stay current with research can result in the continued use of debunked or harmful interventions. For example, a counselor unfamiliar with recent research might continue using psychological debriefing for acute trauma, despite evidence suggesting it may be ineffective or even harmful (Rose et al., 2002).

This lack of up-to-date knowledge can also erode professional credibility. In an era where clients and colleagues increasingly expect EBP, counselors with low research competency may find their professional standing questioned. Gambrill (2012) noted that the inability to articulate the scientific basis for interventions can undermine trust in the therapeutic relationship and may lead to decreased referrals from other professionals.

Ethical concerns arise as well. The ACA's Code of Ethics (2014) emphasized the importance of using techniques, procedures, and modalities that find their footing in theory as well as, or in addition to, an evidence-based foundation. Counselors who lack research skills may inadvertently violate this ethical standard by using interventions without evidence of efficacy or by failing to inform clients about the most effective available treatments.

### COUNSELOR STAGNATION IS ALSO HARMFUL TO CLIENTS

Furthermore, limited research competency can lead to stagnation in professional development and resistance to innovation. Counselors with poor research skills may struggle to meet continuing education requirements, particularly those focused on EBPs, hindering career advancement and limiting opportunities for leadership roles (Kaplan & Gladding, 2011). This can also create skepticism toward new, effective approaches, potentially depriving clients of beneficial innovations in treatment (Dozois, 2013).

The consequences extend to resource allocation and contributions to the field, as well. Without the ability to conduct research like program evaluation or outcome research, counselors and agency leaders may invest time and resources in interventions/treatment programs with limited efficacy, leading to prolonged treatments without significant progress (APA Presidential Task Force on Evidence-Based Practice, 2006). Moreover, counselors with low research competency are less likely to contribute to the growth of their profession through publications, presentations, or participation in research projects, stunting the evolution of counseling as a field (Wester et al., 2018). Addressing these consequences requires a commitment to developing research competency throughout a counselor's career. This involves quality research education in master's programs, ongoing professional development, and a culture that values and promotes EBP (Bezyak et al., 2010).

## WORKING THROUGH PERSONAL RESISTANCE

To mitigate the consequences of low research competency, counselors in training need to receive a quality education about research in their master's programs, and for professionals in the field to seek ongoing education and training in research methods, critical appraisal of literature, and EBPs.

Education dedicated to research literacy not only enhances the quality of care provided to clients but also supports the counselor's professional growth and the advancement of the counseling field as a whole (Wester & Borders, 2014). Again, think about the three levels: you as a professional, the quality of care you provide your client, and the counseling field as a whole.

While these reasons should motivate improvement in research knowledge and understanding, it is natural to encounter some resistance. This resistance often stems from underlying fears or misconceptions about the research process. Some counselors may recognize the importance of research but worry that learning it will be too difficult or that, even after putting in the effort, they still won't fully grasp the material (Steele & Rawls, 2015).

David Burns, MD, well-known for his book *Feeling Good* and other best-selling books, refers to these uncomfortable feelings as *process* and *outcome* resistance (Burns, 2005). Process resistance occurs when the prospect of learning research methods seems daunting and unenjoyable. Outcome resistance, on the other hand, is the fear that the anticipated result of this learning effort will lead to more confusion rather than clarity. Resistance is not uncommon among counselor students; it is normal to feel that way about learning research. Bezyak et al. (2010) found that many counselors report feeling intimidated by research or believe it is not relevant to their clinical practice. Start with acknowledging the resistance; build awareness around it. And then I urge you to think about your ethical obligation to clients because integrating research into practice plays a really important role in providing effective, evidence-based treatments (Norcross & Lambert, 2018).

In *Demystifying Research Methods: Bridging Research and Practice in Counseling*, these concerns are addressed head-on. The book is designed to make the process of learning research not only manageable but also engaging and meaningful. This approach aligns with the recommendations of Gelso et al. (2013), who emphasized the importance of creating a positive research training environment to foster research interest and competence among counselors.

By breaking down complex concepts into digestible parts and relating them directly to clinical practice, the goal is to guide you to a place where research feels like a powerful tool in your clinical tool kit rather than an obstacle. This method of instruction is supported by research on adult learning theories, which suggest that relating new information to practical applications enhances retention and motivation (Knowles et al., 2015). Ultimately, the aim is to transform the perception of research from a daunting academic exercise to an integral part of effective counseling practice. As Betan and Binder (2010) argued, when counselors embrace research as a means to strengthen their clinical skills and client outcomes, it becomes an asset rather than a burden.

## THE AIM OF THIS BOOK

The intention and hope of this book is to (as it says in the title) demystify research by scaling it back to your level. Most importantly, I want to start with a conceptual and an intuitive understanding of research concepts, linking it to practical application in clinical work, and then, you can move on to more technical texts about research methods. As you've read, suffusing research knowledge into your clinical practice enhances your effectiveness, ethical integrity, and theoretical grounding.

The book also highlights the unique contributions that counselors bring to the research community and the challenges and opportunities of modern counseling. The aim is to help you engage with research rather than succumb to process/outcome resistance, so that you can build your research knowledge and competency, able to effectively bridge the gap between theoretical and empirical research findings with clinical practice, develop ethical practices with clients through the use of counseling approaches informed by the best and latest research, foster professional development, address and fill the gaps present in modern social science, cultivate the culture of curiosity in the field of counseling while also maintaining the credibility of our field, and contribute to the body of research, while conducting research from our unique point of view as counselors. Overall, the book's intention is to guide counselors in training on how to effectively integrate research into their practice. By doing so, it seeks to make a positive contribution to the counseling profession, where our field is associated with rigorous research that has an impact and EBP that is client-centered.

1

# The Heart of Research: The Professional Counselor Values and Identity

Research is not a sterile, objective academic exercise conducted in a vacuum, immune to the influences of culture, discipline, or the individual researcher. Quite the opposite! It is a deeply human activity, embedded within specific cultural contexts, disciplinary traditions, and personal worldviews and many other mediating layers that all individually and distinctly play an influential role. In fact, it is a myth to think that research is a completely objective, value-free activity conducted by a researcher devoid of any presuppositions or biases. Every step of the research process—from the initial ideation of your research questions and hypotheses to the analysis of findings—is influenced by the researcher's background, theoretical orientations, and the broader sociocultural context in which the research takes place. These factors shape not only how we approach research but also what we see—and don't see—in our data.

Different approaches to research, grounded in distinct philosophical and theoretical frameworks, yield insights into phenomena that may not be ascertainable through other lenses. A behaviorist approach might uncover patterns of observable actions but miss the rich inner world of subjective experience. A phenomenological approach might shine a light on deep personal meanings but overlook broader social structures. A critical theory perspective shows how power dynamics potentially downplay individual agency.

It is within this framework that research should be considered as a contextually embedded, philosophically grounded activity. This view is emblematic of counseling research, where our approach is shaped by our professional identity, values, and philosophical history, offering a distinct and valuable perspective in the landscape of social science inquiry. Counseling, with its emphasis on holistic wellness, human potential, and the importance of the therapeutic relationship, approaches research questions from a standpoint that differs significantly from more medically oriented or purely psychological perspectives. This approach draws out deep insights into the human experience, mental health, and well-being that might be underexamined by other disciplines.

For instance, a psychiatric approach might focus on symptom reduction through pharmacological interventions and a psychological approach might focus on cognitive processes addressed through manualized treatment; the counseling perspective, on the other hand, might emphasize the role of meaning-making, personal growth, and social context in mental health. These different foci affect practice and lead to different research questions, methodologies, and interpretations of findings.

In this chapter, we will explore the lens through which counselors view and conduct research. We will examine how the professional identity of counselors, constructed through our philosophical, scientific, and professional history, shapes our approach to scientific inquiry. We'll investigate the core values and ethical principles that guide counseling research and how these lead to a research agenda that is both complementary to and distinct from other helping disciplines. We'll first take a historical overview, looking at the medical model of psychiatry, moving through the psychological theories that expanded our understanding of the mind, culminating in the emergence of counseling with its unique focus on wellness, prevention, and human development across the lifespan. We'll look at how counseling carved out its own identity and why this identity impacts our approach to mental health research.

## HISTORY IN A NUTSHELL

### BIRTH OF PSYCHIATRY

The history of psychiatry has seen significant changes over centuries, beginning with the early Greek and Roman writings on psychiatric symptoms around 400 B.C. (Porter, 2003) and continuing with significant developments in the 18th and 19th centuries. These included the establishment of asylums and the development of moral treatment, focusing on the humane treatment of the mentally ill (Shorter, 1997). Fast forward to the 20th century—psychiatry expanded with the introduction of *psychoanalysis* (e.g., Sigmund Freud) and *biological psychiatry* (e.g., Emil Kraeplin) (Barton, 1998), influencing modern therapeutic practices and the conceptualization of mental illnesses primarily as brain disorders (Beer, 1995, 2009; Haslam, 2014). The early iterations of this approach of conceptualizing and treating psychological ailments gave rise to treatments like lobotomies, electroshock therapy, insulin coma therapy, and very primitive and harmful interventions, grounded in views that saw genes as causing defects in the brain (Barton, 1998).

## FROM PSYCHIATRY TO PSYCHOLOGY

The field of psychology, as a distinct discipline from psychiatry, began in the mid-19th century. Pioneers like Wilhelm Wundt established psychology as a laboratory science, focusing on the study of consciousness and the mind (Rieber & Robinson, 2012). Subsequent developments in the 20th century introduced *behaviorism* (think B. F. Skinner, John Watson, Ivan Pavlov), which emphasized observable behaviors and the effects of learning, and later the cognitive revolution, which brought back the focus on mental processes (Miller, 2003). These theorists, and many others, viewed distress as a psychological experience, and therefore, the treatment for distress involved a psychological treatment. Since then, the field has expanded to include diverse approaches like developmental, social, and clinical psychology, each contributing to a broader understanding of human behavior and mental processes (Goodey, 2021).

## CONNECTING THE PAST WITH THE PRESENT

Psychiatry traditionally aligns more with medical sciences given its historical roots we discussed above, focusing primarily on the diagnosis, treatment, and prevention of mental illness primarily from a biological standpoint (Harrington, 2019). The field emphasizes the biochemical processes and physical aspects of mental health disorders, treating these primarily with psychotropic medications. Psychology, on the other hand, is rooted in the science of behavior and mental processes, focusing on understanding psychological experience and distress with a rigor akin to the medical field, with clinical foci on administering psychological assessments and following manualized psychotherapeutic treatments. Psychology's approach is more diverse than psychiatry, incorporating biological, cognitive, and sociocultural perspectives to address mental processes and behavior (Deacon, 2013).

The differences between the two fields become even more apparent when you look at the way they practice. Psychiatrists are medically trained physicians who can prescribe medication, conduct physical examinations, and interpret medical tests along with providing limited psychotherapeutic interventions (however, this is quite variable—some (very few) psychiatrists provide psychotherapy; most do not). Psychologists primarily provide psychological testing and manualized psychotherapy to effect changes in behavior and cognitive processes, with an emphasis on improving overall psychological functioning and well-being (Aftab et al., 2018). Their time is more evenly divided between providing psychotherapy and testing. They may specialize in various subfields such as clinical, educational, or organizational psychology. Furthermore, psychologists often specialize in treating particular psychological issues. For example, 23% of licensed psychologists specialize in clinical child and adolescents, 13% in clinical health, and 9% in clinical neuropsychology, among a number of other specialties (Lin et al., 2017), but only 12% specialize in counseling. Psychologists, also, typically earn a doctoral degree in psychology (PhD or PsyD) focusing extensively on psychological research, testing, and a broad range of psychotherapeutic techniques. Their training does not include medical training or pharmacology unless specifically related to clinical psychopharmacology for prescriptive authority in some states (Arad, 2017).

## FROM PSYCHOLOGY TO COUNSELING

Okay, let's get back to our history lesson. The origins of modern counseling can be traced back to the early 20th century, with Frank Parsons often credited as the father of vocational guidance. In 1908, Parsons founded the Vocation Bureau in Boston and published his seminal work "Choosing a Vocation" in 1909 (Pope, 2000). Parsons' approach emphasized self-understanding, knowledge of the world of work, and the importance of matching individuals to suitable occupations. As the field of vocational guidance evolved, it began to incorporate broader aspects of personal development and mental health.

In 1952, the American Personnel and Guidance Association (APGA) was formed (Herlihy et al., 2018) through the merger of four independent associations: the National Vocational Guidance Association, the American College Personnel Association, the National Association of Guidance and Counselor Trainers, and the Student Personnel Association for Teacher Education (Gladding, 2018). This merger was not without its challenges. The diverse backgrounds and interests of the founding organizations led to initial debates about the association's primary focus and direction. However, these differences also contributed to the richness and breadth of the new organization, reflecting the multifaceted nature of the emerging counseling profession (Gladding & Newsome, 2018).

In the years following its formation, the APGA continued to evolve and expand. New divisions were added to represent emerging specialties within counseling, such as school counseling, rehabilitation counseling, and marriage and family counseling. In 1983, the APGA transitioned in name to the American Association for Counseling and Development to better reflect the breadth of the profession. Finally, in 1992, the organization adopted its current name, the American Counseling Association, further solidifying its identity as the premier organization representing professional counselors (Gladding, 2018). However, the evolution and growth of the counseling field did not occur without resistance, particularly from the field of psychology (Gladding, 2018).

As counseling sought to establish itself as a profession in its own right, it faced significant opposition from the field of psychology. This resistance manifested in several ways. As counselors pushed for state licensure in the 1970s and the 1980s, many psychological associations actively lobbied against counselor licensure laws at the state level, arguing that counselors were not sufficiently trained to provide mental health services (Brooks & Gerstein, 1990). Psychologists argued that counselors should be limited to vocational guidance and not engage in psychotherapy or diagnosis of mental disorders (Hanna & Bemak, 1997). There were also efforts to exclude counselors from insurance panels, with psychologists arguing that only they should be reimbursed for mental health services (Glosoff et al., 1995).

Despite the opposition, in the 1980s, licensure standards were established, helping to define counseling as a distinct professional field (Bloom et al., 1990). What followed was the development of counselor education programs, the establishment of ethical codes and practice standards, and the eventual achievement of licensure in all 50 states solidifying counseling's status as a distinct mental health profession (Remley & Herlihy, 2020). Counseling now encompasses a broad range of practices aimed at supporting individuals across different aspects of life, including emotional, social, and psychological well-being.

## DISTINGUISHING OURSELVES FROM PSYCHOLOGY

As noted above, the cousin fields of psychology and counseling have not always been friendly. Counseling philosophy generally promotes a client-centered, holistic approach, emphasizing personal growth and the therapeutic relationship over diagnostic categorization (Rogers, 1951). This orientation often contrasts with psychology's focus, which can include a more clinical or research-oriented perspective, including assessments and treatments within various subfields[1] (American Psychological Association, n.d.). Counseling philosophy adheres closely to humanistic principles, focusing on clients' strengths and potential rather than the assessment and amelioration of pathology.

### IN PHILOSOPHY

One of the most significant humanistic influences on counseling comes from Carl Rogers' person-centered approach. Rogers (1951) emphasized the inherent tendency of individuals toward growth and self-actualization, a concept he termed the "actualizing tendency." His focus on the therapeutic relationship, characterized by unconditional positive regard, empathy, and congruence, is foundational to the field of counseling practice across treatment models. Counseling also draws on the work of Abraham Maslow's work, particularly his hierarchy of needs and concept of self-actualization, which has also been highly influential in counseling. Maslow (1954) proposed that in-

1. Brain science and cognitive psychology, climate and environmental psychology, clinical psychology, counseling psychology, developmental psychology, experimental psychology, forensic and public service psychology, health psychology, human factors and engineering psychology, industrial and organizational psychology, rehabilitation psychology, school psychology, social psychology, and sports and performance psychology.

dividuals are motivated by a hierarchy of needs, with self-actualization at the apex. This theoretical view encourages counselors to consider the whole person and their unique potential for growth and fulfillment.

Other influences include the following: Existential philosophy, as applied to counseling by theorists like Rollo May and Irvin Yalom, has contributed to the profession's focus on meaning-making and personal responsibility (May, 1981; Yalom, 1980). The work of Viktor Frankl, particularly his logotherapy approach, has influenced counseling's emphasis on finding meaning in life experiences, even in the face of suffering (Frankl, 1959). There's also the contribution from Gestalt therapy, developed by Fritz Perls, Laura Perls, and Paul Goodman, which has contributed to counseling's focus on holistic awareness and personal responsibility (Perls et al., 1951).

These humanistic influences have collectively shaped counseling's core philosophical stance. They have contributed to the profession's emphasis on client autonomy, the importance of the therapeutic relationship, a focus on growth and potential rather than pathology, and a holistic view of the person in context (Ivey et al., 2012). Moreover, these humanistic influences align closely with counseling's wellness orientation. The profession's focus on promoting overall well-being, rather than on simply treating symptoms, is firmly grounded in our humanistic roots. Our field takes a wellness perspective emphasizing prevention, development across the lifespan, and the integration of multiple aspects of a person's life—physical, emotional, social, spiritual, and vocational (Myers & Sweeney, 2008).

## IN PRACTICE

Compare our focus on wellness, life satisfaction, and personal development (Myers & Sweeney, 2008) to psychology's focus that includes a wider range of practices such as experimental, forensic, or neuropsychology that utilize different methodologies and interventions. Counselors' framework of practice seeks to facilitate an individual's functioning across a spectrum of personal and interpersonal levels, providing support that extends beyond mental illness to include personal and career growth, relationship issues, and life transitions (Georges & Tomlinson-Clarke, 2015). The treatment focus is distinctly oriented toward enhancing life skills and coping mechanisms under a less pathological framework than clinical psychology (Corey, 2017). Counseling interventions often incorporate strategies aimed at improving personal insights, emotional acceptance, and behavioral changes through modalities like motivational interviewing (Miller & Rollnick, 2012), solution-focused brief therapy (de Shazer et al., 2007), or mindfulness practices, which are geared more toward life improvement rather than toward clinical symptom reduction (Peluso, 2022). Training for counselors typically focuses on master's level education with an emphasis on skill-building, developing proficiency in techniques, and direct client interactions. This contrasts with psychology where doctoral programs often emphasize research, assessment, and a broad application of psychological principles across different settings. Counseling training includes substantial experiential learning with a strong emphasis on developing interpersonal skills and therapeutic relationships, guided by ethical practices tailored to promoting client welfare and autonomy (McAuliffe & Eriksen, 2010).

The reason I am giving a short history lesson is that the heart of research for counselors has everything to do with our professional identity, values, and philosophical approach to helping people. Counseling, though younger than psychiatry and psychology, has developed a unique professional identity focused on facilitating personal growth and dealing with everyday life challenges. It diverges from psychiatry and psychology by emphasizing client-centered approaches, meaning-making, holistic evaluation and care, taking great care to deeply understand a client's cultural context, personalizing interventions and treatments to the client mediated through a supportive relationship and the development of coping strategies personalized to individual life situation and culture. Counseling promotes a collaborative relationship between the counselor and the client, stressing the importance of a nonpathologizing approach to personal and interpersonal issues (Hansen, 2006). It places a significant value on the development of the whole person, reflecting its roots in humanistic philosophy (Shoben, 1965). Counseling's values, philosophical nuances, and commitments form the basis of our professional identity.

**TABLE 1** Case Study Analysis: Reimagining Research Through a Counseling Lens

### Case Study Analysis: Reimagining Research Through a Counseling Lens

**Instructions:** Read the following psychology research study abstract. Then, analyze how a counselor might approach this research differently. What elements would you add or change to align it more closely with counseling values?

**Abstract**: "This study examined the effectiveness of cognitive-behavioral therapy (CBT) in reducing symptoms of generalized anxiety disorder (GAD) in adults. 100 participants diagnosed with GAD were randomly assigned to either a CBT treatment group or a wait-list control group. Results showed significant reduction in GAD symptoms in the treatment group compared to the control group."

**Questions to consider:**

- How might a counselor expand the focus beyond symptom reduction?
- What holistic or wellness factors could be incorporated?
- How could the study be more inclusive or culturally sensitive?

## COUNSELOR PROFESSIONAL IDENTITY

Counselor professional identity has many dimensions within the overall concept that encompasses values, beliefs, and practices that distinguish counselors from other mental health professionals. This identity is influenced by our education, training, and ongoing professional development. Despite numerous efforts to define counselor professional identity, research highlights a lack of consensus on what precisely constitutes this identity. Woo et al. (2016) found that even among counselor educators in leadership positions, there were varying perspectives on the core elements of professional identity. However, several studies have identified common themes that many in the field recognize as central to counselor identity.

Mellin et al. (2011) noted that counselors often view their profession as distinct in its developmental, prevention, and wellness orientation. This aligns with the findings of Reiner et al. (2013), who observed that counselors frequently emphasize a focus on client strengths and holistic well-being. In addition, multicultural competence and a strong emphasis on the therapeutic relationship are often cited as key components of counselor identity (Woo et al., 2017). However, as Gale and Austin (2003) pointed out, the diversity within the counseling field contributes to the difficulty in establishing a unified professional identity, with the specific components and their relative importance varying depending on different theoretical orientations, practice settings, and individual counselor experiences.

The ongoing dialog about counselor identity within the profession is not just intellectual exercise; it has real implications for how counselors practice, how we are perceived by other fields, and how the public sees us. Nugent and Jones (2009) argued that the lack of a unified definition can lead to confusion both within the profession and in how counseling is perceived externally. Reiner et al. (2013) found that counselors often struggle to articulate a clear, unified professional identity, which can impact their perceived effectiveness and professional standing. As Moss et al. (2014) suggested, the development of professional identity is an ongoing process, reflecting the evolving nature of the counseling field itself. Some have argued that the reason for the lack of a unified definition is due to the diversity of treatment foci in our field. In addition, they suggest that the lack of unity is only true in appearance, but in reality, it is an indicator of our diverse set of voices, specialties, and background of counselors. We have managed to come this far while maintaining a group of diverse professionals, and that is an accomplishment.

But, I don't want to overstate the case about our lack of consensus around a definition. Let's look at how counselor professional identity has been conceptualized in the literature. Table 2 summarizes key perspectives from various scholars and professional organizations. This table highlights some of the common themes and the diversity of viewpoints on what constitutes counselor professional identity.

**TABLE 2** Core Components of Counselor Identity

## Core Components of Counselor Identity

**Developmental Perspective:** Counselors view human growth and change through a developmental lens, focusing on normal and pathological aspects of human development (Remley & Herlihy, 2020).

**Prevention and Early Intervention:** Counselors emphasize preventive approaches and early intervention strategies, focusing on addressing issues before they escalate into more severe problems (Mellin et al., 2011).

**Wellness Orientation:** A key aspect of counselor identity is the emphasis on promoting wellness and optimal functioning, rather than solely focusing on pathology (Myers & Sweeney, 2008).

**Holistic Approach:** Counselors view clients from a holistic perspective, considering the interplay of various life domains including emotional, social, physical, and spiritual aspects (Woo et al., 2017).

**Advocacy and Social Justice:** Counselors are increasingly embracing roles as advocates for clients and social justice, addressing systemic barriers to mental health and well-being (Ratts et al., 2016).

**Multicultural Competence:** A strong counselor identity includes a commitment to developing cultural competence and providing culturally responsive services (Sue et al., 2019).

**Professional Ethics:** Adherence to ethical standards and decision-making processes is a crucial component of counselor identity (ACA, 2014).

**Collaboration and Interdisciplinary Approach:** Counselors often work as a part of interdisciplinary teams, collaborating with other professionals to provide comprehensive care (Mellin et al., 2011).

**Strength-Based Focus:** Counselors emphasize identifying and building upon client strengths and resources, rather than solely focusing on deficits or pathology (Reiner et al., 2013).

**Therapeutic Relationship:** Counselors place a strong emphasis on the importance of the therapeutic relationship as a key factor in facilitating client change and growth (Woo et al., 2017).

**Professional Engagement:** Active participation in professional organizations, continuing education, and contribution to the field's knowledge base are considered as important aspects of counselor identity (Woo et al., 2016).

**Adaptability and Flexibility:** Counselors recognize the need to adapt their approaches to meet diverse client needs and changing societal contexts (Gale & Austin, 2003).

**Ongoing Identity Development:** Counselor professional identity is viewed as a dynamic, ongoing process that evolves throughout one's career (Moss et al., 2014).

**Client Empowerment:** Counselors focus on empowering clients to make their own decisions and take control of their lives, promoting autonomy and self-efficacy (Reiner et al., 2013).

**Research-Informed Practice:** While not always explicitly stated, there is an increasing emphasis on the integration of research into counseling practice as a part of professional identity (Kaplan & Gladding, 2011).

## FORMATION OF COUNSELOR IDENTITY

Having looked at Table 2, stop and reflect. What did you think when looking at the table? What components resonated with you? Your formation, as well as the fields, regarding the professional counselor identity is a dynamic and ongoing process. There is a parallel process going on. The lack of consensus creates a space of uncertainty and the potential for innovation. It is a developmental journey influenced by a variety of factors that shape and refine your professional self-concept. A journey that begins with counselor education and training, which lays the foundation for professional identity (Gibson et al., 2010). Your master's program offers formative experiences that expose aspiring counselors to core theories, ethical principles, and practical skills that form the bedrock of their professional selves. Moreover, counselors in training begin to build and participate in a community of professionals, where they support and encourage one another. As counselors progress in their careers, supervision and mentorship become pivotal in further developing and solidifying their professional identity. Bernard and Goodyear (2019) emphasized the significant impact that supervisory relationships have on a counselor's growth, providing guidance, support, and opportunities for reflection that contribute to a more robust professional identity.

Engagement with professional associations also plays a substantial role in identity formation. Luke and Goodrich (2010) noted that involvement in these organizations offers counselors opportunities for networking, leadership development, and exposure to diverse perspectives within the field. This involvement can broaden a counselor's understanding of the profession and their place within it. In addition, continuing education and professional development activities, as discussed by Neukrug (2016), are essential for maintaining and expanding counselor identity. These ongoing learning experiences allow counselors to stay current with evolving best practices, theories, and ethical considerations, thereby continually refining their professional identity in response to new knowledge and changing societal needs.

The importance of developing a strong professional identity cannot be overstated. Research conducted by Woo et al. (2017) has demonstrated that counselors with a well-established professional identity tend to experience greater job satisfaction, exhibit more consistent ethical behavior, and demonstrate increased overall effectiveness in their counseling practice. This finding underscores the critical nature of identity development not just for the individual counselor, but for the quality of care provided to clients and the overall integrity of the profession. As such, the formation of counselor identity should be viewed as a career-long endeavor, requiring intentional effort, reflection, and engagement with the broader counseling community.

## VALUES UNDERGIRDING COUNSELING

Counselor values form the foundation of the profession counselor identity. These values reflect the profession's commitment to client welfare, social justice, and professional excellence. They are long-standing principles that shape how counselors approach their work, interact with clients, navigate complex ethical situations, and approach research. Moreover, counselor values are not static but continue to evolve in response to changing societal needs, emerging ethical challenges, and advances in our understanding of mental health and human development. They serve as a compass, guiding counselors in their research questions and in their broader roles as advocates for mental health and social justice. To provide a more comprehensive overview of the key values that underpin the counseling profession, let's examine Table 3 that outlines these core values and their implications for practice. This table will highlight the fundamental principles that guide counselors in their work and illustrate how these values translate into ethical and effective counseling practice.

**TABLE 3** Core Counselor Values

| Core Counselor Values |
| --- |
| **Respect for Human Dignity:** Counselors uphold the inherent worth and value of all individuals, respecting client autonomy and promoting self-determination (ACA, 2014). |
| **Promotion of Social Justice:** Counselors work to address societal inequities and promote equal access to opportunities and resources (Ratts et al., 2016). |
| **Commitment to Diversity and Inclusion:** Counselors value and respect individual differences, striving to provide culturally responsive services (Sue et al., 2019). |
| **Integrity:** Counselors maintain high standards of personal and professional conduct, adhering to ethical principles in all aspects of their work (ACA, 2014). |
| **Competence:** Counselors are committed to ongoing professional development and maintaining competence in their areas of practice (Neukrug, 2016). |
| **Empowerment:** Counselors aim to facilitate client growth and development, empowering individuals to overcome challenges and achieve their goals (McWhirter, 1991). |
| **Holistic Approach:** Counselors view clients as whole persons, considering the interplay of physical, emotional, social, and spiritual factors in well-being (Myers & Sweeney, 2008). |

The counseling professional identity and counseling values guide researchers in conducting ethical, humble, and culturally sensitive studies that uphold human dignity and promote social justice. The values of respect for human dignity and integrity translate into rigorous ethical protocols, informed consent procedures, and confidentiality measures. The commitment to diversity and inclusion drives researchers to use representative sampling and culturally responsive methodologies. Research standards in counseling reflect the profession's values of competence and integrity. These standards emphasize the importance of methodological rigor, transparency in reporting, and the ethical treatment of research participants. The value of a holistic approach encourages research that considers multiple facets of human experience and well-being. Counselor values also shape research topics. The promotion of social justice and commitment to diversity often lead to studies on marginalized populations, health disparities, and culturally adaptive interventions. The value of empowerment inspires research on client resilience, growth, and self-determination. The holistic approach encourages studies that examine the interplay of various factors in mental health and well-being. Kernes and Kinnier (2008) found that counselors' personal values were positively correlated with their therapeutic effectiveness and job satisfaction. Fuertes et al. (2006) demonstrated that counselors' multicultural values and competencies were associated with stronger therapeutic alliances and improved client outcomes.

**TABLE 4** Values-Driven Research Question Development

## Values-Driven Research Question Development

Instructions: This exercise will help you explore how counselor professional identity and values shape the research questions we ask and the problems we choose to focus on in our research.

**Step 1**: Review the following core values of the counseling profession in Table 3.

**Step 2:** For each of the following broad research areas, develop a research question that reflects one or more of these counseling values. Then, briefly explain how your question embodies these values.

**Research Areas:** a) Adolescent mental health; b) Career development; c) Trauma and resilience; d) Multicultural counseling; e) Technology in counseling

**Example Research Area:** Adolescent mental health

**Value-Driven Research Question:** "How do school-based mindfulness programs impact holistic well-being, including academic performance, social relationships, and emotional regulation, among diverse groups of high school students?"

**Explanation:** This question reflects the counseling values of holistic wellness, prevention, and multicultural competence. It looks beyond just mental health symptoms to consider overall well-being across multiple domains of an adolescent's life. The focus on school-based programs emphasizes prevention and early intervention. By specifically mentioning diverse groups, it acknowledges the importance of multicultural competence in counseling research.

**Step 3:** Choose one of your developed research questions and expand on it by considering:

- What problem or gap in current knowledge does this question address?
- How might answering this question contribute to counseling practice or advocacy efforts?
- What potential barriers or ethical considerations might arise in pursuing this research?

**Step 4:** Reflect on the process. How did consciously applying counseling values change the way you approached formulating research questions? How might this approach lead to research that is distinct from other mental health disciplines?

# BRINGING IT ALL TOGETHER: CONNECTING PROFESSIONAL IDENTITY AND VALUES TO RESEARCH

Counseling research serves as both a reflection of our professional identity and a means to shape and refine it. The unique perspective that counselors bring to the research process—emphasizing wellness, holistic approaches, and social justice—distinguishes counseling research from other disciplines and contributes valuable insights to the broader field of mental health. Let's explore a few key examples of how counselor professional identity manifests in research:

Counselors' commitment to holistic wellness often leads to research that explores the interconnectedness of physical, psychological, social, and spiritual aspects of well-being (Myers & Sweeney, 2008). For instance, a counseling researcher might investigate how social support networks, physical exercise, and spiritual practices collectively contribute to mental health outcomes in cancer survivors. This holistic perspective provides a more comprehensive understanding of health that transcends traditional medical models.

Aligned with counseling's emphasis on health promotion, research often focuses on preventive measures, strength-based interventions, and resilience factors. A study might examine how positive coping strategies developed in adolescence contribute to mental health resilience in adulthood, shifting the narrative from treating illness to promoting lifelong well-being (Cutuli et al., 2020).

Counseling research frequently adopts an intersectional approach, recognizing the complex interplay of multiple identities and social contexts (Crenshaw, 2013). A researcher might investigate how racial identity, socioeconomic status, and gender interact to influence access to mental health services and treatment outcomes.

## APPLYING PROFESSIONAL IDENTITY TO YOUR RESEARCH

As a counselor in training, your professional identity can shape your research in several ways: When formulating research questions, consider how they reflect counseling's holistic, strength-based, and inclusive values. Instead of asking, "What are the symptoms of depression in college students?" you might ask, "How do college students' support systems and coping strategies contribute to their mental well-being?" Reflect on how your choice of methodology aligns with counseling's focus on individual experiences and contexts. Mixed-methods approaches, for example, can provide both generalizable data and rich, contextual insights.

When testing interventions, consider incorporating measures of well-being and personal growth alongside symptom reduction scales. As you develop or apply theories, consider how they align with

counseling's developmental and wellness-oriented perspective. Make sure your research design reflects counseling's strong ethical foundation, particularly in areas like informed consent, confidentiality, and respect for diversity. The conscious alignment of your research with counseling's professional identity contributes to a body of knowledge that is distinctly counseling-oriented, enhancing the field's unique contributions to mental health research and practice.

**TABLE 5** Reflection Exercise: Connecting Identity to Research

**Reflection Exercise: Connecting Identity to Research**

**Instructions:** Take 15 min to reflect on your understanding of counselor professional identity. Consider the core values, perspectives, and approaches that distinguish counseling from other mental health professions. Then, brainstorm three potential research topics that align with this identity. For each topic, explain how it reflects counseling values and approaches.

**Example:** Counselor Identity Reflection: Counseling emphasizes holistic wellness, focusing on strengths and resilience rather than on pathology. It values cultural competence and social justice.

**Research Topic 1**: The impact of community gardening programs on mental well-being in urban neighborhoods. Alignment: This topic reflects counseling's holistic approach by examining how engagement with nature and community affects mental health. It also addresses social justice by focusing on urban areas that may have limited access to green spaces.

## CONCLUSION

The unique identity and values of the counseling profession shape our research agenda that is not only distinct from but complementary to other mental health disciplines. As we've explored throughout this chapter, counselors bring a perspective to research that emphasizes holistic wellness, strength-based approaches, and social justice. This lens, formed through a rich historical and philosophical tradition, allows counselors to contribute valuable insights to the broader field of mental health research and practice. By integrating core professional values such as respect for human dignity, promotion of social justice, and commitment to diversity and inclusion into their research, we can advocate for practices that honor the richness and intersectionality of the human experience. This bridges a key gap in the delivery of mental health services and simultaneously addresses critical areas that may be overlooked by more medically oriented approaches.

Moreover, the counseling profession, as a whole, puts a strong emphasis in understanding individuals within their sociocultural contexts, which promotes research that explores how various life domains interact to influence mental health and well-being. The shift from a deficit-focused, disease model to one of wellness and personal growth represents an evolution in counseling research. Furthermore, as we learn more regarding the impact of trauma, the mental health implications of global events such as pandemics and climate change and the growing awareness of the importance of mental health in overall well-being present opportunities for counseling research to lead the way in developing innovative, holistic approaches.

The integration of professional values into research remains essential for developing treatments that are grounded in science and humanistic philosophy. This focus allows counselors to contribute to the scientific community in a relevant, impactful, and true manner to the profession's commitment to fostering human dignity and well-being in all its diverse forms. As counselors-in-training embarking on your research journey, remember that your professional identity is not just a backdrop to your work, but a powerful lens through which you can view, question, and explore the complexities of human experience and mental health. By grounding your research in the values and principles of counseling, you have the opportunity to contribute to a body of knowledge that is uniquely positioned to address the mental health challenges of our time. The intersection of counselor professional identity and research offers a rich terrain for exploration and innovation. As you move forward in your studies and careers, embrace the opportunity to conduct research that not only advances the field but also embodies the core values that make counseling a distinct and vital profession in the landscape of mental health care.

# 2

# Fixing the Potholes: Navigating the Challenges in Social Science

Research serves as the backbone for evidence-based practice and informs the ethical and effective treatment of clients. However, the research landscape in social science, yes even counseling, has some proverbial potholes, which make for a bumpy ride. Issues such as the replication crisis, the research–practice gap, idea laundering, and a hyperfocus on counselor experiences at the expense of client outcomes significantly impact the reliability and applicability of research findings. These challenges are not merely academic concerns; they have real-world implications for counseling practice. The replication crisis, for instance, has called into question the legitimacy of many foundational studies in psychology and counseling, potentially undermining the evidence base for common therapeutic approaches. Understanding these issues is crucial for counselors in training and practicing professionals alike. By critically examining the challenges in our field's research, we can become more discerning consumers and producers of research, make more informed clinical decisions, and ultimately provide better care for our clients.

## THE REPLICATION CRISIS

The replication crisis refers to researchers inability of many psychological studies, revealing problems in how research is conducted, reported, and interpreted. As counselors rely on these findings to guide their practice, the inability to replicate studies poses a challenge to the foundation of counseling as an evidence-based discipline (Open Science Collaboration, 2015). But I'm getting ahead of myself; I should probably explain what the replication crisis is first.

The replication crisis has something to do with researchers' inability to reproduce or replicate the findings of key studies that served as foundational pieces of knowledge in various fields, including psychology. If you can't replicate the findings of the study, it calls into question the legitimacy of the initial findings. The original study's findings may have been due to any number of systematic or random errors that are present in the research process. Findings found in only one study should be treated with great skepticism until replication studies have been done. That is one reason, among many for replication. Since I can't go into all the reasons why replication is important, please see Table 1 below for a quick overview.

**TABLE 1** 8 Reasons Why Replication Is Important

### 8 Reasons Why Replication Is Important

**Verification of findings:** Replication helps confirm that the original results were not due to chance, error, or unique circumstances. It increases confidence in the validity and reliability of research findings.

**Generalizability:** Successful replications across different contexts, populations, or settings demonstrate that findings are more broadly applicable and not limited to specific conditions of the original study.

**Detecting errors or fraud:** Replication can uncover mistakes, methodological flaws, or even fraudulent practices in the original research.

**Refining theories and methods:** Failed replications can lead to improvements in research methods, refinement of theories, or identification of important variables that weren't considered in the original study.

**Building cumulative knowledge:** Science progresses through the accumulation of replicated, reliable findings. Replication contributes to this process by solidifying or challenging existing knowledge.

**Informing practice:** In fields like counseling, where research informs clinical practice, replication ensures that interventions and approaches are based on robust, reproducible evidence.

**Addressing publication bias:** Replication studies can help counteract the tendency to publish only positive or novel findings, providing a more balanced view of research outcomes.

**Enhancing scientific credibility:** A culture of replication demonstrates the self-correcting nature of science, enhancing public trust and confidence in scientific findings.

A study conducted in 2015 found that only 36% of studies in the field of psychology were successfully replicated (Open Science Collaboration, 2015). The worry about replication extends to counseling research as well, where similar concerns about reproducibility have been raised (Heppner et al., 2016). Think of the ways nonreplicable research could have a ripple effect throughout the field of counseling. That research could find its way into textbooks, which will influence counselors in training. It could be the basis of further research, which wastes time and money and comes with opportunity costs since researchers could have been devoting their focus elsewhere. And lastly, faulty research may get caught in the cycle of idea laundering (another pothole we'll discuss later).

## WHAT THE REPLICATION CRISIS MEANS FOR COUNSELORS

The replication crisis in psychology, characterized by a significant proportion of studies that cannot be reliably replicated, casts a long shadow over the counseling field. We can't stand at a distance and say "That's psychology's problem, not ours." As we discussed in the last chapter, the counseling field grew out of the fields of psychiatry and then psychology. Much of counseling's theories, philosophies, interventions, and ethics are shaped by psychology. We cannot extricate ourselves from the historical influence of psychology on our field to avoid the replication crisis. The replication crisis is as much of a problem as it is for psychology, as it is for counseling. For instance, a study by Sakaluk et al. (2019) found that many popular psychological interventions have not been rigorously tested or replicated, potentially leading counselors to use techniques that may not be as effective as believed.

A systematic review of literature found that despite facing similar incentive structures, psychology (including the field of economics) exhibited different practices and approaches to replication. Psychology reported higher replication success rates, but these rates are likely inflated due to methodological and reporting issues (Hensel, 2021). This suggests a need for greater scrutiny and improvement in research practices within counseling to assess whether findings are reliable and applicable in practice. Beyond methodological and scientific issues, what lies at the heart of the replication crisis is ethics.

If practice is based on shaky research, the ethics of our practice is called into question. How can we, with any confidence, provide an evidence-based treatment, when the treatment is founded in questionable evidence? Are we really guarding client welfare? Are we really offering the best possible treatment? What if ineffectual treatment discourages a client and they drop out of counseling? What if it wastes time and money? Or what if the absence or delay of improvement due to ineffectual treatment worsens a mental health condition? And leads to a client relapsing, self-harming, or harming another?

Counselors conduct their practice within an ethical framework that emphasizes the client–counselor relationship, autonomy, and beneficence, making it crucial for research in counseling to reflect these core principles uniquely (Lenz, 2015). How can clients trust the results of the research which forms the basis of our practice, if we can't also trust our own research?

High-impact journals such as *Nature* and *Science* have brought the reproducibility of empirical findings into the spotlight, labeling the phenomenon as a "replication crisis" (Lösel, 2018). The spotlight on the issue of reproducibility is encouraging a broader conversation about the practices and methodologies in fields like criminology, psychology, and counseling. The crisis stems from various factors, including methodological flaws, biases in study designs, and the underreporting of null or negative findings (Munafò et al., 2017). In response to the crisis, some have called for developing enhanced methodologies, greater transparency, and increasing replication efforts across disciplines (Open Science Collaboration, 2015). But what do enhanced methodologies, transparency, and replication efforts mean for counseling? The replication crisis is just the tip of the iceberg. There are a number of other crucially important threats to the trustworthiness of social science.

## THE RESEARCH–PRACTICE GAP

Compounding the replication crisis is the research–practice gap, a divide between what research shows to be effective and what practices are actually implemented in clinical settings. This gap often results from the inaccessibility of research to practitioners, the perceived irrelevance of research findings to practical counseling scenarios, and the slow pace of translating research into practice. Bridging this gap is important for ensuring that the most current and effective therapies are available to clients (Beutler et al., 2016).

The research–practice gap in counseling has been well documented. A survey by Cook et al. (2017) found that only 47% of counselors reported regularly using evidence-based practices in their work. This disjunction can be attributed to several factors. First, the research literature can be complex and inaccessible (Horigian et al., 2016). Research journal articles are often behind paywalls, and supposing counselors invested the money into purchasing an article, the technical language may make it difficult for the counselor to understand the results and implications of those results to their practice. The second factor is time constraints in clinical practice (Beidas et al., 2016). Most counselors, if they are working full-time, see on average 35 clients or more. Those 35 client contact hours come with billing, documenting, scheduling, consulting, and supervising commitments. There simply is not enough time in the week to do what counselors need to do, on top of reading research articles.

Third, counselors may hold some skepticism about the relevance of research to individual clients (Lilienfeld et al., 2013). Potentially, and correctly, the research finding was based on a sample population who is not representative of the client a counselor is working with. Or, they feel dubious about the statistical analysis, unsure how the researcher reached their conclusion. Or, in more complex studies, the findings are nuanced and don't conclude with nice, neat, and straightforward results. There is insufficient training in interpreting and applying research findings. Research has also shown that time, motivation, and practice are also important factors in applying research to practice (Abu-Odah et al., 2022). Reading research articles is one thing, but knowing how to translate that finding into your own clinical practice is another thing.

## IDEA LAUNDERING

Idea laundering refers to the process by which unverified, nonempirical, or ideologically driven claims are published in academic journals and subsequently cited as if they are factual or scientifically validated truths. This phenomenon can occur through several mechanisms: the establishment of journals with low peer-review standards, echo chambers within certain academic communities, or the circumvention of rigorous scientific methodology in favor of advancing specific agendas. The impact of idea laundering is significant and complex, affecting both the broader field of social scientific research and specific disciplines like counseling (Dickersin, 2005; Joober et al., 2012).

The phenomenon of idea laundering is particularly problematic in counseling and psychology due to the field's reliance on theoretical constructs that can be difficult to empirically verify. For example, Lilienfeld et al. (2014) identified several widely accepted psychological interventions that lack strong empirical support, highlighting the need for more rigorous evaluation of therapeutic approaches.

The implications of idea laundering are particularly concerning due to the direct impact on client care and therapeutic outcomes. For example, if counseling practices are based on ideologically driven research that has bypassed rigorous empirical testing, there is a risk that these practices may be ineffective or, worse, harmful. Counselors relying on such research may use interventions that do not have a sound scientific basis, potentially leading to poor outcomes for clients (Lilienfeld et al., 2014). Furthermore, idea laundering can lead to a situation where counselors unknowingly adopt practices that are not truly evidence-based, thereby compromising their ethical commitments (Kaplan et al., 2014).

There are also ethical implications regarding resources, relative to practice and counselor training. When counseling practices informed by laundered ideas are implemented, resources (time, money, and effort) may be wasted on interventions that do not benefit clients. This not only affects individual client care but can also impact broader mental health services by diverting resources away from more effective treatments (Boisvert & Faust, 2006). Regarding counselor education, counseling students and new professionals may learn and internalize ineffective or misguided theories and practices if their education is influenced by laundered ideas. This can perpetuate a cycle of poor practice that is difficult to correct (Tracey et al., 2014).

## OVEREMPHASIS ON COUNSELOR EXPERIENCES IN COUNSELING RESEARCH

The predominance of counseling research focuses on counselors' perceptions and lived experiences. While it is important to understand the practitioner's viewpoint, counseling research is inundated with research that examines counselors perceptions, leaving rigorous investigation into client outcomes ignored. Richard Balkin, an educator, a journal editor, and a leading researcher in the field of counseling, said "I believe we are sorely lacking our clients' experiences in our research. The hyper-focus on our own perceptions—not of those in counseling, but those who are enrolled in graduate programs--at the expense of those we serve is not healthy, in my opinion" (private communication, 2022). This imbalance not only restricts the breadth of counselor education and practice but also hampers our understanding of what truly benefits clients within the therapeutic process.

Balkin's observation is supported by recent literature reviews. For instance, Yates et al. (2017) found that only 23% of articles published in major counseling journals focused primarily on client outcomes. Similarly, Wester and Wachter Morris (2018) noted a significant underrepresentation of client voices in counseling research, with most studies relying on counselor reports or standardized measures rather than on in-depth client perspectives.

The overrepresentation of research that focuses on counselor's experiences can lead to a research bias, where the subjective experiences of the practitioner are prioritized over objective, measurable client outcomes. This skew can result in a limited evidence base for what constitutes effective therapy, making it difficult for counselors to identify and apply the most effective treatments. It may also challenge the profession's ability to innovate and evolve therapeutic practices based on solid evidence (Wampold & Imel, 2015).

Research that does examine counseling outcomes, but still from the counselor's perspective, still runs the risk of being biased and dubious. A meta-analysis by Cooper (2008) found that studies focusing on counselor experiences tended to report more positive outcomes than those focusing on client-reported measures, suggesting a potential overestimation of treatment effectiveness when relying solely on counselor perspectives.

The primary ethical obligation of counselors is to benefit their clients and do no harm. A discipline overly focused on the experiences of its practitioners, rather than on those they serve, becomes narcissistic and risks compromising client outcomes. Counselors are at a disadvantage due to the dearth of client outcome research. This misalignment with ethical standards could lead to practices that, while enriching for the counselor, may not be in the best interest of the client or may overlook what is truly therapeutic (Kaplan et al., 2014). Furthermore, the American Counseling Association Code of Ethics (2014) emphasizes the importance of using techniques/procedures/modalities that are grounded in theory and/or have an empirical or a scientific foundation. An overconcentration on the counselor's perspective can detract from a truly client-centered practice. This shift away from the client's experience and needs may reduce the effectiveness of counseling and the potential for clients to achieve their therapeutic goals (Duncan et al., 2010). Research by Norcross and Lambert (2018) has shown that client factors and the therapeutic alliance account for a significant portion of therapy outcomes. However, again, an *overemphasis* on counselor experiences may lead to an *underemphasis* on these crucial client-centered factors.

## NARROWED EDUCATIONAL SCOPE

Counseling training programs rightly focus on developing self-awareness through self-reflection in order to better understand one's impact on the therapeutic relationship (Schmidt & Adkins, 2012). However, an education lacking a strong emphasis on measurable client outcomes may produce counselors less equipped to apply the most effective interventions (Wester, 2007). Counselors would do well to learn about the research that informs the models they practice and to learn why those models and interventions produce positive outcomes for clients. Additionally, they could learn how to use psychometrically validated instruments to measure client outcomes.

Research has shown that counselor education programs often prioritize counselor development over client outcomes. A study by Barden et al. (2017) found that only 35% of Council for Accreditation of Counseling and Related Educational Programs–accredited programs had a specific course dedicated to outcome research and evaluation. In comparison, the field of psychology puts a greater emphasis on practitioners' learning and following manualized treatments, where clinicians follow protocols. Part of the uniqueness of counseling is a conscious break with manualized treatments, yet there is something to learn from the field of psychology. Clinical psychologists are trained in the manualized treatments and the evidential basis for those treatments. They learn the *why* in addition to the *what.*

## PROFESSIONAL CREDIBILITY AND PUBLIC TRUST

The quality of counseling research also directly impacts the perception of counseling among the public and across other disciplines. We want counseling to be recognized for what it is, a science-based profession. However, we must demonstrate a commitment to rigorous research and evidence-based practice. A discipline that has poor replication, with a wide research–practice gap, based on faulty idea laundered research and weak research education, and that is more interested in introspecting than in focusing on client outcomes may struggle to maintain its professional credibility and public trust. This perception can impact the profession's ability to attract funding for research, influence policy, and expand its role within the broader health-care ecosystem (Laska et al., 2014). As Mellin et al. (2011) argued, the counseling profession's identity is closely tied to its ability to demonstrate effectiveness through empirical research. A lack of focus on client outcomes and evidence-based practices can lead to skepticism from other health-care professionals, policymakers, and the public.

Furthermore, public trust in mental health professions is crucial for our ability to affect social impact. A study by Jorm (2000) found that public beliefs about the effectiveness of mental health treatments significantly influence help-seeking behaviors. Therefore, maintaining and enhancing public trust through rigorous, outcome-focused research are essential for the counseling profession to effectively serve its clients and society at large.

## OTHER CONCERNS IN COUNSELING RESEARCH

There are two other concepts I want to make you aware of before discussing solutions. The first is *concept creep*, as described by Haslam (2016), which poses a unique challenge for counseling research. As psychological concepts expand over time to include milder phenomena, it can affect how we define and measure constructs central to counseling, such as trauma, anxiety, or resilience. For instance, what was once considered a normal life stressor might now be classified as trauma, potentially inflating prevalence rates and complicating comparisons across studies conducted at different time points (Levine & Safer, 2022). This expansion, while potentially increasing awareness and access to treatment, may also risk pathologizing normal human experiences (Lilienfeld, 2017). For counseling researchers, this means being vigilant about how constructs are defined and operationalized and being aware of how these definitions might have shifted over time.

The second issue is *jingle–jangle fallacies*, which highlight the importance of precise construct definition and measurement in counseling research (Block, 1995). The jingle fallacy, where different constructs are given the same name, can lead to false equivalences in research. For example, studies on "therapeutic alliance" might be measuring fundamentally different aspects of the client–therapist relationship, leading to inconsistent or contradictory findings (Marsh, 1994). Conversely, the jangle fallacy, where the same construct is given different names, can result in redundant research efforts and a fragmented literature base. This is particularly problematic in a field like counseling, where nuanced understanding of psychological constructs is crucial for effective intervention (Marsh et al., 2019).

These issues compound the challenges already present in counseling research, such as the difficulty in standardizing interventions across diverse client populations and the ethical constraints on experimental designs. They contribute to the broader problem of replication crisis and can hinder the development of a cohesive, evidence-based foundation for counseling practice (Weidman et al., 2017).

## SOLUTIONS AND FORWARD MOVEMENT

To address these challenges, the counseling profession must strive for a more balanced research agenda that equally values the insights from counselors' experiences and rigorous investigations into client outcomes, engages in replication research, and educates its students well.

This balance can be achieved by encouraging an increase in outcome-based research within counseling journals. While counselor experiences and perceptions are valuable, there needs to be a renewed emphasis on client outcomes and evidence-based practices in both research and clinical work (Norcross & Lambert, 2018). Please see Table 2 for information about a key counseling journal that publishes research about clinical outcomes. Journals could implement policies that prioritize studies focusing on client outcomes, and editors could actively solicit research that addresses gaps in outcome literature (Heppner et al., 2016; Wester & Wachter Morris, 2018).

**TABLE 2** Counseling Research Journal Highlight

| Counseling Research Journal Highlight |
|---|
| *The Counseling Outcome Research and Evaluation* (CORE) journal is a significant publication in the field of counseling. Published by SAGE Publications in partnership with the Association for Assessment and Research in Counseling (AARC), CORE is dedicated to advancing the science of counseling by publishing research on the outcomes and effectiveness of counseling approaches and programs. The journal encompasses a wide range of research methodologies, including quantitative, qualitative, and mixed methods studies. It covers topics such as counseling outcomes, program evaluation, methodological advancements, and innovations in counseling practice. CORE serves a diverse audience, including counselor educators, practitioners, researchers, and students in counseling and related mental health fields. Its primary goal is to bridge the gap between research and practice, providing evidence-based insights that can inform and improve counseling interventions. |

Developing training programs that emphasize evidence-based practices and the critical appraisal of research literature is also crucial. This can be accomplished by integrating more research methodology and critical thinking courses into counselor education programs and providing continuing education opportunities focused on research literacy and application (Umstead, 2019; Wester & Borders, 2014).

Fostering collaborations between researchers and practitioners is essential to evaluate whether research questions are relevant to practice and focused on client outcomes. This can be achieved by establishing practice–research networks to facilitate ongoing collaboration and encouraging practitioner involvement in research design and implementation (McLeod, 2016; Bager-Charleson, 2014).

In addition to greater collaboration, counseling training programs could improve the rigor of research training for counseling students, improving the research literacy among students. With the development of practice–research networks, the field can draw attention to new empirical findings that could inform clinical practice more effectively (Bager-Charleson, 2014). Improved training will encourage counselors to approach both research and practice with a critical, enquiring mindset that can help combat issues like idea laundering and the uncritical acceptance of unproven theories (Huber & Kuncel, 2016).

**TABLE 3** Counseling Research Journal Highlight

**Counseling Research Journal Highlight**

*The Measurement and Evaluation in Counseling and Development* (MECD) journal is another crucial publication in the counseling field. Also published by SAGE Publications in partnership with the Association for Assessment and Research in Counseling (AARC), MECD focuses specifically on issues related to assessment in counseling. This journal is devoted to the advancement of assessment practices, publishing articles that explore the development and use of assessment tools and techniques in counseling contexts. The content of MECD includes research on test development, validation studies, innovative assessment methods, and the practical application of assessment in various counseling settings. It caters to a readership of counselors, psychologists, educators, and other professionals interested in measurement and evaluation in counseling and related fields. MECD plays a vital role in ensuring that assessment practices in counseling are grounded in solid scientific research, contributing to more accurate and effective client evaluations and interventions.

It is important for counselors to not become siloed in their own field. Engaging with related fields such as psychology, social work, and neuroscience, counseling can broaden its perspectives and strengthen its research base (Kaplan & Gladding, 2011). Interdisciplinary research allows for new perspectives, theoretical paradigms, research questions, and viewpoints to strengthen our research processes.

Advocating for funding and support for large-scale, empirical studies focused on determining the effectiveness of specific therapeutic interventions is another important step. This involves engaging with policymakers to highlight the importance of counseling research and collaborating with other mental health professions to advocate for increased research funding (Kaplan & Gladding, 2011). Replication studies foster transparency in research processes, allowing the field to build a more reliable knowledge base (Munafò et al., 2017).

Establishing clear guidelines and ethical standards that prioritize client welfare and the importance of evidence-based practice is crucial. This can be accomplished by regularly updating ethical codes to reflect the latest research on best practices and developing and promoting practice guidelines based on robust research evidence (ACA, 2014; Kaplan et al., 2014). As the profession evolves, it must continually update its ethical guidelines to reflect the latest research findings and best practices, ensuring that client welfare remains at the forefront of all counseling activities (Kaplan et al., 2014).

## GRAB A SHOVEL

You, as a counselor in training, are positioned to effect change and make a significant contribution to counseling research. This small section on solutions is broad in focus, discussing what the field can do to fix the potholes. You might be wondering what you can do. You as a counselor in training are actually in a unique position to effect change and really address these challenges. Below are a few ideas where I think you can metaphorically grab a shovel, and start filling in the potholes:

First, cultivate a critical mindset. As you engage with research literature, don't simply accept findings at face value. Question methodologies, consider sample sizes, and look for potential biases. Analyze whether the study has been replicated or if it's just a one-off. If it is a one-off, don't immediately discount or accept the findings, but hold out for additional studies to replicate the findings. This critical approach will help you identify robust studies and recognize limitations in weaker ones.

Second, prioritize research literacy. Develop a strong foundation in research methods and statistical analysis. Evaluate whether the studies' claims are based on evidence or idea laundered claims. Furthermore, evaluate whether the findings of the study support the conclusions of the study. This knowledge will enable you not only to consume research more effectively but also to contribute to it. Consider taking additional courses or workshops in research design and analysis to bolster your skills.

Third, bridge the research–practice gap in your own work. As you begin your clinical practice, strive to integrate research findings into your approach. Simultaneously, document your observations and outcomes systematically. This practice-based evidence can provide valuable insights that complement traditional research.

Fourth, advocate for client-centered research. When you have the opportunity to participate in or conduct research, make sure that client outcomes and experiences are at the forefront. This focus can help shift the field toward more relevant and impactful studies. Understanding the counselor's experience and perspective is important, but there needs to be balance in counseling research.

Fifth, engage in replication efforts. As you progress in your career, consider participating in or initiating replication studies of important findings in the field. This contribution is crucial for building a more reliable knowledge base in counseling.

Sixth, practice transparency in your own research endeavors. If you conduct research, commit to open science practices such as preregistration of studies, sharing data when possible, and reporting all results, not just those that are statistically significant.

Seventh, collaborate across disciplines. Counseling can benefit greatly from insights in related fields such as psychology, neuroscience, and social work. Seek out interdisciplinary collaborations to bring fresh perspectives to counseling research.

Lastly, stay informed about evolving research practices and ethical guidelines. The field of research methodology is continually advancing, and staying current will help you contribute to and advocate for high-quality, ethical research in counseling.

## CONCLUSION

As we've explored throughout this chapter, the field of counseling faces significant challenges in its research practices and the application of research findings to clinical work. The replication crisis has called into question the reliability of many foundational studies in psychology and counseling, undermining confidence in the evidence base for many therapeutic approaches. The research–practice gap continues to be a persistent issue, with many counselors struggling to integrate current research findings into their clinical practice due to accessibility issues, time constraints, and perceived lack of relevance. Moreover, the phenomenon of idea laundering poses a serious threat to the integrity of counseling research and practice. It can lead to the propagation of unverified or ideologically driven ideas, potentially resulting in the adoption of ineffective or even harmful therapeutic practices.

These challenges are not insurmountable, but addressing them requires a concerted effort from all stakeholders in the counseling profession. Researchers must commit to more rigorous methodologies, increased transparency, and a focus on replication studies. Practitioners need to cultivate a stronger sense of research literacy and actively seek ways to incorporate evidence-based practices into their work. Educators must equip students with the skills to critically evaluate research and apply it effectively in clinical settings.

Furthermore, professional organizations and journal editors have a crucial role to play in maintaining high standards for research quality and relevance. They can promote practices such as preregistration of studies, open data sharing, and the publication of null results to combat publication bias.

Addressing challenges head-on, the counseling profession can strengthen its scientific foundation, enhance its credibility, and most importantly improve the quality of care provided to clients. As counselors, researchers, and educators, we have a responsibility to continually question, evaluate, and improve our practices. Only through this ongoing process of critical reflection and evidence-based improvement can we truly fulfill our commitment to promoting mental health and well-being in the communities we serve.

The progression toward more robust, reliable, and relevant counseling research is ongoing. It requires dedication, critical thinking, and a willingness to challenge established norms. However, the potential rewards—in terms of improved client outcomes, enhanced professional credibility, and the advancement of the field—make this endeavor not just worthwhile, but essential. As we move forward, let us commit to fostering a culture of scientific rigor, ethical practice, and client-centered care in counseling research and practice.

# 3

# Philosophical Foundations of Research Design

John and David Creswell, a father–son duo who are both leading researchers in their respective fields, said "Research approaches are philosophically based and stem from different scientific traditions" (Creswell & Creswell, 2018, p. 3). Research in counseling, like in all social sciences as Creswell and Creswell pointed out, is grounded in philosophical assumptions that shape how we approach knowledge, truth, and reality. Understanding these philosophical foundations matters for how we develop a coherent and an effective research design.

The philosophical grounding of research goes way beyond an intellectual exercise; it is the bedrock upon which all meaningful inquiry is built. Our philosophical stance informs every aspect of the research process, from the questions we ask to the methods we choose and the ways we interpret our findings. By understanding these foundations, counselors in training, learning to be researchers, can make sure that their work is not only methodologically sound but also philosophically coherent and ethically grounded. This assurance comes from having done "the work" and by that I mean you have explored the philosophical issues and more importantly reflected on your own personal philosophical precommitments. Self-awareness is important for the practice of counseling and conducting counseling research. To assist with this self-reflection, please take a moment to complete the self-inventory in Appendix C.

Additionally, as you read this chapter, think of Chapters 3 and 4 as being one unit: Chapter 3 focuses on the philosophical underpinning of the different research methodologies; Chapter 4 focuses on how to conduct research using the various methodologies. This chapter lays the groundwork for understanding the "why" behind different research approaches. It will explore the ontological and epistemological assumptions that guide our research, helping you to critically reflect on your own worldviews and how they might influence your research decisions. By the end of this chapter, you will have a solid foundation in the philosophical principles that underpin various research methodologies.

Chapter 4 will then build on this foundation, translating these philosophical concepts into practical research strategies. It will provide you with the tools and techniques to design and conduct research that is not only methodologically rigorous but also philosophically sound. Together, these two chapters will equip you with an understanding of both the theoretical underpinnings and practical applications of research in counseling.

## UNDERSTANDING DIFFERENT RESEARCH PARADIGMS

Research paradigms, models, theories, methodologies, and approaches hold an enormous sway over our perspectives, methodologies, and interpretations. These paradigms—positivism, post-positivism, interpretivism, critical theory, and constructivism, among others—come from philosophical traditions that offer unique lenses through which we view the world and approach our inquiries (Guba & Lincoln, 1994).

To illustrate, imagine a stage light shining down on a stage in a dark theater. The stage lights are doing exactly what they were designed to do, illuminate the object of focus. When the light is directed to shine on an object, it is by that choice NOT shining on other objects. There is, if you will, an opportunity cost inherent to research design. By choosing one design to capture information about a phenomenon, we are choosing to NOT capture data about a different phenomenon. And to go one step further, design also determines particular kinds of data about the phenomenon. Let's say, for example, there are 1,000 unique and different ways we can understand a phenomenon of interest, but we only have the instrumentation and the capacity to understand 10 of those 1000 ways. But, the problem is even worse than that. In a research project, for example, I can only choose one way. That leaves nine ways, nine aspects, or angles of the phenomenon that could be captured by other methodologies, unaccounted for. And that is important to acknowledge. In every study, there are limitations. With every design choice, there are trade-offs that come with strengths and weaknesses—opportunities and missed opportunities. And this is why we need lots of research, using different methodological tools in order to fully capture the complexity and dimensionality of a construct. So, let's talk about a stage light often used in social science that has to do with numbers and measurements of variables.

Quantitative research is a powerful tool, a stage light among many, for gathering information about the prevalence of a disorder in a population, the likelihood of someone relapsing, and how effective an intervention is, but there are certain valuable pieces of information, highly relevant to understand the human experience that lies just beyond that threshold.

Qualitative research, on the other hand, is designed to gather information about people's direct experiences and perception by gathering rich, dense, descriptive textual data (that may also include objects like photos, poems, and keepsakes). These data allow the participant to speak and to verbalize according to their understanding the *whys* and the *hows* of their experience. And so there is an important and a creative tension between these two approaches that are absolutely vital for gathering information, which covers the nuances and various facets of a phenomenon.

When all the various quantitative and qualitative facets of information are gathered, if the research is strong, the various stage lights will start to shine down on proximate areas of the stage. You will start to see an agreement between the different kinds of data, they will converge. That is to say, the various kinds of data, streaming in from different methodologies, will center on similar, robust descriptions of the human experience. The data will cohere in a tapestry of rich descriptive data directly from participants and outcome data from complex, multivariate quantitative research.

Hopefully, that gives you a sense of the *why* behind the need for different research methodologies and for understanding not only the methodological, but also the philosophical distinctives behind the various approaches to research. So, without further ado, let's jump right in starting with the philosophical underpinnings for quantitative research.

## PHILOSOPHICAL FRAMEWORKS TO RESEARCH

### POSITIVISM

Positivism, rooted in the scientific method, asserts that objective reality exists and can be measured and understood through empirical observation and logical reasoning (Aliyu et al., 2014). This paradigm emphasizes empirical evidence and measurable phenomena, advocating for a value-free, neutral stance of the researcher. Positivist research typically employs deductive reasoning and hypothesis testing. In counseling research, a positivist approach might involve using standardized assessments to measure the effectiveness of a specific intervention, assuming that the intervention's impact can be objectively quantified (Barkham et al., 2010). The positivist speaks the language of numbers and precisely defined constructs, assuming that what they see (observe and measure) corresponds with reality.

### POST-POSITIVISM

Post-positivism emerged as a response to criticisms of positivism, acknowledging that while an objective reality exists, our understanding of it is imperfect and probabilistic (Phillips & Burbules, 2000). This paradigm recognizes researcher bias and its potential impact on observations, emphasizing the importance of multiple measures and observations. Post-positivism also stresses the importance of falsifiability in scientific theories and often employs both qualitative and quantitative methods. A post-positivist counseling study might combine quantitative measures of therapeutic outcomes with qualitative interviews to gain a more comprehensive understanding of the therapy process (Ponterotto, 2005). The post-positivists also speak the language of numbers and precisely defined constructs, yet they recognize that what they see (observe and measure) is clouded by their own sociocultural perceptions (the researchers' situatedness) and biased instruments (error and method effects) so that what they observe may partially correspond with reality.

## INTERPRETIVISM

Interpretivism, also known as constructivism, posits that reality is socially constructed and that multiple realities can coexist based on individual experiences and interpretations (Schwandt, 1994). This paradigm focuses on understanding and interpreting human behavior, recognizing the researcher's role in coconstructing meaning. Interpretivist research emphasizes context and subjective experiences, primarily utilizing qualitative methodologies. An interpretivist approach in counseling research might involve in-depth interviews with clients to understand their unique experiences of the therapeutic process (McLeod, 2011). The interpretivist speaks the language of language, recognizing that words and their meanings are a product of social interactions with others, further recognizing that the mechanism by which we describe reality falsely assumes an objective relationship to reality, which in fact is culturally situated.

## CRITICAL THEORY

Critical theory focuses on critiquing and changing society, rather than on merely understanding or explaining it (Kincheloe & McLaren, 2011). This paradigm examines power structures and social inequalities, with an emancipatory goal of research. Critical theory often employs participatory and action-oriented methodologies, integrating theory and practice. A critical theory approach in counseling research might explore how societal power structures influence access to mental health services and work toward developing more equitable systems (Prilleltensky & Nelson, 2002). The critical theorist speaks the language of power, calling attention to how socially dominant groups protect the corpus of knowledge based on their political and economic interests, rather than an objective pursuit of the truth.

## PRAGMATISM

Pragmatism focuses on the practical consequences of research findings and the "what works" approach (Morgan, 2013). This paradigm emphasizes the research question over the method or paradigm, recognizing both singular and multiple realities. Pragmatism takes a value-oriented approach to research and often combines different research methods as needed. A pragmatic approach in counseling research might use whatever methods are best suited to answer the research question, potentially combining quantitative outcome measures with qualitative exploration of client experiences (Feilzer, 2010).

Understanding these paradigms is crucial for researchers as they inform the entire research process, from problem formulation to data interpretation. For example, a positivist approach might lead a researcher to conduct controlled experiments to test hypotheses, while an interpretivist approach might favor in-depth interviews or ethnographic studies to explore lived experiences (Creswell & Creswell, 2018). Please see Table 1 for an overview of each philosophical approach.

**TABLE 1**

| ASPECT | POSITIVISM | POST-POSITIVISM | INTERPRETIVISM | CRITICAL THEORY | PRAGMATISM |
|---|---|---|---|---|---|
| View of Reality | Objective reality exists and can be measured. | Objective reality exists, but our understanding is imperfect. | Reality is socially constructed; multiple realities exist. | Reality is shaped by social, political, cultural, and economic factors. | Both singular and multiple realities; focuses on practical consequences |
| Research Approach | Deductive; hypothesis testing | Deductive and inductive; falsification of hypotheses | Inductive; understanding and interpretation | Participatory; action-oriented | Mixed methods; "what works" approach |
| Researcher's Role | Neutral, value-free observer | Recognizes potential for bias | Coconstructor of meaning | Advocate for change | Value-oriented; adapts to research needs |
| Methodology | Primarily quantitative | Quantitative and qualitative | Primarily qualitative | Often participatory and qualitative | Mixed methods based on research question |
| Data Analysis | Statistical analysis; measurable phenomena | Statistical analysis with the recognition of probabilistic nature | Interpretive analysis; focus on context and subjective experiences | Analysis of power structures and inequalities | Varied, based on research question and chosen methods |
| Goal of Research | Explain and predict | Explain and predict with acknowledgment of limitations | Understand and interpret | Critique and transform | Solve problems; inform practice |

| | | | | | |
|---|---|---|---|---|---|
| Example in Counseling Research | Using standardized assessments to measure intervention effectiveness | Combining quantitative outcome measures with qualitative interviews | In-depth interviews to understand client experiences | Examining how societal power structures influence access to mental health services | Using mixed methods to answer specific research questions about therapy effectiveness |
| Language/ Perspective | Speaks the language of numbers and precisely defined constructs | Recognizes limitations in measurements and observations | Speaks the language of language; recognizes cultural situatedness | Speaks the language of power; critiques dominant knowledge structures | Focuses on practical outcomes and applications |

## ONTOLOGY, EPISTEMOLOGY, AND METHODOLOGY

To fully grasp the implications of different research paradigms, it is essential to understand three key philosophical concepts: ontology, epistemology, and methodology.

### ONTOLOGY

Ontology refers to the nature of reality and what can be known about it (Crotty, 1998). It asks questions like the following: Is there a single, objective reality, or are there multiple realities? Is reality fixed, or is it in constant flux? Different paradigms have different ontological positions. Positivism and post-positivism assume a single, objective reality, while interpretivism and constructivism assume multiple, socially constructed realities (Denzin & Lincoln, 2011). Critical theory assumes a reality shaped by social, political, cultural, and economic values (Kincheloe & McLaren, 2011).

In counseling research, ontological considerations might influence how a researcher conceptualizes mental health. A positivist might view mental health as an objective state that can be measured, thinking of how the medical field conceptualizes disease. Whereas an interpretivist might see it as a subjective experience that varies between individuals and cultures (Ponterotto, 2005), thinking of an anthropologist or a sociologist who studies cultures and different groups in how they make meaning.

## EPISTEMOLOGY

Epistemology concerns the nature of knowledge and how we can acquire it (Crotty, 1998). It addresses questions such as the following: What is the relationship between the knower and what can be known? How do we know what we know? Epistemological positions vary across paradigms. Positivism and post-positivism, for example, assume an objective, detached researcher stance (Guba & Lincoln, 1994). Researchers gather facts through the use of different tools. Interpretivism and constructivism assume that knowledge is cocreated between researcher and participants (Schwandt, 1994). From this point of view, the researcher and the participant collaborate or coconstruct "facts," and those facts are partially composed of the coconstruction, but are also shaped by the history, culture, and social situatedness of the researcher and the participant. Critical theory assumes that knowledge is mediated by power relations and should be used to empower the oppressed (Kincheloe & McLaren, 2011). The researcher comes from a particular social group, and that group occupies a privileged or an oppressed position in society. That privilege extends beyond economic and political power, but also to the means of producing and interpreting research facts.

In counseling research, epistemological considerations might influence how a researcher approaches data collection. A positivist might use standardized questionnaires to gather "objective" data, while an interpretivist might engage in in-depth interviews to coconstruct understanding with participants (Ponterotto, 2005). A critical theorist may view knowledge not as neutral but as something influenced by power dynamics in society. Therefore, research should have an emancipatory goal, aiming to empower marginalized groups. Counseling research from a critical theory view may pursue concrete actions or policy recommendations. The aim is to use research as a tool for social change and improved mental health services.

## METHODOLOGY

Methodology refers to the process and procedures of the research (Creswell & Poth, 2018). It is influenced by ontological and epistemological assumptions and addresses questions like the following: How can we go about acquiring knowledge? What procedures can we use to acquire knowledge? Methodological approaches vary across paradigms. Positivism and post-positivism often employ experimental or quasi-experimental designs (Shadish et al., 2002). Interpretivism and constructivism typically use qualitative methods like phenomenology or grounded theory (Charmaz, 2014). Critical theory often uses participatory action research or other emancipatory methodologies (Kemmis & McTaggart, 2005).

In counseling research, methodological considerations might influence the choice between a randomized controlled trial to test a new intervention (positivist) versus an in-depth case study to explore a client's therapeutic journey (interpretivist) (McLeod, 2010), for example.

Understanding these philosophical concepts helps researchers align their research design with their underlying assumptions about reality, knowledge, and how to acquire it. This alignment enhances the coherence and credibility of the research (Carter & Little, 2007).

**TABLE 2**

| ASPECT | POSITIVISM | POST-POSITIVISM | INTERPRETIVISM | CRITICAL THEORY | PRAGMATISM |
|---|---|---|---|---|---|
| Ontology (Nature of Reality) | Single, objective reality exists. | Single, objective reality exists, but our understanding is imperfect. | Multiple, socially constructed realities | Reality shaped by social, political, cultural, and economic values | Both singular and multiple realities; focuses on practical consequences |
| Epistemology (Nature of Knowledge) | Objective, detached researcher stance | Objective, detached researcher stance, but recognizes potential for bias | Knowledge is cocreated between the researcher and the participants. | Knowledge is mediated by power relations and should empower the oppressed. | Knowledge is derived from experience and should solve practical problems. |
| Methodology (Research Approach) | Experimental or quasi-experimental designs; quantitative methods | Experimental designs with recognition of limitations; may include qualitative methods | Qualitative methods like phenomenology or grounded theory | Participatory action research or other emancipatory methodologies | Mixed methods based on research question; "what works" approach |
| Example in Counseling Research | Randomized controlled trial to test a new intervention | Combining quantitative outcome measures with qualitative interviews to test and understand an intervention | In-depth case study to explore a client's therapeutic journey | Examining how societal power structures influence access to mental health services | Using mixed methods to answer specific research questions about therapy effectiveness |

## BEYOND QUALITATIVE VERSUS QUANTITATIVE RESEARCH

As you can see from the abovementioned discussion regarding the philosophical distinctions, researchers coming from different philosophical stances are often, but not always, critical of other approaches. The contention historically falls between qualitative and quantitative research. The debate between these two approaches has long been a cornerstone of scholarly discourse. However, it is increasingly recognized that these approaches are not mutually exclusive but can be complementary (Johnson & Onwuegbuzie, 2004). Understanding the strengths and limitations of each approach can help researchers make informed decisions about their research design.

## QUANTITATIVE RESEARCH

Quantitative research emphasizes measurement, objectivity, and statistical analysis (Creswell & Creswell, 2018). If you were to imagine a spectrum, quantitative research would harmonize with the philosophical traditions of *naive realism*, *structural realism*, and *critical realism* that assumes one reality experienced universally by all (Moon & Blackman, 2014). In practice, it is characterized by large sample sizes, standardized data collection methods, statistical analysis, and generalizability of findings. The strengths of quantitative research include its ability to test hypotheses and establish causal relationships and to generalize findings to larger populations and replicability of studies (Shadish et al., 2002). However, it also has limitations, such as potential oversimplification of complex phenomena, limited ability to capture context and subjective experiences, and the risk of overlooking important variables not included in the study design (Yilmaz, 2013).

In counseling research, quantitative methods are often used to measure the effectiveness of interventions, examine relationships between variables (e.g., the correlation between attachment style and relationship satisfaction), or track changes in symptoms over time (Barkham et al., 2010). For instance, a researcher might use a standardized depression inventory to measure the impact of a new cognitive behavioral therapy protocol on depressive symptoms across a large sample of clients (Hunsley & Lee, 2007).

## QUALITATIVE RESEARCH

Qualitative research focuses on understanding the depth and complexity of human experiences (Denzin & Lincoln, 2011). Going back to the imaginary spectrum, you would final qualitative research on the opposite side, harmonizing with the philosophical traditions of *bounded relativism* and *relativism*, which assumes that multiple realities are experienced by individual subjects and groups (Moon & Blackman, 2014). In practice, it typically involves small, purposefully selected samples; in-depth, open-ended data collection methods; inductive analysis; and rich, detailed descriptions. The strengths of qualitative research include its ability to capture complex, nuanced experiences, flexibility to explore unexpected findings, and deep understanding of context and meaning (Patton, 2015). However, it also has limitations, including limited generalizability, potential for researcher bias, and time-intensive data collection and analysis processes (Yilmaz, 2013).

In counseling research, qualitative methods are often used to explore clients' experiences of therapy, understand the process of change, or investigate complex phenomena like resilience and post-traumatic growth (McLeod, 2011). For example, a researcher might conduct in-depth interviews with clients who have successfully overcome addiction to understand their personal journeys and the factors that contributed to their recovery (Morrow, 2005).

## MOVING BEYOND THE DICHOTOMY

Rather than viewing qualitative and quantitative research as opposing approaches, many researchers now recognize them as complementary (Teddlie & Tashakkori, 2009). Each approach has its strengths and can address different aspects of research questions. For example, in studying the effectiveness of a new counseling intervention, quantitative methods could measure changes in symptoms and functioning, while qualitative methods could explore how clients experienced the intervention and what aspects they found most helpful. By combining these approaches, researchers can gain a more comprehensive understanding of the intervention's impact (Hanson et al., 2005).

Moreover, the distinction between qualitative and quantitative research is not always clear-cut. Many researchers argue for a continuum rather than a dichotomy, recognizing that elements of both approaches can be present in a single study (Johnson & Onwuegbuzie, 2004). This perspective has paved the way for the development of mixed-methods research, which we'll explore in the next section. For a breakdown of the distinctions between quantitative and qualitative research, see Table 3.

**TABLE 3**

| ASPECT | QUANTITATIVE RESEARCH | QUALITATIVE RESEARCH |
|---|---|---|
| Focus | Measurement, objectivity, statistical analysis | Understanding depth and complexity of human experiences |
| Sample Size | Large | Small, purposefully selected |
| Data Collection | Standardized methods | In-depth, open-ended methods |
| Analysis | Statistical analysis | Inductive analysis |
| Results | Generalizability of findings | Rich, detailed descriptions |
| Strengths | Tests hypotheses and establishes causal relationships<br>Generalizes findings to larger populations<br>Ensures replicability of studies | Captures complex, nuanced experiences<br>Flexible to explore unexpected findings<br>Provides deep understanding of context and meaning |
| Limitations | Potential oversimplification of complex phenomena<br>Limited ability to capture context and subjective experiences<br>Risk of overlooking important variables not included in study design | Limited generalizability<br>Potential for researcher bias<br>Time-intensive data collection and analysis processes |
| Example in Counseling Research | Using a standardized depression inventory to measure the impact of a new cognitive behavioral therapy protocol on depressive symptoms across a large sample of clients | Conducting in-depth interviews with clients who have successfully overcome addiction to understand their personal journeys and factors contributing to recovery |

## MIXED-METHODS RESEARCH: THE BEST OF BOTH WORLDS

Mixed-methods research has emerged as a "third paradigm" that integrates quantitative and qualitative approaches (Johnson & Onwuegbuzie, 2004). This approach recognizes the value of both numerical and narrative data in understanding complex phenomena.

## DEFINING MIXED-METHODS RESEARCH

Creswell and Plano Clark (2018) defined mixed-methods research as a design that collects and analyzes both qualitative and quantitative data, integrates the two forms of data, and uses distinct designs that may involve philosophical assumptions and theoretical frameworks. The goal of mixed-methods research is to draw on the strengths of both quantitative and qualitative approaches to provide a more comprehensive understanding of the research problem than either approach alone could offer (Teddlie & Tashakkori, 2009).

## PHILOSOPHICAL UNDERPINNINGS OF MIXED METHODS

The philosophical underpinnings of mixed methods allow for flexibility and adaptability in research design. Mixed methods often adopt a pragmatic ontological stance, which allows for both singular and multiple realities. Instead of saying it is one or the other, in a philosophical sense, mixed methods research says "both/and." This approach acknowledges that there may be a single reality (as in post-positivism) for some research questions, while accepting multiple, constructed realities (as in constructivism) for others. Mixed methods research typically embraces both objective and subjective knowledge. It recognizes that some knowledge can be objectively measured, while other forms of knowledge are subjectively constructed. This aligns with the pragmatic view that different types of knowledge are valuable depending on the research question.

Pragmatism is the most common philosophical orientation for mixed-methods research. The pragmatic approach focuses on "what works" to answer research questions, rather than adhering strictly to one paradigm. It allows researchers to use both deductive (typically quantitative) and inductive (typically qualitative) reasoning. Mixed methods, by definition, combine quantitative and qualitative methodologies. This integration can occur at various stages of the research process—data collection, analysis, or interpretation.

## TYPES OF MIXED-METHODS DESIGNS

There are several common mixed-methods designs. The *convergent parallel design* involves collecting quantitative and qualitative data concurrently, analyzing them separately, and then merging the results (Creswell & Plano Clark, 2018). The *explanatory sequential design* begins with quantitative data collection and analysis, followed by qualitative data collection and analysis to help explain the quantitative results (Ivankova et al., 2006). Conversely, the *exploratory sequential design* starts with qualitative data collection and analysis, informing the subsequent quantitative phase (Morgan, 2013).

Other designs include the *embedded design*, where one dataset provides a supportive, secondary role in a study based primarily on the other data type; the *transformative design*, which uses a theoretical lens (e.g., feminist theory) as an overarching perspective within a design that collects both quantitative and qualitative data; and the multiphase design, which combines concurrent and/or sequential strategies in multiple phases of a study (Creswell & Plano Clark, 2018).

### STRENGTHS AND CHALLENGES OF MIXED-METHODS RESEARCH

Mixed-methods research offers several strengths. It provides a more comprehensive understanding of research problems, allows for triangulation of findings, can offset weaknesses of single methods, and provides stronger evidence for conclusions (Johnson et al., 2007). However, it also presents challenges. It requires expertise in both quantitative and qualitative methods, can be time-consuming and resource-intensive, may be challenging to integrate different types of data, and has the potential for conflicting results between methods (Teddlie & Tashakkori, 2009).

### APPLICATION IN COUNSELING RESEARCH

Mixed-methods research is particularly valuable in counseling, where understanding both the measurable outcomes and the lived experiences of clients is crucial (Hanson et al., 2005). For example, a mixed-methods study on the effectiveness of group therapy for depression might use quantitative measures to track changes in depression symptoms over time, conduct qualitative interviews to understand participants' experiences of the group and what aspects they found most helpful, and then integrate these findings to provide a comprehensive evaluation of the therapy's effectiveness and mechanisms of change (Barkham et al., 2010).

By leveraging both quantitative and qualitative data, such a study can provide rich insights that inform both theory and practice in counseling. This approach allows researchers not only to determine whether an intervention is effective but also to understand why and how it works, providing valuable information for refining and improving counseling practices (Lewin et al., 2009).

## THINKING PHILOSOPHICALLY WHEN CHOOSING A RESEARCH DESIGN

Selecting the most appropriate research design is a crucial decision that shapes the entire research process. This choice should be guided by several factors, including the nature of the research question, the purpose of the research, the researcher's philosophical stance, and practical considerations (Creswell & Creswell, 2018). However, it is paramount to understand that while we are exploring various approaches to research design in Chapters 3 and 4, and aiming to help you find a methodology that aligns with your philosophical stance and comfort level (please take a moment to take the self-inventory in Appendix C), there are a number of factors that determine which research design you should choose, the first being the research question itself.

## RESEARCH QUESTION

The pursuit of truth and knowledge is the fundamental goal of research, and the methodology that is best suited to address the research question should take precedence over personal preferences or philosophical leanings. A well-crafted research question serves as the North Star of any study, guiding all subsequent methodological decisions. It defines what you're trying to understand, measure, or explore, and therefore, it should be the primary factor in determining how you go about conducting your research. The nature of the research question is the primary factor in determining the appropriate design (Bryman, 2006).

For instance, if your research question seeks to understand the lived experiences of individuals dealing with a specific phenomenon, a qualitative approach such as phenomenology might be most appropriate, regardless of whether you personally feel more comfortable with quantitative methods. Conversely, if your question aims to test a specific hypothesis about the relationship between variables across a large population, a quantitative approach would likely be more suitable, even if you typically lean toward interpretive paradigms.

So, for example, if your research question aims to test a hypothesis or establish a causal relationship, quantitative methods might be more suitable. A question like "Does cognitive behavioral therapy reduce symptoms of anxiety more effectively than mindfulness-based stress reduction?" would typically call for a quantitative approach, possibly an experimental or a quasi-experimental design (Shadish et al., 2002).

Some research questions require both breadth and depth of understanding, suggesting a mixed-methods approach (Tashakkori & Teddlie, 2010). For example, "How effective is a new online counseling platform for treating depression, and what factors contribute to its effectiveness?" This question could be addressed through a combination of quantitative outcome measures and qualitative exploration of user experiences.

It is also worth noting that many complex research questions may require a mixed-methods approach, combining elements of both qualitative and quantitative research. The key is to let the question drive the method, not vice versa. Forcing a preferred method onto a research question that it is not suited for can lead to flawed results and missed opportunities for genuine insight.

While your philosophical stance and methodological preferences are important and can inform your research approach, they should not constrain your ability to address your research question effectively. As a researcher, it is necessary to be flexible and open to using whatever methods are best suited to answer your specific question, even if it means stepping out of your comfort zone or learning new skills.

## PURPOSE OF THE RESEARCH

The second factor in determining which research design you should choose is the aim of the study. Exploratory research, for example, which seeks to discover new insights, often uses qualitative methods (Patton, 2015). Let's take a closer look at an example. A study exploring the experiences of counselors working with clients during a global pandemic might use in-depth interviews or focus groups to uncover new themes and challenges.

Descriptive research, aiming to profile a phenomenon, might use quantitative or mixed methods (De Vaus, 2001). A study describing the prevalence and characteristics of anxiety disorders among college students could use surveys (quantitative) supplemented by interviews (qualitative) for a more comprehensive picture.

Explanatory research, seeking to explain relationships between variables, often uses quantitative or mixed methods (Punch, 2013). A study investigating the relationship between childhood attachment styles and adult relationship satisfaction might use quantitative measures of attachment and relationship quality, possibly supplemented by qualitative interviews to explore the nuances of this relationship.

## PHILOSOPHICAL STANCE

Third, you must consider your own philosophical stance. That's right, you have to engage in some self-reflection and analyze your own presuppositions. We're familiar with this process when it comes to counseling, understanding the culture, worldview, and background that informs perspective, but we must also do so with research. We have to reflect on our ontological and epistemological beliefs in order to determine whether they are aligned with our research questions and chosen methodology (Carter & Little, 2007). For example, a researcher who believes that depression is an entity that can be objectively measured and quantified might choose to use standardized depression inventories in a large-scale survey and would likely be working from positivist assumptions (Beck et al., 1996).

A view of reality as multiple and constructed aligns with qualitative methods (Denzin & Lincoln, 201_). A researcher who believes that the experience of depression is deeply personal and culturally influenced might choose to conduct in-depth interviews or ethnographic research to explore these subjective experiences (Kleinman, 2004).

A pragmatic stance might lead to mixed methods (Morgan, 2013). A researcher who believes that both objective measures and subjective experiences are valuable in understanding a phenomenon might choose to combine quantitative and qualitative methods to gain a more comprehensive understanding.

Table 4 illustrates how these philosophical paradigms typically align with quantitative and qualitative approaches, providing a framework for understanding the interplay between a researcher's worldview and their methodological choices. It is important to note, however, that these alignments are not rigid; researchers may choose methods that best suit their specific research questions, sometimes diverging from traditional paradigm-method associations.

**TABLE 4**

| RESEARCH PARADIGM | TYPICAL METHODOLOGICAL ALIGNMENT | RATIONALE |
|---|---|---|
| Positivism | Strongly aligned with quantitative | Emphasis on objective measurement and statistical analysis aligns with positivist belief in single, knowable reality |
| Post-positivism | Primarily quantitative, may include qualitative | Recognizes limitations in measurements, may use qualitative methods to supplement quantitative data |
| Interpretivism | Strongly aligned with qualitative | Focus on subjective experiences and multiple realities aligns with qualitative methods |
| Critical Theory | Primarily qualitative, may include quantitative | Emphasis on power structures and societal change often requires in-depth qualitative exploration, but may use quantitative data to support arguments |
| Pragmatism | Mixed methods (both quantitative and qualitative) | "What works" approach allows for flexible combination of methods based on research question |

## RESPONDING AND REDIRECTING TYPICAL STUDENT RESPONSES

I've had many counseling students, when discussing quantitative research, who say they can't imagine how the methodology is at all useful. They'd rather hear someone's story and learn about their experiences. To them, quantitative research seems so cold and impersonal. To these students, I applaud them sharing their honest reaction, and instead of making it my mission to convince them they are wrong, and that quantitative is superior, or to at least consider mixed methods, I gladly direct them to the *Qualitative Inquiry and Research Design: Choosing Among Five Approaches* by Creswell and Poth. They are demonstrating a self-awareness that is absolutely vital to be an effective researcher. Some research methods you simply will not agree with based on philosophical considerations. In those cases, I encourage students to pursue what they agree with, with an open mind: to at least learn about the approach they disagree with to understand why.

On the other hand, I've experienced students who have equal and opposite reactions—who say that merely listening to one person's story doesn't shed much of any light on a psychological phenomenon. They'd rather see the empirical evidence, rather than that subjective narrative, that supports whether X effects Y. Again, rather than trying to convince them that quantitative is inferior to qualitative, I direct them to *Quantitative Research in Counseling: A Primer on Research Methods and Analysis* by Jason T. Lambie and Glenn W. Lambie, for example. I would praise their philosophical self-awareness in their identification of what they agree with and feel strongly about, and encourage them to learn everything they can about the approach they resonate with, than going on a crusade to convince them of something they have philosophical issues. I'd rather use Socratic questions, and education, to encourage an open mind and to assist them with understanding what they disagree with and why. For those who have a strong reaction to mixed methods, they seem to see a place for both quantitative and qualitative research, and I typically point them in the direction of *A Concise Introduction to Mixed Methods Research* by John W. Creswell.

## CONCLUSION

Research design in counseling is a complex and an evolving field, shaped by philosophical assumptions, methodological innovations, ethical considerations, and interdisciplinary influences. By understanding the range of available approaches and carefully considering the alignment between research questions, methods, and theoretical frameworks, researchers can design studies that contribute meaningfully to both the science and practice of counseling (Heppner et al., 2016).

The philosophical foundations discussed in this chapter, from positivism to critical theory, provide the bedrock upon which research designs are built. These paradigms influence not only how we conceptualize reality and knowledge but also how we approach the research process itself (Guba & Lincoln, 1994). As counseling researchers, it is crucial to reflect on our own philosophical stances and how they shape our research choices. The traditional dichotomy between qualitative and quantitative research has generated nuanced understanding of these approaches as complementary rather than oppositional (Johnson & Onwuegbuzie, 2004), where multiple lines of evidence, from different research methodologies, converge on one phenomenon, offering a multifaceted, multidimensional perspective. Mixed-methods research, in particular, offers exciting possibilities for addressing complex research questions in counseling, allowing for both breadth and depth of understanding (Creswell & Plano Clark, 2018).

Ethical considerations, as we've seen, must be at the forefront of research design in counseling. The sensitive nature of counseling research, often involving vulnerable populations, necessitates a thorough understanding and application of ethical principles throughout the research process (ACA, 2014). From informed consent to data protection, ethical considerations should inform every stage of research design and implementation.

Keep in mind that there is no one-size-fits-all approach to research design. The key is to thoughtfully consider your research goals, the nature of your research question, and the context in which you're working and to choose methods that best address these factors. The field of counseling research is rich with possibilities. By understanding philosophical foundations of our research methods, employing rigorous and innovative research approaches, maintaining high ethical standards, and remaining open to interdisciplinary perspectives, we can continue to advance both the science and practice of counseling. As researchers, our ultimate goal should be to produce knowledge that not only contributes to academic discourse but also improves the lives of those we seek to help through counseling (Wampold & Imel, 2015). As you apply the principles and approaches discussed in this chapter, you join a community of scholars and practitioners dedicated to enhancing the field of counseling through thoughtful, rigorous, and impactful research.

# 4

# Navigating the Methodological Pathways

In the previous chapter, we explored the philosophical foundations that underpin research methods. We explored the ontological, epistemological, and methodological considerations that shape our approach to knowledge, truth, and reality. This exploration of the "what" and "why" of research methodologies sets the stage for moving from the abstract into the practical aspects, focusing our attention to the "how," "where," and "who" of research. This chapter aims to guide you through the practical aspects of various research methodologies, providing a roadmap for designing and conducting studies. We will bridge the gap between philosophical understanding and practical application, translating theoretical concepts into concrete research strategies.

As we discussed in Chapter 3, the choice of methodology is intrinsically linked to the nature of the research question and the philosophical stance of the researcher. There is a degree of self-exploration and self-awareness necessary in order to be an effective counseling researcher regarding your personal philosophical presuppositions discussed in Chapter 3 and in a broader sense the philosophical commitments attached to the professional counselor identity discussed in Chapter 1. Understanding these connections is crucial for making informed decisions that align philosophical foundations, research goals, and meaningful contributions to the field of counseling.

Specifically, this chapter will explore quantitative, qualitative, and mixed-methods approaches. For each, we will detail specific research designs and provide step-by-step guidance for implementation. We'll explore data collection techniques, sampling strategies, and data analysis methods. Throughout, I'll point out considerations for safeguarding research quality and maintaining ethical integrity.

# QUANTITATIVE RESEARCH METHODS

Quantitative research in counseling focuses on measuring variables, testing hypotheses, and identifying patterns or causal relationships through statistical analysis. This approach is particularly useful when seeking to generalize findings to larger populations or when aiming to establish the effectiveness of specific interventions (Creswell & Creswell, 2018). There are, though, varying degrees of causality that can be established by the design we use.

## EXPERIMENTAL DESIGNS

Experimental designs are seen as the gold standard in determining the causal relationships between variables. In counseling research, these designs often involve comparing the effects of different interventions or treatments. But when we say causal relationship, what do we mean? Causation refers to the idea that changes in one variable (the independent variable) directly lead to changes in another variable (the dependent variable). Unlike correlational studies, which can only show that variables are related, experimental designs allow researchers to manipulate the independent variable and observe its effects on the dependent variable while controlling for other factors.

This ability to demonstrate causation is crucial in counseling research, as it allows us to determine whether specific interventions or treatments actually cause improvements in client outcomes. For example, an experimental design might randomly assign clients to either a new therapy technique or a control condition, allowing researchers to conclude that any observed differences in outcomes are caused by the therapy itself, rather than by other factors.

However, it is important to note that establishing true causation requires meeting several conditions. The conditions below (partial list) were first developed in 1965 by Sir Austin Bradford Hill:

1. *Temporal precedence*: The cause (independent variable) must occur before the effect (dependent variable).
2. *Covariation*: Changes in the independent variable must be associated with changes in the de-*pendent variable.*
3. *Nonspuriousness*: The relationship between the variables must not be better explained by other factors.

Experimental designs, particularly randomized controlled trials (RCTs), are specifically structured to meet these conditions, making them powerful tools for establishing causal relationships in counseling research.

*Randomization* is a key element of experimental designs, particularly in randomized controlled trials (RCTs). It involves the *random assignment* of participants to different treatment conditions or groups within the study. This process helps ensure that each participant has an equal chance of being placed in any group, reducing the likelihood of systematic differences between groups that could influence the results.

The primary purpose of randomization is to control for potential confounding variables, both known and unknown. By randomly distributing these variables across groups, researchers can be more confident that any observed differences in outcomes are due to the experimental manipulation rather than preexisting group differences.

Randomization strengthens the internal validity of a study, allowing researchers to make stronger causal inferences about the relationship between the independent and dependent variables. It is a powerful tool in counseling research for evaluating the effectiveness of interventions, as it helps isolate the impact of the treatment being studied from other factors that might influence client outcomes.

RCTs randomly assign participants to experimental and control groups, minimizing the influence of confounding variables. For example, a study comparing the efficacy of cognitive behavioral therapy (CBT) versus mindfulness-based stress reduction (MBSR) for treating anxiety would randomly assign participants to a CBT group, an MBSR group, or a control group (Hofmann et al., 2010).

### Key considerations for experimental designs

- True randomization to create equivalent groups and reduce selection bias
- Controlling for potential confounding variables through study design and statistical analysis
- Addressing ethical concerns about withholding treatment from control groups, such as using wait-list controls or standard treatment comparison groups
- Maintaining treatment fidelity across experimental conditions
- Determining appropriate sample size to achieve adequate statistical power
- Minimizing attrition and handling missing data appropriately
- Considering the generalizability of findings to real-world settings

## QUASI-EXPERIMENTAL DESIGNS

When true randomization is not feasible or ethical, quasi-experimental designs offer an alternative. These designs lack random assignment but still aim to establish causal relationships. Quasi-experimental designs have elements of observational research with experimental research. For example, a researcher may work with individuals or groups in a community, introducing an educational program (experimental element, since the educational program was not previously present in the community without the researcher's intervention), yet the researcher is not randomly assigning who joins the educational program (observational element). The researcher may gather data from the participants in the education program and can make within-group comparisons or between-group comparisons if he were to also gather data from the community members who did not receive the educational program. This design has strong external validity (generalizability) since the setting is the representative of real life (as opposed to an artificial laboratory setting), yet there is less control; therefore, the internal validity is weakened. There are many quasi-experimental designs to consider, for example:

*Nonequivalent Group Designs*: This approach compares naturally occurring groups. For instance, a study might compare the outcomes of students who voluntarily participate in a school counseling program with those who do not (Cook & Campbell, 1979).

*Time-Series Designs*: These designs involve multiple observations before and after an intervention. For example, a researcher might measure anxiety levels in clients multiple times before, during, and after a new therapy intervention to assess its impact over time (Kazdin, 2020).

**Key considerations for quasi-experimental designs**

- Selecting appropriate comparison groups that are as similar as possible to the treatment group
- Controlling for preexisting differences between groups through matching or statistical adjustment
- Addressing potential threats to internal validity, such as history and maturation effects
- Considering the trade-offs between internal and external validity
- Using multiple baseline designs or interrupted time series when appropriate
- Interpreting results cautiously, acknowledging the limitations of causal inference

## OBSERVATIONAL RESEARCH DESIGNS

Observational research is where researchers systematically observe and record behavior, events, or phenomena in their natural setting without direct intervention. This approach allows for the study of subjects in real-world contexts, providing insights that may not be accessible through other research methods. In observational research, data collection typically occurs in the subject's natural environment, with researchers taking a noninterventional stance (so no experimental elements). Observations are conducted and recorded in a structured, consistent manner, although the approach can be flexible, ranging from highly structured to more open-ended formats, and may involve participant or nonparticipant observation. This method yields rich, detailed data about behavior and interactions, capturing contextual information that might be missed in more controlled settings (helpful for external validity). Observational research can be particularly valuable in counseling for studying client–therapist interactions, group dynamics in therapy sessions, or behavioral patterns related to mental health conditions. However, researchers must be mindful of potential observer bias and ethical considerations, especially regarding privacy and consent. While powerful on its own, observational research can also be combined with other research approaches to provide a comprehensive understanding of the phenomena under study.

*Survey Research:* Survey research is widely used in counseling to gather data on attitudes, behaviors, and characteristics of large populations. This method can be cross-sectional (data collected at one point in time) or longitudinal (data collected over an extended period). For instance, a national survey on counselor job satisfaction might explore factors such as work environment, client load, and professional development opportunities (Mullen et al., 2018).

*Correlational Studies:* Correlational research examines relationships between variables without manipulating them. While this approach cannot establish causation, it can identify important associations and patterns. For example, a study might explore the relationship between attachment styles and therapeutic alliance in counseling sessions (Mallinckrodt et al., 1995). Researchers could use standardized measures of attachment and therapeutic alliance, calculating correlation coefficients to determine the strength and direction of the relationship.

**Key considerations for observational research**

- Clearly defining the population and sampling frame
- Addressing potential sources of bias, such as selection bias and information bias
- Controlling for confounding variables through study design and statistical analysis
- Considering the temporal sequence of exposure and outcome in cohort studies
- Addressing recall bias in case–control studies
- Using appropriate statistical methods to analyze observational data
- Interpreting associations cautiously, avoiding causal language when not warranted

## EXPERIMENTAL, QUASI-EXPERIMENTAL, AND OBSERVATIONAL RESEARCH: BALANCING VALIDITY, CAUSATION, AND GENERALIZABILITY

Experimental, quasi-experimental, and observational studies each offer unique approaches to understanding phenomena, with varying degrees of control over variables and different strengths in establishing causal relationships and generalizability (Shadish et al., 2002). Experimental designs, characterized by random assignment of participants to conditions, offer the strongest basis for causal inference (RCTs) (Cartwright, 2007). By controlling for confounding variables through randomization, these designs maximize internal validity—the extent to which we can confidently attribute observed effects to the manipulated variable (Campbell & Stanley, 1963). However, the highly controlled nature of experiments can sometimes limit their external validity or generalizability to real-world settings (Jiménez-Buedo & Miller, 2010). See Table 1 below to know about the internal validity issue related to the selected samples. The randomization of selection and assignment in experimental design eliminates that concern.

TABLE 1

| TYPE OF VALIDITY | THREAT | DESCRIPTION | EXAMPLE |
|---|---|---|---|
| Internal Validity | History | External events occurring between pretest and posttest | A major news event affecting participants' stress levels during a stress reduction study |
| Internal Validity | Maturation | Natural changes in participants over time | Cognitive development in children during a long-term educational intervention study |
| Internal Validity | Testing | Effects of taking a pretest on posttest scores | Participants becoming familiar with anxiety measures in a therapy effectiveness study |
| Internal Validity | Instrumentation | Changes in measurement instruments or observers | Using different raters for pre- and postintervention assessments |
| Internal Validity | Statistical regression | Tendency of extreme scores to regress toward the mean | Selecting participants with very high depression scores for an intervention study |
| Internal Validity | Selection | Differences between groups prior to the study | Self-selection bias in volunteering for a weight loss program |
| Internal Validity | Experimental mortality | Differential loss of participants from comparison groups | Higher dropout rates in a more intensive therapy condition |
| External Validity | Population validity | Limited generalizability to other populations | Studying college students and generalizing to all adults |
| External Validity | Ecological validity | Limited applicability to real-world settings | Conducting a therapy study in a highly controlled laboratory environment |
| External Validity | Temporal validity | Limited generalizability across time | Studying coping strategies during a pandemic and generalizing to nonpandemic times |
| Construct Validity | Inadequate preoperational explication | Poor definition or measurement of constructs | Using a single-item measure for a complex construct like "well-being" |
| Construct Validity | Mono-operation bias | Using only one operationalization of a construct | Measuring depression solely through self-report questionnaires |
| Statistical Conclusion Validity | Low statistical power | Insufficient sample size to detect true effects | Conducting a study with too few participants to detect small effect sizes |
| Statistical Conclusion Validity | Violated assumptions of statistical tests | Using tests that are inappropriate for the data | Using parametric tests with non-normally distributed data |

Quasi-experimental designs, which lack random assignment but still involve manipulation of an independent variable, occupy a middle ground (Cook & Campbell, 1979). While they may have lower internal validity than true experiments due to potential confounds, they often have higher external validity as they're frequently conducted in more naturalistic settings (Shadish et al., 2002).

Observational studies, including correlational research, have the lowest capacity for establishing causation but often excel in external validity (Rosenbaum, 2002). These studies examine phenomena as they naturally occur, potentially offering high generalizability, but limited ability to rule out alternative explanations for observed relationships (Grimes & Schulz, 2002).

The evidentiary strength for causation generally decreases from experimental to quasi-experimental to observational designs (Concato et al., 2000). However, this hierarchy doesn't necessarily hold for generalizability. An observational study in a real-world setting might offer more generalizable findings than a tightly controlled laboratory experiment, despite its lower ability to establish causation (Rothwell, 2005). One of the key issues that accounts for this asymmetry of internal versus external validity has to do with group equivalence discussed in Table 2.

**TABLE 2**

| METHOD | DESCRIPTION | ADVANTAGES | LIMITATIONS |
|---|---|---|---|
| Random Assignment | Participants are randomly allocated to groups. | Ensures probabilistic equivalence of groups; controls for most confounding variables | May be unethical or impractical in some situations; doesn't guarantee perfect equivalence, especially in small samples |
| Matched Groups | Participants are matched on key variables before assignment. | Controls for known confounding variables; useful when random assignment isn't possible | Time-consuming; may not control for unknown confounds; can reduce sample size |
| Stratified Random Sampling | Population is divided into strata; then, random sampling occurs within each stratum. | Ensures representation of important subgroups; combines benefits of matching and randomization | Requires prior knowledge of important stratifying variables; can be complex to implement |
| Analysis of Covariance (ANCOVA) | Statistical control for preexisting differences | Can adjust for initial differences post hoc; useful in quasi-experimental designs | Assumes linear relationships; may not fully compensate for lack of randomization |

| | | | |
|---|---|---|---|
| Propensity Score Matching | Statistical technique to equate groups on likelihood of receiving treatment | Can create equivalent groups in observational studies; useful for large datasets | Complex to implement; relies on observed variables only |
| Regression Discontinuity | Assigns participants to groups based on a cut-off score | Useful when random assignment is not possible; can provide strong causal inferences | Limited to situations where a clear cut-off point exists; requires large sample sizes |

It is helpful to note that these research approaches don't exist in isolation. Each has its place in the scientific process, and researchers often use a combination of methods to build a comprehensive understanding of phenomena (Creswell & Plano Clark, 2017). For instance, observational studies might identify patterns that inform hypotheses for experimental testing, while field experiments might validate laboratory findings in real-world contexts (Leichsenring, 2004).

In selecting a research design, investigators must carefully consider their research questions, the nature of the variables involved, ethical considerations, and practical constraints (Parahoo, 2014). The goal is to balance internal and external validity while maximizing the potential for meaningful, applicable findings (Slack & Draugalis, 2001). Understanding the strengths and limitations of each approach allows researchers to make informed decisions and interpret results appropriately, contributing to the cumulative growth of knowledge in their field (Robson & McCartan, 2016).

## QUALITATIVE RESEARCH METHODS

Qualitative research is a research approach that seeks to understand and interpret human experiences, behaviors, and social phenomena in their natural contexts. In contrast to quantitative research, which gathers numerical data in order to perform statistical analysis, qualitative research looks into the depth and complexity of human experiences, aiming to capture the nuances, meanings, and contexts that numbers alone cannot convey (Denzin & Lincoln, 2018). One of the defining characteristics of qualitative research is its preference for naturalistic inquiry. Qualitative researchers study phenomena in their natural contexts, trying to understand, make sense of, and interpret these phenomena through a lens that aligns with that of the participants (Patton, 2015). This means that the researcher has to get their hands dirty so to speak. They have to leave the confines of the "lab" and be with, among and a part of those who they are researching. This approach stands in contrast to the controlled environments often used in quantitative studies—a *deductive process* of testing hypotheses formulated before any data has been gathered—and allows for a more holistic understanding of complex social realities.

While quantitative research often tests preexisting hypotheses, qualitative research typically employs an inductive approach. This means that themes, patterns, and even theories are allowed to emerge from the data, rather than being imposed from the outset (Charmaz, 2014). This *inductive process* enables researchers to discover new insights and generate theories grounded in the lived experiences of participants. Qualitative data are characterized by their rich, descriptive nature. Instead of relying on numbers and statistics, qualitative researchers collect and analyze detailed descriptions, direct quotations, and careful observations (Merriam & Tisdell, 2016).

Another distinctive feature of qualitative research is the role of the researcher as the *primary instrument* for data collection and analysis. The researcher's own perspective, experience, and interpretation play a determinative role in the research process (Stake, 2010), as opposed to psychometrically validated instruments used in quantitative research. This subjective element is acknowledged and often embraced in qualitative research, with researchers practicing reflexivity to understand and account for their own influence on the research process.

Qualitative research designs are often characterized by their flexibility and emergent nature. Unlike the fixed designs typical of quantitative research, qualitative studies can evolve as the researcher gains new insights and understanding throughout the research process (Creswell & Poth, 2018). This flexibility allows researchers to adapt their methods and focus as they learn more of their subject matter.

The emphasis on context is another hallmark of qualitative research. Qualitative researchers recognize that human behavior and experiences are deeply influenced by the contexts in which they occur. Therefore, they strive to understand phenomena within their specific social, cultural, and historical contexts, rather than attempting to isolate variables or generalize findings across all situations (Maxwell, 2013).

Now that we've general distinctives of qualitative research, let's look at some specific qualitative approaches in the following sections. It's important to keep these overarching characteristics in mind, as they inform and shape the various methodologies within the qualitative tradition. The following is a brief overview of several qualitative research approaches.

## PHENOMENOLOGY

Phenomenology aims to describe and interpret the lived experiences of individuals around a specific phenomenon. This method is particularly useful in counseling research for understanding clients' experiences of therapy or mental health conditions. For example, a phenomenological research study seeks to understand the lived experience of recovery from substance abuse, providing rich, thick descriptions of participants' life stories (Shinebourne & Smith, 2011). Key features of phenomenological research include the following: in-depth interviews with a small number of participants; bracketing of researcher assumptions; and thematic analysis to identify common experiences.

## GROUNDED THEORY

Grounded theory is an inductive approach that aims to develop theory from data. This method is valuable when existing theories are inadequate to explain a phenomenon or when exploring new areas of inquiry in counseling. A grounded theory study might investigate the process of developing resilience in adolescents who have experienced trauma, resulting in a theoretical model of resilience development (Ungar et al., 2007). Key aspects of grounded theory include the following: theoretical sampling; constant comparative analysis; and memo-writing.

## ETHNOGRAPHY

Ethnography involves immersive study of a particular cultural group or setting. In counseling research, this approach can be used to understand the cultural contexts of mental health and help-seeking behaviors. An ethnographic study might explore the mental health beliefs and practices in a specific immigrant community, providing insights for culturally sensitive counseling interventions (Chung et al., 2011). Ethnographic research typically involves participant observation; field notes; and in-depth interviews with key informants.

## CASE STUDIES

Case study research involves an in-depth examination of a particular case or unit of analysis (e.g., an individual participant, a group, or an agency/organization) within its actual context. This method is useful for exploring complex issues in counseling practice. For instance, a case study might examine the implementation of a new counseling program in a school system, detailing the challenges and successes encountered (Yin, 2018). Case studies often incorporate multiple data collection methods; triangulation of data sources; and rich, contextual description.

## NARRATIVE INQUIRY

Narrative inquiry focuses on the stories participants share about their experiences. This approach is particularly relevant in counseling research, where clients' narratives are central to the therapeutic process. A narrative study might explore the stories of individuals who have overcome eating disorders, examining how they construct and make meaning of their recovery experiences (Papathomas

& Lavallee, 2012). Key features of narrative inquiry include the following: in-depth interviews; analysis of narrative structure and content; and attention to the coconstruction of narratives between the researcher and the participant.

**Key considerations for qualitative research**

- Selecting an appropriate qualitative approach (e.g., phenomenology, grounded theory, and ethnography)
- Ensuring rich, detailed data collection through methods like in-depth interviews or participant observation
- Maintaining reflexivity and acknowledging the researcher's role in data collection and interpretation
- Using rigorous data analysis techniques, such as constant comparison or thematic analysis
- Establishing trustworthiness through strategies like member checking, peer debriefing, and thick description
- Considering ethical issues, particularly around confidentiality and participant anonymity
- Balancing depth of inquiry with breadth of experiences captured
- Articulating how findings contribute to theory or practice in the field of counseling

## COMPARING AND CONTRASTING QUANTITATIVE AND QUALITATIVE RESEARCH

Quantitative and qualitative research approaches represent two distinct paradigms in counseling research, each rooted in different epistemological and ontological assumptions as we discussed in Chapter 3. While both aim to contribute to our understanding of human behavior and mental health, they differ significantly in their methods, goals, and the type of knowledge they produce.

Quantitative research, grounded in positivist and post-positivist philosophies, emphasizes objective measurements and statistical analysis of numerical data. It seeks to test hypotheses, establish causal relationships, and generalize findings to broader populations (Creswell & Creswell, 2018). This approach is characterized by its use of standardized measures, large sample sizes, and statistical techniques to analyze data. Quantitative researchers often aim for reliability and validity in their measurements, striving to minimize bias and maximize the generalizability of their findings (Shadish et al., 2002).

In contrast, qualitative research, often associated with interpretivist and constructivist paradigms, focuses on exploring and understanding the depth and complexity of human experiences through non-numerical data (Denzin & Lincoln, 2018). Qualitative researchers aim to generate rich, contextual insights and new theoretical perspectives, often working with smaller sample sizes but looking deeply into individual experiences and meanings. This approach values the subjective nature of human experience and recognizes the researcher as an integral part of the research process (Merriam & Tisdell, 2016).

The nature of the research question often determines which approach is most appropriate. Quantitative research is well suited for questions about prevalence, causality, and the effectiveness of interventions. For instance, "What is the efficacy of cognitive behavioral therapy in reducing symptoms of depression?" would typically be addressed through a quantitative approach. Qualitative research, on the other hand, is ideal for exploring complex phenomena, understanding lived experiences, and generating new theories. A question like "How do individuals experience and make meaning of their recovery from substance abuse?" would be better suited to a qualitative approach.

The data collection methods also differ significantly between these two approaches. Quantitative research typically employs structured methods such as surveys, experiments, and standardized assessments. These methods allow for systematic collection of numerical data that can be statistically analyzed. Qualitative research, however, uses methods like in-depth interviews, focus groups, participant observation, and document analysis to gather rich, descriptive data (Patton, 2015).

The role of the researcher also varies between these approaches. In quantitative research, the researcher aims to remain objective and separate from the subject of study to avoid influencing the results. In qualitative research, the researcher is often seen as a key instrument in the research process, with their own subjectivity acknowledged and often embraced as part of the interpretive process (Stake, 2010).

Analysis techniques differ as well. Quantitative data are typically analyzed using statistical methods, ranging from descriptive statistics to complex multivariate analyses. Qualitative data, on the other hand, are often analyzed through methods like thematic analysis, content analysis, or grounded theory approaches, which involve identifying patterns and themes in the data (Braun & Clarke, 2006).

Despite these differences, it is important to note that quantitative and qualitative approaches are not mutually exclusive. Many researchers advocate for mixed-methods approaches that combine elements of both, leveraging the strengths of each to provide a more comprehensive understanding of complex phenomena (Creswell & Plano Clark, 2018).

## TABLE 3

**Control groups:** Experimental and quasi-experimental designs often include control groups that do not receive the intervention or treatment being studied. This allows researchers to compare the outcomes between treated and untreated groups. Qualitative research generally does not use control groups.

**Manipulation of variables:** In experimental and quasi-experimental research, researchers deliberately manipulate independent variables to observe their effects on dependent variables. Qualitative research is typically observational and does not involve manipulation of variables.

**Randomization:** True experimental designs use random assignment of participants to different conditions. While quasi-experimental designs may not always include randomization, they often attempt to approximate it. Qualitative research does not typically involve randomization.

**Quantitative measurement:** Experimental and quasi-experimental designs rely on quantitative measurements of variables, often using standardized instruments or scales. Qualitative research primarily deals with non-numerical data.

**Statistical analysis:** These designs employ statistical techniques to analyze data and test hypotheses. Qualitative research uses different analytical approaches, such as thematic analysis or content analysis.

**Hypothesis testing:** Experimental and quasi-experimental research often starts with specific hypotheses that are then tested. Qualitative research is typically more exploratory and may generate hypotheses rather than testing them.

**Emphasis on causality:** These designs aim to establish causal relationships between variables. Qualitative research is more focused on understanding meanings, experiences, and processes.

**Structured protocols:** Experimental and quasi-experimental research typically follows structured protocols to ensure consistency across participants. Qualitative research often uses more flexible, emergent designs.

**Large sample sizes:** These quantitative approaches often require larger sample sizes to achieve statistical power. Qualitative research typically uses smaller, purposively selected samples.

**Generalizability:** Experimental and quasi-experimental designs often aim for findings that can be generalized to broader populations. Qualitative research is more focused on the depth of understanding in specific contexts.

Understanding these differences is critical for counseling researchers as they design studies and interpret findings. Each approach offers unique insights: Quantitative research provides statistical rigor and generalizability, while qualitative research offers depth, context, and nuanced understanding of individual experiences.

Increasingly, researchers recognize the value of integrating both approaches through mixed-methods designs, leveraging the strengths of each to provide a more comprehensive understanding of complex phenomena in counseling and mental health.

## MIXED-METHODS RESEARCH

Mixed-methods research represents a distinct methodology that bridges the divide between quantitative and qualitative approaches, offering a more holistic and nuanced understanding of complex phenomena in counseling and mental health. This approach, which has gained significant traction in recent decades, involves the intentional integration of quantitative and qualitative data collection, analysis, and interpretation within a single study or a series of related studies (Creswell & Plano Clark, 2018).

The fundamental premise of mixed-methods research is that the combination of quantitative and qualitative approaches provides a more comprehensive understanding of research problems than either approach alone. This integration allows researchers to harness the strengths of both methodologies while mitigating their individual limitations (Johnson & Onwuegbuzie, 2004).

Mixed-methods research is grounded in pragmatism, a philosophical worldview that focuses on the consequences of research and the importance of the research question over the methods used. This pragmatic foundation allows researchers to move beyond the traditional paradigm wars between quantitative and qualitative purists, embracing a more flexible and practical approach to addressing complex research questions (Morgan, 2007).

One of the key strengths of mixed-methods research is its ability to address a broader and more complete range of research questions. It allows researchers to simultaneously gather both numeric trends and detailed views of participants, providing a fuller picture of the phenomenon under study. For instance, in a study on the effectiveness of a new counseling intervention, quantitative methods might be used to measure changes in symptom severity, while qualitative methods could explore clients' lived experiences of the intervention and factors contributing to its effectiveness (Fetters et al., 2013).

Mixed-methods research also offers the advantage of offsetting the weaknesses inherent to using only quantitative or qualitative methods. The limitations of one method can be compensated for by the strengths of the other. For example, while quantitative methods may lack the depth to fully capture the context of a phenomenon, qualitative methods can provide rich, detailed descriptions. Conversely, while qualitative findings may be criticized for lack of generalizability, quantitative methods can provide statistical power and representativeness (Greene et al., 1989). Furthermore, mixed-methods research allows for triangulation, where findings from different methods can be used to corroborate, elaborate, or illuminate the research problem. This can lead to increased validity and a deeper understanding of the phenomenon being studied (Tashakkori & Teddlie, 2010).

However, it is important to note that mixed-methods research is not simply a matter of collecting both quantitative and qualitative data. It requires a thoughtful and purposeful integration of the two types of data to generate insights that go beyond what could be obtained by treating the data sources separately. This integration can occur at various stages of the research process, including data collection, analysis, and interpretation (Bazeley, 2018).

In the following section, we'll examine specific mixed-methods designs. Keep in mind that the choice of design should be driven by the research question and the purpose of mixing methods. Whether it is a convergent design that merges quantitative and qualitative data for a comprehensive analysis, an explanatory sequential design that uses qualitative data to explain quantitative results, or an exploratory sequential design that uses quantitative methods to extend qualitative findings, each approach offers unique benefits and challenges (Creswell & Plano Clark, 2018).

In the context of counseling research, mixed methods can be particularly valuable. The complexity of human behavior and mental health processes often requires multiple perspectives to be fully understood. Mixed methods allow counseling researchers to not only measure the effectiveness of interventions but also understand the mechanisms through which they work and how they are experienced by clients. This comprehensive approach can lead to more nuanced and applicable findings, bridging the gap between research and practice in meaningful ways. The following is a brief overview of several mixed-methods research approaches.

*Convergent Parallel Design:* In this design, quantitative and qualitative data are collected concurrently, analyzed separately, and then merged for interpretation. For example, a study on the effectiveness of a new anxiety intervention might combine quantitative measures of anxiety symptoms with qualitative interviews about participants' experiences of the intervention (Fetters et al., 2013).

*Explanatory Sequential Design:* This design begins with quantitative data collection and analysis, followed by a qualitative inquiry to help explain the quantitative results. A study using this design might first survey counselors about their use of evidence-based practices and then conduct follow-up interviews to understand the factors influencing their adoption of these practices (Ivankova et al., 2006).

*Exploratory Sequential Design:* Starting with qualitative data collection and analysis, this design uses the qualitative findings to inform subsequent quantitative research. For instance, a study might begin with focus groups exploring barriers to mental health help-seeking among college students and then use these findings to develop and administer a quantitative survey to a larger sample (Creswell & Plano Clark, 2018).

### Key considerations for mixed-methods designs

- Clearly articulating the rationale for using a mixed-methods approach
- Selecting an appropriate mixed-methods design (e.g., convergent parallel, explanatory sequential, and exploratory sequential)
- Ensuring integration of qualitative and quantitative components at appropriate stages (design, data collection, analysis, or interpretation)
- Addressing potential philosophical tensions between qualitative and quantitative approaches
- Developing skills in both qualitative and quantitative methods or collaborating with researchers from different methodological backgrounds
- Considering the timing and priority of qualitative and quantitative components
- Addressing potential challenges in merging or connecting data from different methods
- Ensuring that sample sizes are appropriate for both qualitative and quantitative components
- Managing the complexity and time demands of conducting both types of research
- Addressing potential discrepancies between qualitative and quantitative findings
- Presenting mixed-methods results in a coherent and an integrated manner
- Adhering to quality criteria for both qualitative and quantitative components, as well as specific mixed-methods quality criteria

## DATA COLLECTION TECHNIQUES

Selecting appropriate data collection techniques is related to the reliability and validity of your methods for gathering information. The choice of technique depends on the research design, the nature of the inquiry, and the type of data required.

### INTERVIEWS

Interviews are widely used in qualitative counseling research to gather in-depth information about participants' experiences, perceptions, and feelings. Types of interviews include the following:

- Structured interviews: Use predetermined questions in a fixed order.
- Semi-structured interviews: Follow a guide, but allow for flexibility in question order and follow-up probes.
- Unstructured interviews: Use open-ended questions to explore topics in depth.

For example, a semi-structured interview might be used to explore clients' experiences of online counseling during the COVID-19 pandemic (Wind et al., 2020). Key considerations for interviews include building rapport with interviewees; developing effective questioning techniques; and managing researcher bias.

## FOCUS GROUPS

Focus groups involve facilitated discussions with small groups of participants, allowing researchers to gather data on collective views and group dynamics. This technique can be particularly useful for exploring shared experiences or generating ideas for interventions. A focus group study might examine counselors' perspectives on integrating technology into their practice (Anthony, 2015). Important aspects of focus group research include the following:

- Facilitating group interaction
- Managing group dynamics
- Analyzing both individual- and group-level data

## OBSERVATIONS

Observational techniques involve systematically watching and recording behavior in natural settings. In counseling research, observations might be used to study counselor–client interactions or group therapy processes. For instance, an observational study might examine nonverbal communication patterns in successful therapy sessions (Dowell & Berman, 2013). Considerations for observational research include the following:

- Deciding between participant and nonparticipant observation
- Developing systematic observation protocols
- Addressing potential observer effects

## SURVEYS AND QUESTIONNAIRES

Surveys and questionnaires are efficient tools for collecting data from large samples, often used in quantitative counseling research. They can gather information on attitudes, behaviors, and characteristics of populations. A survey might be used to assess job satisfaction among school counselors across a state or region (Mullen et al., 2018). Key aspects of survey research include the following:

- Designing clear and unambiguous questions
- Choosing appropriate response formats (e.g., Likert scales and multiple-choice)
- Addressing potential response biases

## SAMPLING STRATEGIES

The sampling strategy you choose impacts whether your findings are valid and generalizable. The choice of sampling method depends on the research design, population characteristics, and practical considerations.

### PROBABILITY SAMPLING

Probability sampling techniques give each member of the population a known, nonzero chance of being selected. These methods are preferred when aiming for generalizability in quantitative research.

*Simple Random Sampling*: Each member of the population has an equal chance of selection, for example, randomly selecting counselors from a professional association's membership list for a survey on continuing education practices.

*Stratified Sampling*: The population is divided into subgroups (strata) based on specific characteristics, with random sampling within each stratum. This method increases the representation of important subgroups, for instance, stratifying a sample of counselors by specialization (e.g., school, clinical, and rehabilitation) before random selection.

*Cluster Sampling*: The population is divided into clusters (often geographic), and a random sample of clusters is selected. This can be efficient for large, dispersed populations. An example might be randomly selecting schools from different districts for a study on school counseling programs.

### NONPROBABILITY SAMPLING

Nonprobability sampling techniques are often used in qualitative research or when probability sampling is not feasible. While these methods limit generalizability, they can be valuable for in-depth exploration of specific phenomena.

*Purposive Sampling*: Participants are selected based on specific characteristics or experiences relevant to the research question, for example, selecting clients who have undergone online counseling for a study on virtual therapy experiences (Etikan et al., 2016).

*Convenience Sampling*: Participants are selected based on their accessibility and willingness to participate. While often criticized for potential bias, this method can be practical for pilot studies or when resources are limited.

*Snowball Sampling*: Initial participants recruit additional participants from their networks. This can be useful for reaching hidden or hard-to-access populations, such as individuals with rare mental health conditions.

### SAMPLE SIZE CONSIDERATIONS

Determining an appropriate sample size affects your recruitment efforts and strategy for both quantitative and qualitative research: For quantitative studies, sample size is often determined through power analysis, considering factors such as effect size, significance level, and desired power (Cohen, 1992). In qualitative research, sample size is often guided by the principle of data saturation, where data collection continues until no new themes or insights emerge (Guest et al., 2006).

## DATA ANALYSIS

Data analysis is the process of systematically applying statistical and/or logical techniques to describe, illustrate, and evaluate data. The method of analysis depends on the type of data collected and the research questions being addressed.

### QUANTITATIVE DATA ANALYSIS TECHNIQUES

Quantitative data analysis in counseling research often involves statistical methods to identify patterns, test hypotheses, and draw conclusions.

*Descriptive Statistics*: These techniques summarize and describe the basic features of a dataset. Common measures include mean, median, mode, standard deviation, and frequency distributions. For example, a study might report the average anxiety scores of participants before and after a counseling intervention (Tabachnick & Fidell, 2019).

*Inferential Statistics*: These methods allow researchers to make inferences about populations based on sample data. Common techniques include the following:

- T tests: Used to compare means between two groups, for instance, comparing depression scores between a treatment group and a control group.
- Analysis of Variance: Used to compare means among three or more groups. An example might be comparing the effectiveness of three different counseling approaches on reducing stress levels.
- Regression Analysis: Used to examine relationships between variables, for example, exploring how factors like social support and coping strategies predict resilience in trauma survivors (Field, 2018).
- Factor Analysis: This technique is used to identify underlying constructs or dimensions in a set of variables. It is often employed in the development and validation of psychological assessments used in counseling (Thompson, 2004).

## QUALITATIVE DATA ANALYSIS APPROACHES

Qualitative data analysis involves systematically examining and interpreting textual data to understand meanings, identify patterns, and develop explanations.

*Thematic Analysis*: This method involves identifying, analyzing, and reporting patterns (themes) within data. It is widely used in counseling research to understand client experiences. For example, a study might use thematic analysis to explore themes in clients' narratives about their experiences of grief counseling (Braun & Clarke, 2006).

*Content Analysis*: This approach involves systematically coding and categorizing textual data to identify patterns and themes. It can be used to analyze interview transcripts, open-ended survey responses, or counseling session notes (Krippendorff, 2018).

*Grounded Theory Analysis*: This method involves a systematic, inductive approach to developing theory from data. It is particularly useful when existing theories don't adequately explain a phenomenon in counseling. The analysis typically involves open coding, axial coding, and selective coding to develop a theoretical framework (Charmaz, 2014).

*Narrative Analysis*: This approach focuses on the stories people tell, examining both content and structure. It is particularly relevant in counseling research, where client narratives are central. For instance, a study might use narrative analysis to explore how clients construct their recovery stories in addiction counseling (Riessman, 2008).

## MIXED-METHODS ANALYSIS STRATEGIES

Mixed-methods analysis involves integrating quantitative and qualitative data analysis techniques. Common strategies include the following: *Data Transformation*: Qualitative data are converted into quantitative data (or vice versa) for analysis. *Parallel Mixed Analysis*: Quantitative and qualitative analyses are conducted separately and then compared. *Sequential Mixed Analysis*: The analysis of one type of data informs the analysis of the other type.

For example, a mixed-methods study on the effectiveness of a new counseling intervention might use statistical analysis to measure changes in symptom scores, while thematic analysis of interview data explores clients' perceptions of the intervention's impact (Creswell & Plano Clark, 2018).

## KEEPING THE QUALITY IN RESEARCH

Maintaining the quality and rigor of research is key for producing trustworthy and valuable findings in counseling research.

### VALIDITY AND RELIABILITY IN QUANTITATIVE RESEARCH

Validity refers to the extent to which a measure accurately represents the concept it is intended to measure. Types of validity include the following:

- Content Validity: The extent to which a measure represents all facets of a given construct.
- Construct Validity: The degree to which a test measures what it claims to measure.
- External Validity: The extent to which results can be generalized to other settings or populations.

Reliability refers to the consistency and precision of a measure. It includes the following:

- Test–Retest Reliability: The consistency of a measure over time.
- Interrater Reliability: The degree of agreement among raters.
- Internal Consistency: The consistency of results across items within a test.

Researchers can enhance validity and reliability through careful instrument selection, pilot testing, and statistical analyses (Shadish et al., 2002).

## TRUSTWORTHINESS IN QUALITATIVE RESEARCH

Lincoln and Guba (1985) proposed four criteria for establishing trustworthiness in qualitative research:

*Credibility*: Confidence in the "truth" of the findings. Techniques include prolonged engagement, persistent observation, and triangulation.

*Transferability*: Showing that the findings have applicability in other contexts. This is enhanced through thick description of the research context and participants.

*Dependability*: Showing that the findings are consistent and could be repeated. This involves maintaining an audit trail of research decisions and processes.

*Confirmability*: The extent to which the findings are shaped by the respondents and not researcher bias. Reflexivity is key to enhancing confirmability.

For example, a qualitative study on the experiences of LGBTQ+ clients in counseling might use member checking (having participants review and confirm the accuracy of interview transcripts and interpretations) to enhance credibility (Morrow, 2005).

## QUALITY CRITERIA FOR MIXED-METHODS RESEARCH

Assessing quality in mixed-methods research involves considering the quality of both quantitative and qualitative components, as well as the integration of these components. Criteria proposed by Teddlie and Tashakkori (2009) include the following: *design quality*: The extent to which the research design is appropriate for addressing the research questions; *interpretive rigor*: The degree to which interpretations are credible and consistent with the data; and *inference transferability*: The extent to which conclusions can be applied to other settings or populations.

For instance, a mixed-methods study on the efficacy of a new counseling approach might demonstrate quality by using validated quantitative measures, conducting rigorous qualitative analysis, and effectively integrating these findings to provide a comprehensive understanding of the approach's impact.

**TABLE 4**

### Choosing the Appropriate Methodology for Your Research Question

Selecting the most appropriate methodology for your research question is a critical decision that shapes the entire research process. This choice should be guided by several factors:

1. Nature of the Research Question: The type of question you're asking should inform your methodological approach. For example:
   - "What is the relationship between X and Y?" might suggest a quantitative approach.
   - "How do individuals experience X?" might be better suited to a qualitative approach.
   - "To what extent does X impact Y, and how do individuals perceive this impact?" might call for a mixed-methods approach.
2. Existing Knowledge: Consider the current state of knowledge in your area of inquiry. If little is known about a phenomenon, an exploratory qualitative approach might be appropriate. If substantial theory exists, a quantitative approach to test hypotheses might be more suitable.
3. Practical Considerations: Factors such as time, resources, access to participants, and your own methodological expertise should be considered when choosing a research approach.
4. Ethical Implications: Some research questions or populations might necessitate certain methodological approaches due to ethical considerations.
5. Intended Application of Findings: Consider how you intend to use your research findings. For example, if you aim to generalize results to a larger population, a quantitative approach might be more appropriate.

Remember that there is no one "best" methodology; rather, the strength of your research lies in choosing a method that aligns well with your research questions and objectives. As you embark on your research journey, remain flexible and open to adapting your approach as you gain new insights and encounter challenges.

## CONCLUSION

As we've explored throughout this chapter, the field of counseling research offers a rich array of methodological pathways, each with its own strengths and applications. From the rigorous hypothesis testing of experimental designs to the deep, contextual insights of qualitative approaches and the comprehensive perspective offered by mixed methods, these methodologies provide counselors with the tools to investigate human behavior and mental health. The choice of research methodology is not merely a technical decision, but a strategic one that shapes the entire research process and the nature of the knowledge produced. This choice should be guided by the research question, the existing body of knowledge, practical considerations, ethical implications, and the intended application of findings.

Quantitative methods offer the ability to test hypotheses, establish causal relationships, and generalize findings to broader populations. They provide statistical rigor and the potential for wide-reaching implications. Qualitative methods, on the other hand, allow for in-depth exploration of individual experiences, uncovering nuances and generating new theoretical insights. Mixed-methods research bridges these approaches, offering a more comprehensive understanding of complex phenomena. Regardless of the chosen methodology, making sure your study has ethical integrity is key. This involves considerations of validity, reliability, and trustworthiness, as well as attention to ethical standards throughout the research process. It enables you not only to conduct your own research but also to critically evaluate existing studies, informing evidence-based practice. Remember, the goal is not to become an expert in every methodology (as much as we may want to), but to develop a broad understanding that allows you to choose the most appropriate approach for your research questions.

# 5

# Ethical Frameworks in Counseling Research

In Chapter 3, we discussed important philosophical topics such as ontology and epistemology. These two philosophical issues are usually followed by the third pillar of research philosophy: axiology. Axiology, derived from the Greek words "axios" meaning "worth" or "value" and "logos" meaning "study" or "theory," is the philosophical study of value. In the context of research, axiology refers to the role of values and ethics in the research process.

While ontology asks "What is the nature of reality?" and epistemology questions "How can we know that reality?", axiology invites us to consider "What is the role of values in research?" and "What are the ethical principles that guide research?" Ethical considerations permeate every stage of the research process, from the initial formulation of research questions to the dissemination of findings. They guide our decisions about methodology, participant recruitment, data collection, analysis, and reporting. As counselor–researchers, we have a dual responsibility: to advance knowledge in our field and protect the well-being of our research participants.

In other words, ethics are more than afterthought. They are more than a box you check after you have sorted out all the interesting parts of your research design. Rather, ethics is to be considered first and foremost in the research-design process. It is the foundation; the principles that guide the entire research process. Counseling research seeks to explore individuals' innermost thoughts, feelings, and experiences. The kind of research we conduct demands sensitivity and a commitment to principles that protect clients and research participants' rights, dignity, and welfare.

However, this commitment to individual rights and welfare has not always been evident throughout the evolution of research. Our ethical principles have been forged out of a long history of mistakes and errors, punctuated by events demonstrating the potential harm research can lead to. Our ugly past also tells the story of human progress, where ethical codes have been identified and purposefully baked into research practices. This chapter reviews the historical development of research ethics, exploring the key events that have shaped our current understanding and the evolution of ethical guidelines that govern our work today. We will examine examples of ethical violations from the past, not to cast judgment, but to learn from these cautionary tales that outline the *why* behind the principles.

The discussion of ethics is especially relevant for our field since the vast majority of counselors-in-training, licensed counselors, and counselor educators work directly with clients in various clinical contexts; therefore, there is a potential for blurred boundaries to occur between clinician and researcher. Application of ethical principles in these contexts, where there is a potential for dual roles, presents unique challenges and opportunities. We will explore how informed consent, confidentiality, and minimizing harm avoid situations where lines may be inadvertently crossed between researcher and therapist. Additionally, we will cover cultural humility and a multicultural framework, specifically looking at how cultural context, researcher bias, and cultural sensitivity are implemented in research methods

## HISTORICAL DEVELOPMENT OF RESEARCH ETHICS

The evolution of research ethics is a testimony to the human capacity for both great scientific achievement and profound moral failure. Reflecting on our history of moral and ethical failures, done in the name of science, helps us draw bright, clear boundaries, so that the consequences that follow, when lines are crossed, are obvious and avoidable.

### KEY EVENTS SHAPING ETHICAL UNDERSTANDING

#### The Nuremberg Code (1947)

The atrocious acts committed by Nazi physicians during World War II led to the creation of the Nuremberg Code, widely regarded as the first international document to set out ethical principles for human subjects research. The code emphasized voluntary consent as absolutely essential, stating that participants should have the legal capacity to consent, situated to be able to exercise free power of choice, and have sufficient knowledge and comprehension of the research to make an informed decision (Shuster, 1997). The code's first principle declared, "The voluntary consent of the human subject is absolutely essential," setting a new standard for research ethics that would influence all subsequent guidelines (Annas & Grodin, 1992, p. 2). The development of voluntary consent signaled a shift from previous research practices where subjects were often uninformed or coerced.

### The Declaration of Helsinki (1964)

Building on the Nuremberg Code, the World Medical Association adopted the Declaration of Helsinki. This declaration introduced the concept of independent committee review of research protocols, a precursor to modern Institutional Review Boards (IRBs). It also emphasized the importance of balancing risks and benefits in research, stating, "Medical research involving human subjects may only be conducted if the importance of the objective outweighs the risks and burdens to the research subjects" (World Medical Association, 2013, p. 2191). The declaration has undergone multiple revisions, yet its influence extends beyond medicine, informing ethical practices in counseling and other social science research.

### The Tuskegee Syphilis Study (1932–1972)

Perhaps no single event has had a more profound impact on research ethics in the United States than the Tuskegee Syphilis Study. This 40-year study, conducted by the U.S. Public Health Service, observed the natural progression of untreated syphilis in African American men under the guise of providing free health care. The study continued even after penicillin was established as an effective treatment for syphilis, deliberately withholding treatment from participants (Jones, 1981). The public outcry following the exposure of this study led to the National Research Act of 1974, which established the National Commission for the Protection of Human Subjects of Biomedical and Behavioral Research. This commission was tasked with identifying basic ethical principles that should underlie human subjects research along with the development of guidelines so that research is congruent with those principles (National Commission for the Protection of Human Subjects of Biomedical and Behavioral Research, 1979).

## EVOLUTION OF ETHICAL GUIDELINES

### The Belmont Report (1979)

The National Commission work led to development of the Belmont Report, one of the most formative documents that guide research in the present day. The report identified three fundamental ethical principles: respect for persons, beneficence, and justice. These principles have since formed the basis for most ethical guidelines in human subjects research, including counseling research (National Commission for the Protection of Human Subjects of Biomedical and Behavioral Research, 1979). The principle of respect for persons emphasizes the autonomy of participants and the necessity to safeguard individuals with diminished autonomy. Beneficence requires researchers to maximize potential benefits while minimizing potential harms. Justice demands the fair distribution of the benefits and burdens of research across different populations.

## DEVELOPMENT OF PROFESSIONAL CODES OF ETHICS

In response to these developments, professional organizations developed their own ethical codes specific to their fields. The American Psychological Association (APA) first published its code ethics in 1953, which has been regularly revised to reflect evolving ethical standards and new challenges in psychological research and practice (Smith, 2003). The American Counseling Association (ACA) followed suit, publishing its first code of ethics in 1961. The ACA Code of Ethics has since undergone multiple revisions, with the most recent version emphasizing the importance of cultural sensitivity, social justice, and the use of technology in counseling research and practice (ACA, 2014). See Table 1 for a brief overview of the ACA ethical codes.

**TABLE 1.**

| SECTION | TITLE | KEY POINTS |
|---|---|---|
| A | The Counseling Relationship | Respecting client welfare and rights; Informed consent; Confidentiality and privacy; Maintaining appropriate boundaries |
| B | Confidentiality and Privacy | Respecting client confidentiality; Exceptions to confidentiality; Record-keeping and documentation |
| C | Professional Responsibility | Competence and boundaries of competence; Professional development; Advertising and soliciting clients; Technology applications |
| D | Relationships with Other Professionals | Interdisciplinary teamwork; Relationships with employers and employees |
| E | Evaluation, Assessment, and Interpretation | Proper use of assessment tools; Interpreting assessment results; Sharing results with clients |
| F | Supervision, Training, and Teaching | Counselor supervision and training responsibilities; Student welfare and rights; Dual relationships in academic settings |
| G | Research and Publication | Research responsibilities; Rights of research participants; Reporting research results; Publication and authorship |
| H | Distance Counseling, Technology, and Social Media | Benefits and limitations of technology-assisted counseling; Informed consent in online counseling; Maintaining online privacy and security |
| I | Resolving Ethical Issues | Ethical decision-making models; Suspected violations; Cooperation with ethics committees |

These professional codes serve a dual function; they provide ethical guidelines and enforceable standards for practitioners and researchers. Put in another way, they offer assistance to researchers, helping them conduct their studies in accord with the highest ethical principles and address field-specific concerns as clinicians face ethical questions and dilemmas in their work.

# FUNDAMENTAL ETHICAL PRINCIPLES IN RESEARCH

The ethical principles that guide counseling research find their grounding in a broader framework of research ethics, drawing heavily from the Belmont Report (as we discussed above). These principles provide guideposts for ethical decision-making in research design, implementation, and dissemination.

## RESPECT FOR PERSONS

The principle of respect for persons encompasses two fundamental ethical convictions: first, participants ought to be regarded as autonomous agents; second, participants with diminished capacity or autonomy are in a vulnerable position and need to be protected (Chamberlain, 2007; National Commission for the Protection of Human Subjects of Biomedical and Behavioral Research, 1979). Research ought not to violate or infringe on someone's agency in deciding what is best for them. It ought not also ignore and exploit a person's limited agency. What is in the interest of the researcher may not be in the interest of the participant, and the participants' well-being always trumps the researchers' agenda.

### Autonomy in Research Participation

Now that we have an idea of what the principle is, what does this look like in practice? In counseling research, respect for persons manifests primarily through the process of informed consent. This process protects participants' information and capacity to make a voluntary decision about their participation in research. As Beauchamp and Childress (2001) note, "Respect for autonomy is a norm of respecting the decision-making capacities of autonomous persons" (p. 101). For counseling researchers, this principle extends beyond mere compliance at the outset of the study, but an ongoing process of protecting participant autonomy. This might involve, for example, *ongoing consent processes* in longitudinal studies or careful consideration of power dynamics in research with clients (Fisher, 2012).

### Protection of Vulnerable Populations

The second aspect of this principle—protecting those with diminished autonomy—is particularly relevant in counseling research, where participants may be experiencing mental health challenges or other vulnerabilities. Levine et al. (2004) argue that vulnerability in research is context-dependent and can arise from various factors, including cognitive capacity, institutional settings, and socioeconomic status. In practice, this principle might necessitate additional safeguards for certain populations. For instance, when conducting research with individuals experiencing severe depression, researchers might need to employ more rigorous consent procedures and provide additional support resources (Appelbaum et al., 1987). If working with children, for example, parental consent and child assent are needed. If working with a person with an intellectual disability, getting consent from a guardian or authorized research representative (ARR) is needed.

The concept of capacity to consent in research typically encompasses four key elements: the ability to comprehend relevant information, recognize the implications of this information for one's personal circumstances, rationally consider available options, and communicate a decision (Appelbaum, 2007). Because of the additional steps regarding capacity and consent, researchers have historically avoided researching these populations, which, some have argued, excludes these populations from full participation in research.

### Racial and Political Power Dynamics

It is important that researchers approach their work with cultural sensitivity and humility when conducting research with diverse populations. Recognition and respect for cultural differences in beliefs, values, customs, and communication styles, while avoiding imposing one's own cultural worldview on participants is essential for multiculturally competent counselors. Researchers must develop awareness of their own cultural biases and assumptions, approaching cross-cultural interactions with an attitude of openness, respect, and willingness to learn. As Sue et al. (2019) note, "Cultural humility involves an ongoing process of self-reflection and self-critique, recognizing one's own biases and acknowledging that cultural learning is a lifelong process" (p. 45).

Equally important is the understanding how privilege and power dynamics may creep into the research process, particularly when working with marginalized or vulnerable populations. It is helpful for researchers to acknowledge their own social position and how it may influence interactions with participants regardless of their philosophical and methodological approach to research. Researchers are encouraged to develop awareness of historical contexts of oppression (also referred to as critical consciousness) and how they may impact the relationships between themselves and their participants and the communities they come from. Fisher et al. (2002) emphasize that "Researchers have an ethical obligation to be aware of their relative power and privilege and to take steps to minimize power differentials in research relationships" (p. 1025).

Culturally responsive methods should be considered in order to conduct research that is truly respectful of cultural diversity. This may include community-based participatory research approaches, indigenous research methodologies, culturally adapted assessment tools and measures, use of cultural brokers or consultants, providing materials in participants' preferred languages, and incorporating culturally relevant concepts and frameworks. As Ponterotto et al. (2010) argue, "Culturally responsive research methods acknowledge the central role of culture in people's lives and seek to honor cultural worldviews throughout the research process" (p. 583). By practicing cultural humility, examining power dynamics, and employing culturally responsive methods, counseling researchers can conduct more ethical, equitable, and meaningful research with diverse populations. This requires ongoing learning, self-reflection, and a commitment to conducting research in ways that respect and empower participants from all cultural backgrounds.

## BENEFICENCE

The principle of beneficence obligates researchers to act in ways that benefit research participants and/or society, while minimizing potential harms. This principle is often summarized as "do no harm," but it extends beyond merely avoiding harm to actively promoting good (Dutka & Astroth, 202[illegible]; National Commission for the Protection of Human Subjects of Biomedical and Behavioral Research, 1979). Providing tangible benefits to participants and their communities entails a long-term, ongoing relationship, not a relationship where researchers gather their data and then vanish. In fact, responsible and ethical research often involves ongoing engagement and follow-up with participants and communities.

### Maximizing Benefits

In counseling research, potential benefits might include improved therapeutic techniques, better understanding of mental health conditions, or enhanced training for counselors. However, as Emanuel et al. (2000) point out, "The ethical requirement to maximize the benefits and minimize the risks of research has been criticized as too unspecific to be helpful" (p. 2703). Thus, it is key for researchers to clearly articulate the potential benefits of their research and how these benefits will be realized.

### Minimizing Risks

Assessing and mitigating risk are highly important components of ethical research design. In counseling research, risks might include psychological distress, breach of confidentiality, or stigmatization. Sieber and Tolich (2013) suggest considering the probability and magnitude of potential harms. Researchers must implement appropriate safeguards to minimize these risks. This might involve measures such as debriefing sessions, secure data-management protocols, or the availability of mental health support for participants who experience distress (Becker-Blease & Freyd, 2006).

# JUSTICE

The principle of justice in research ethics concerns not only the fair allocation of the benefits but also the burdens of research. It raises questions about who receives the benefits of research and at what cost to others (National Commission for the Protection of Human Subjects of Biomedical and Behavioral Research, 1979). In a very straightforward way of looking at it, participating in research takes time with little to no financial reward for participants, yet the research results may be hugely beneficial to others. Is this just?

**Fair Selection of Participants**

Justice in participant selection involves ensuring that the burdens and potential benefits of research are equitably distributed. This principle guards against the exploitation of vulnerable groups and promotes inclusivity in research. In counseling research, this might mean carefully considering the demographics of study participants and ensuring that certain groups are not unfairly excluded or overrepresented. For instance, Corbie-Smith et al. (1999) highlight how historical injustices have led to underrepresentation of certain minority groups in medical research, a concern that extends to counseling research as well. Representation in research is a social justice issue. Sample populations need to include diverse samples.

**Equitable Access to Research Benefits**

The justice principle also demands that the benefits of research be accessible to those who bear its risks. In counseling research, this might involve ensuring that communities or populations involved in research have access to any interventions or knowledge generated from the study. For example, if a study develops a new counseling intervention for a specific community, ethical considerations of justice would suggest making efforts to implement this intervention in that community after the study concludes (Trickett et al., 2011).

By carefully applying these ethical principles, counseling researchers can conduct studies that not only advance knowledge but also respect and protect the rights and well-being of participants. This approach ensures that research in the field of counseling maintains high ethical standards while contributing valuable insights to the discipline (ACA, 2014; APA, 2017). See Table 2 for a summary of the ethical principles and the research practices they inform.

TABLE 2

| ETHICAL PRINCIPLE | RESEARCH PRACTICE |
|---|---|
| Respect for Persons: Autonomy | Implement a thorough informed consent process that ensures participants fully understand the research and can make voluntary decisions about participation. |
| Respect for Persons: Protection of Vulnerable Populations | Develop additional safeguards for vulnerable participants, such as simplified consent forms or the involvement of participant advocates. |
| Beneficence: Maximizing Benefits | Clearly articulate the potential benefits of the research in the study design and communicate these to participants and stakeholders. |
| Beneficence: Minimizing Risks | Conduct a comprehensive risk assessment and implement appropriate safeguards, such as confidentiality measures and provision of mental health support for participants, if needed. |
| Justice: Fair Selection of Participants | Design recruitment strategies that ensure diverse representation and avoid unfair exclusion or overrepresentation of certain groups. |
| Justice: Equitable Access to Research Benefits | Develop plans for disseminating research findings and implementing interventions in the communities that participated in the research. |

## RESPONSIBLE RESEARCH PRACTICES

Now that we have an overview of ethics in research, let us discuss how these principles are translated into practices. Responsible research practices (RRPs) are practices, grounded in ethics, that maintain the integrity, reliability, and ethical standards of scientific inquiry. They include a range of behaviors and decisions that researchers make throughout the research process, from the initial study design all the way to data collection, analysis, and dissemination of findings. The National Academies of Sciences, Engineering, and Medicine (2017) define RRPs as "behavior that meets or exceeds the professional norms and ethical principles essential to the responsible conduct of research" (p. 23). This includes adherence to ethical guidelines, transparency in methods and reporting, respect for research participants, and commitment to scientific rigor. In contrast, irresponsible research practices (IRPs), sometimes referred to as research misconduct or questionable research practices, violate these norms and principles. The Office of Research Integrity (Steneck, 2007) defines research misconduct as "fabrication, falsification, or plagiarism in proposing, performing, or reviewing research, or in reporting research results" (para. 1). Between RRPs and IRPs lies a spectrum that Steneck (2006) describes as a continuum from ideal research practices down to questionable research practices, and ultimately research misconduct. The identification of the spectrum is helpful since a researcher may take a number of small steps that from the outside do not appear to be misconduct, but by degree, are moving in the direction of irresponsibility. Steneck argues that while outright misconduct is relatively rare, questionable practices that fall short of responsible conduct are more common and can significantly undermine research quality and credibility.

RRPs are critical in counseling research, where studies sample from vulnerable populations and gather sensitive personal data from participants. The American Counseling Association (ACA, 2014) emphasizes the importance of ethical research practices in its Code of Ethics, stating that counselors have a responsibility to "conduct research in an ethical manner and report results of research accurately" (section G.1.a).

Understanding and implementing RRPs is essential for counseling researchers to strengthen the validity of their findings, protecting the rights and well-being of participants, and contributing meaningfully to the field's knowledge base. The following sections will explore specific aspects of RRPs in counseling and strategies for promoting their adoption.

Wester et al. (2013) conducted a comprehensive review of research practices in counseling journals. They found that while many studies adhered to ethical guidelines, there were areas of concern. For instance, only 54% of the studies reported obtaining institutional review board (IRB) approval, which is a fundamental aspect of responsible research. This suggests a significant gap in reporting, if not in actual practice. On a positive note, Balkin et al. (2014) found that counseling researchers generally demonstrated good practices in terms of protecting participant confidentiality and providing clear information about the nature of their studies. However, they also noted inconsistencies in how researchers addressed potential conflicts of interest and power differentials with participants.

In terms of cultural sensitivity, Leong et al. (2011) reviewed multicultural research in counseling and found improvements over time in the consideration of cultural factors. However, they also highlighted ongoing challenges in developing truly culturally responsive research methodologies. Regarding statistical and methodological practices, Sink and Mvududu (2010) found that counseling researchers were increasingly adopting more sophisticated analytical techniques. However, they also noted concerns about the proper reporting of effect sizes and the handling of missing data, which are critical pieces of information to include for the accurate interpretation of results. A study by Woo et al. (2016) examined publication practices in counseling research. They found that while the field has made strides in promoting transparency, issues such as selective reporting of outcomes and lack of data sharing remain challenges.

It is worth noting that the counseling field has been proactive in addressing research ethics. For instance, the Association for Counselor Education and Supervision (ACES) has developed specific research guidelines to promote responsible practices (Wester & Borders, 2014).

## CONTINUAL ETHICAL REFLECTION

The nature of RRPs is an ongoing, continual practice of ethical reflection. To be fair, counselors are great at reflecting on ethical considerations in their clinical work. Wester (2011) found that counselors demonstrate strong ethical awareness in clinical practice. That is something to celebrate. Yet, ethical reflection does not stop at the counseling office door; it must also extend to research. Wester also found that ethical awareness does not always translate fully to research contexts, specifically observing gaps in counselors' understanding of nuanced ethical issues, struggles with implementing ongoing consent processes in longitudinal studies, and difficulties navigating the complexities of confidentiality in the digital age. Wester also found that some researchers struggled with the full transparent reporting of methods and results, particularly when findings were unexpected or null. There was a general understanding of the importance of the Institutional Review Board (IRB) approval, but some researchers viewed it as a bureaucratic hurdle rather than an opportunity for ethical reflection.

Ethical considerations in research are not a one-time checklist to be completed at the outset of a study. Researchers must regularly pause to consider whether they are continuing to uphold their ethical commitments, whether new ethical considerations have emerged as the research progresses, and whether their practices remain aligned with their ethical principles. Levitt et al. (2017) argued that ethical decision-making in qualitative research, for example, is a dynamic process that requires researchers to be responsive to evolving ethical challenges throughout their studies. This requires constant monitoring of personal biases. Researchers must be aware that their own experiences, beliefs and cultural backgrounds can influence every aspect of their research, from the questions they ask to how they interpret data. Hays et al. (2016) emphasize the importance of researcher reflexivity in maintaining ethical integrity, particularly in qualitative research, but quantitative researchers would be wise to follow this practice as well. They suggest that researchers engage in regular self-reflection exercises, seek diverse perspectives from colleagues and participants, and consider using tools like reflexive journaling to document and examine potential biases.

## WHAT IS THE VALUE OF ETHICALLY QUESTIONABLE RESEARCH?

While the pursuit of knowledge is a noble goal, it is key to remember that a research product based on unethical practices is not worth the knowledge gained. Ethical integrity should always take precedence over research outcomes. This means being willing to alter or even abandon research plans if ethical concerns cannot be resolved, prioritizing participant well-being over data collection, and maintaining transparency about ethical challenges and how they were addressed in research reports. Mohatt and Thomas's (2006) study argues for the importance of prioritizing community well-being and relationships over research goals.

It is not uncommon for ethical principles to sometimes come into tension with one another, creating complex dilemmas for researchers. For example, beneficence might suggest including vulnerable populations in research that could benefit them, while respect for persons might caution against their inclusion due to concerns about autonomy. Similarly, the pursuit of knowledge (a form of beneficence) might conflict with the need to protect participants from potential harm. When these tensions occur, and they undoubtedly will, we need to proceed with caution, carefully considering all perspectives and consulting with colleagues, ethicists, and the community members involved in the research. And ultimately, one must be willing to adjust research plans if ethical concerns cannot be adequately addressed. Fisher (2012) provides a framework for ethical decision-making in such complex scenarios, emphasizing the importance of collaborative problem-solving and transparency. See Table 3 for a framework often used in the counseling field developed by Forester-Miller and Davis (1996), which was later updated and expanded by the ACA.

**TABLE 3** ACA Ethical Decision-Making Model

| |
|---|
| **Identify the problem:** Gather information and define the ethical issue at hand. |
| **Apply the ACA Code of Ethics:** Consult the ACA Code of Ethics and identify relevant sections. |
| **Determine the nature and dimensions of the dilemma:** Consider all parties involved and potential consequences. |
| **Generate potential courses of action:** Brainstorm various possible solutions. |
| **Consider potential consequences of all options:** Evaluate the potential impact of each option on all stakeholders. |
| **Evaluate the selected course of action:** Determine if the chosen action is consistent with ethical principles and the ACA Code of Ethics. |
| **Implement the course of action:** Put the decision into practice. |

## CONCLUSION

Ethical considerations provide the skeletal system for conducting research with integrity, guided by the values present in the counseling profession. As researchers, we have a responsibility to uphold the highest ethical standards, protecting the rights and well-being of our participants, while contributing to the advancement of knowledge in our field. So, staying informed about ethical guidelines, remaining vigilant to potential ethical issues, and cultivating a commitment to ethical practice, we can conduct research that is not only scientifically rigorous but also morally sound. Our field is constantly evolving, shaped by new technologies, changing social norms, and emerging challenges. As such, ethical competence is not a destination but a progression of continuous learning and reflection. With all the shifts and changes, we need to maintain research that not only adheres to ethical standards but also contributes positively to the lives of those we study and the broader society we serve. To that end, maintain an attitude that sees research as more than just following rules or guidelines. It is about embodying a commitment to respect, beneficence, and justice in every aspect of our work. As counselors and researchers, we have the unique opportunity to contribute to knowledge while also upholding the dignity and well-being of those we study. By keeping a strong ethical foundation, we work toward producing research that advances our field and honors our participants and the wider community.

# 6

# Crafting Research Questions: From Curiosity to Scholarly Inquiry

Imagine, for a moment, constructing a house without first laying a proper foundation. The walls might stand for a while, but they would soon begin to crack and crumble, unable to withstand the pressures of time and external forces. A research project, much in the same way as a house, built on a weak or poorly defined research question may initially appear sound, but it will inevitably falter under scrutiny, failing to provide the robust insights and contributions that characterize valuable scholarly work. Like a foundation that supports the entire structure above it, a precise, researchable, and significant research question guides every aspect of your study, from methodology to data analysis and interpretation.

Research questions are constructed, starting with *broad* curiosity, serving as a springboard into a more *narrow* and well-defined research question. Constructing or building good research questions is an art and a science. In this chapter, we will begin by understanding the importance of a good research question, getting into its characteristics and how it sets the stage for your research process. Then, we will explore a step-by-step guide to transform your initial curiosity into a focused and actionable research question, making sure it meets the essential criteria of specificity, researchability, significance, and feasibility. To aid in this process, this chapter will include interactive exercises designed to help you refine your research question through deeper inquiry and peer feedback.

Additionally, this chapter offers practical tips and strategies customized for counselors in training. We will explore how to integrate your clinical experiences into your research and vice versa. Furthermore, we will discuss how to balance intuition with evidence and utilize reflective practices in your research. By the end of this chapter, you will have a comprehensive understanding of how to craft a research question that not only guides your study but also contributes to the field of counseling in a significant way.

## UNDERSTANDING THE IMPORTANCE OF A GOOD RESEARCH QUESTION

So, why is the research question so important? For counselors in training, the ability to formulate a clear, focused, and meaningful research question is like setting up the first domino. If the first domino is set up properly, all other dominos will follow suit. In other words, the research question provides clarity and focus for your aims, methods, results, discussion, and conclusion sections. By state your research question with precision and specificity, you are setting the direction and purpose, which simultaneously limits you from pursuing other non-relevant aims. Now, imposing a limitation may sound like a bad thing, but in fact, it is a good thing. Trying to accomplish too much or addressing too many foci will create confusion and water down your results. It is better to have a laser-focused research question that sets out to address one issue and one issue only.

### CLARITY AND FOCUS: THE GUIDING LIGHT OF RESEARCH

A focused research question is directly connected to a clear problem present in a defined population. Creswell and Creswell (2018) state, "A research problem is an issue or concern that needs to be addressed" (p. 88). Ideally, the research question addresses the research problem and allows for data to be gathered that can answer the question. Therefore, in a research paper, there is information you ought to be looking for, or if writing one, information you ought to include prior to stating your research question, namely the population of interest and significant problems present in that group. This is oversimplified since there are a lot of moving pieces in a research paper's introduction. But your job is to decode those elements and evaluate whether they all logically connect to one another. See Table 1 for common pieces of information you typically find in the introduction of a research paper.

**TABLE 1.**

**Introduction of the Population of Interest**
- A clearly defined specific group or population the research focuses on
- Relevant demographic details (e.g., age range, gender, ethnicity)
- Specific geographical location or setting (if applicable)
- Unique characteristics that define this group

**Identification of Problems and Needs**
- Primary issues or challenges faced by this population
- The significance of these problems and their impact on the population
- Statistics or data that support the prevalence or severity of these issues
- Problems connected to potential counseling interventions or approaches

**Social, Cultural, and Contextual Factors**
- Broader societal influences on the population (e.g., historical, economic, political)
- Cultural factors that may contribute to or mitigate the identified problems
- Intersectionality considerations in how they affect the population's experiences
- Relevant theoretical frameworks that help explain these contextual factors

**Existing Solutions and Research Literature**
- Key findings from recent, peer-reviewed research
- Critical evaluation of existing research for strengths and limitations
- Effective interventions or approaches that have been used with this population

Once that information has been laid out, the research question should be self-evident. As an exercise, find a well-written research article. Then, without looking, cover the research question and hypotheses section. Read the introduction and see if you can guess what the research questions and hypotheses are. If the paper is well written, argued, and evidence-based, you should be able to anticipate what the aims and purposes of the study are.

But sadly, not all research papers are equal. Some studies are poorly conceived, or the writing does not have a strong logical structure. So, let us look at an example. Review the questions below and evaluate the difference between a broad, unfocused question and a clear, focused one:

> *Broad*: "How does counseling affect mental health?"
>
> *Focused*: "How does cognitive-behavioral therapy impact anxiety levels in college students aged 18–22 over a 12-week treatment period?"

Do you see the difference? The broad question was very open-ended and they lead to ambiguous, often uninterpretable findings. Broad questions imperil the validity of your study by allowing other explanations for your results to creep in. On the other hand, focused questions are precise and clear. You know exactly what is in the mind of the researcher. You know exactly what they intend to do and accomplish in the study.

Focused questions provide clear boundaries for the study, specifying the type of therapy, the mental health concern, the population, and the time frame. It is the precision, the clarity, and the specificity that afford the researcher confidence that the results found are due to the solution they are testing having an effect on the problem. This clarity allows researchers to design appropriate methodologies, select relevant participants, choose suitable measurement tools, and analyze data with precision. Each one of these elements is governed by the research question and must agree with each other. Then when you do get data, a focused research question increases the likelihood of producing results that clearly answer the quest (Punch, 2016).

## DIRECTION AND PURPOSE: CHARTING THE COURSE OF INQUIRY

Imagine a car driving down a road without guardrails. Without those boundaries, you are liable to drive off the road or into oncoming traffic. Precise, specific, and concrete research questions demarcate what you are studying and what you are not studying; this gets to what I mentioned earlier about limitations being a good thing. Young researchers often dream up ambitious research projects (which is not wrong) with big research questions. The bigger the question, the more difficult it is to find evidence to confirm or disconfirm your question. Therefore, there is a practical ruthlessness to research. Researchers have to ask themselves, am I able to gather evidence for my research question? There may be some amazing, valid, and legitimately important research questions that are simply not investigatable due to the challenges associated with gathering evidence. As noted by Agee (2009), "The reflective and interrogative processes required for developing research questions can give shape and direction to a study in ways that are often underestimated" (p. 431).

So, learning to ask precise research questions is critical for epistemic reasons (will the data I gather provides knowledge sufficient to address the research question?), but it also has practical implications as well. Remember, a research question is like the first domino in a chain of dominos. If your first domino is set up correctly, then all that follows falls into place. For example, your research question influences:

**Literature review focus:** It helps you identify relevant literature and gaps in current knowledge.

**Methodology selection:** The nature of your question often dictates whether a qualitative, quantitative, or mixed-methods approach is most appropriate.

**Data-collection strategies:** Your question informs what type of data you need to collect and how to collect it.

**Analysis techniques:** The framing of your question can suggest appropriate analytical approaches.

Here are a few more examples of how research questions affect the research process: "What are the lived experiences of first-generation college students accessing mental health services?" clearly indicates a qualitative approach, likely using phenomenological methods. In contrast, "To what extent does online counseling reduce depressive symptoms compared to in-person therapy?" suggests a quantitative, comparative study.

**TABLE 2.**

| RESEARCH QUESTIONS | LITERATURE REVIEW FOCUS | METHODOLOGY SELECTION | DATA-COLLECTION STRATEGIES | ANALYSIS TECHNIQUE |
|---|---|---|---|---|
| What are the lived experiences of first-generation college students accessing mental health services? | First-generation college students<br>Mental health services in higher education<br>Barriers to accessing mental health care | Qualitative, likely phenomenological approach | In-depth interviews<br>Focus groups<br>Narrative inquiry | Thematic analysis<br>Interpretative phenomenological analysis |
| To what extent does online counseling reduce depressive symptoms compared to in-person therapy? | Online counseling efficacy<br>Depression treatment modalities<br>Comparative studies of therapy delivery methods | Quantitative, comparative study | Randomized controlled trial<br>Surveys<br>Standardized depression scales | Statistical analysis (e.g., *t*-tests, ANOVA)<br>Effect size calculations |
| How do socioeconomic factors influence childhood obesity rates in urban areas? | Childhood obesity<br>Social determinants of health<br>Urban health disparities | Mixed-methods approach | Demographic data collection<br>BMI measurements<br>Surveys<br>Interviews with families and health professionals | Regression analysis<br>Correlation studies<br>Thematic analysis of qualitative data |

| | | | | |
|---|---|---|---|---|
| What is the impact of gamification on employee engagement in corporate training programs? | Gamification in education<br>Employee engagement theories<br>Corporate training effectiveness | Quantitative, potentially with qualitative elements | Pre- and post-intervention surveys<br>Training completion rates<br>Performance metrics<br>Focus groups | Statistical analysis of engagement metrics<br>Content analysis of qualitative feedback |
| How do cultural beliefs influence end-of-life care decisions among elderly Asian immigrants? | End-of-life care practices<br>Cultural competence in healthcare<br>Asian immigrant health beliefs | Qualitative, ethnographic approach | In-depth interviews<br>Participant observation<br>Document analysis (e.g., advance directives) | Grounded theory analysis<br>Cross-cultural comparative analysis |
| What is the relationship between social media use and academic performance among high school students? | Social media effects on adolescents<br>Academic performance factors<br>Digital literacy | Quantitative, correlational study | Social media usage surveys<br>Academic records<br>Time-use diaries | Correlation analysis<br>Multiple regression<br>Path analysis |

## ENGAGEMENT AND RELEVANCE: CONNECTING RESEARCH TO PRACTICE

So, you have put a lot of effort into developing a precise, bounded research question that will (hopefully) yield very specific results. But… even though you have put effort into drafting a technically strong question, it is important to evaluate whether it addresses a real-world clinical issue. Your research question should bridge the gap between academic inquiry and practical application, and the findings should be relevant and impactful in clinical settings.

Engagement is achieved when the question resonates with your professional experiences and curiosities. Gelso (2006) made the interesting comment that "Research training in counseling psychology should help students develop a research identity that complements and enhances, rather than competes with, their identity as practitioners" (p. 5). Think of Gelso's comment in light of what we discussed in chapter 1, where we discussed the professional counselor identity serving as a conceptual framework that marries together practitioner and researcher interests, grounded in counseling's unique philosophical tradition. The professional counselor identity allows for you to think like a practitioner *and* like a researcher, where the two are not mutually exclusive. And, when you can get the two identities talking to each other, amazing things happen.

Research that is informed by actual clinical experiences, questions, and concerns is relevant and useful. Research ultimately has to serve the needs of practitioners and clients. If we are just spinning our wheels, writing overly academic papers that will only be read by academics, what have we really accomplished? So, try to keep things relevant. Think about the current trends in counseling practice, emerging challenges faced by clients, gaps in evidence-based treatments, and ethical considerations in counseling. Have these in mind when you consider research questions that start with, but extend beyond what is of personal interest to you, but will have broad significance and impact. For instance, a question like "How do teletherapy interventions compare to in-person therapy in treating social anxiety among rural adolescents?" addresses a current trend (teletherapy), a specific population (rural adolescents), and a common clinical issue (social anxiety). This kind of question not only engages the researcher but offers findings that could directly inform clinical practice.

## PUTTING IT ALL TOGETHER: A STEP-BY-STEP GUIDE

Now that you have got some basic principles about research questions, let us switch gears to actually writing some research questions. The following section will provide a comprehensive step-by-step guide to help you transform your initial interests into a focused and actionable research question. By following this process, you can develop research questions that are not only academically rigorous but also personally meaningful and relevant to the field.

### STEP 1: IDENTIFY YOUR AREA OF INTEREST

Start with your curiosity. I know I said do not just consider questions of personal interest; but, do not completely rule out your personal interests. Focused research questions start with what is of personal interest to you and how else are you going to care about answering the question? So consider the following questions to help stimulate your thinking: What do you want to know more about? What do you see as a concern or problem among your clients or the populations that you serve? This can be broad. Research questions begin with identifying your area of interest. Your interests, like I said, will not be the ultimate basis of your question, but they are a starting point. If you are not passionate about what you are investigating, you might as well not do it. Research is difficult and challenging; your passion will help you fight through all the barriers that the process will throw at you.

#### Self-reflection

Self-reflection is also a helpful starting point in the research process. As noted by Gelso (2006), "The seeds of good research often lie in the researcher's own experiences and observations" (p. 6). Reflect on what genuinely excites you about the field of counseling. Think about your personal and professional experiences that have shaped your interests. What moments in your practice or studies have sparked questions or curiosity? Align your research interests with your long-term career aspirations. How might exploring certain topics advance your knowledge and skills in areas you are passionate about or wish to specialize in? For example, if you have a strong interest in adolescent mental health due to your experiences working in a high school setting, this could be a potential area of focus for your research.

**Literature Review**

A preliminary literature review helps you understand the current state of knowledge in your area of interest and identify potential gaps. As emphasized by Booth et al. (2016), "A good literature review is the foundation of a good research question" (p. 10). Conduct a review of existing literature to understand what is already known about your area of interest. Identify key themes, theories, and findings. Use academic databases, journals, and recent publications to gather this information. Look for gaps in the literature where further research is needed. Identify areas that have not been explored or where conflicting results suggest a need for more investigation. Pay attention to calls for future research in recent studies. For instance, through your literature review, you might find that while there is substantial research on adolescent anxiety, there is less focus on the impact of social media on adolescent anxiety levels. This gap could inform your research direction.

## STEP 2: NARROW DOWN YOUR FOCUS

Once you have identified your broad area of interest, the next step is to narrow down your focus to a more specific topic or question. To help with conceptualizing how this works, think of a funnel. At the top of the funnel, the opening is wide, but as you descend down the funnel, it gets narrower and narrower. Your research questions start broad, but the more you think about the question and the more you learn about your population, theory, and the existing literature, your research question will evolve and develop, until it is very precise. But let us start with the top of the funnel first and work our way down.

**Brainstorming**

Start by brainstorming to generate multiple ideas and potential research directions. As suggested by Alvesson and Sandberg (2013), "Problematization is key to generating novel research questions" (p. 12). Compile a list of potential topics and corresponding questions related to your area of interest. Allow yourself to think broadly and creatively without immediate judgment. Consider different angles, populations, or contexts within your broader interest area. Consider using concept mapping techniques (I use a whiteboard, but there are also apps and websites that help you do this) to visually represent your thoughts and see connections between different ideas. This can help you identify potential relationships or areas of overlap that might lead to interesting research questions.

For example, from your interest in adolescent mental health and the literature gap on social media, you might brainstorm questions like:

- "How does social media usage affect anxiety levels in adolescents?"
- "What role do parental controls on social media play in adolescent mental health?"
- "How do different types of social media platforms impact self-esteem in teenagers?"
- "What are the differences in social media effects on mental health between urban and rural adolescents?"

**Prioritization**

After generating a range of ideas, prioritize and select the most promising ones. Evaluate each potential topic based on its relevance to current issues in the field and its potential to contribute meaningful insights. As noted by Tracy (2010), "Relevant research is timely, significant, interesting, or evocative" (p. 840). Consider the practical aspects of conducting research on each topic, including time, resources, and access to participants or data. Punch (2016) emphasizes, "Feasibility is a key criterion in assessing research questions" (p. 19). Reflect on which topics resonate most with your passions and professional goals. Choose questions that you are genuinely excited about exploring. Keep your enthusiasm high—that energy will sustain you through the challenges of the research process. After evaluating your brainstormed ideas, you might prioritize the question "How does social media usage affect anxiety levels in adolescents?" because it is relevant to current mental health concerns, feasible to study within your constraints, and aligns with your interest in adolescent mental health.

## STEP 3: FORMULATE YOUR RESEARCH QUESTION

As we move down the funnel, the narrowed focus of your research question will begin to emerge.

**Drafting**

Drafting involves writing down several versions of your research question to explore different phrasings and scopes. As Agee (2009) suggests, "Qualitative research questions are often refined and sometimes reformulated as the study proceeds" (p. 432). Quantitative questions on the other hand are usually anchored in evaluating the type of relationship between variables. It may seem simpler, in some respects, to write a quantitative research question; some statistical models can be quite complex, therefore, making a precise research question rather difficult to write.

Write down several versions of your research question. Play with different phrasings and scopes to see which one best captures your inquiry. Consider variables, populations, and contexts you might include or exclude. Make sure each version of your question is specific and clearly defined. Avoid vague or overly broad questions that would be difficult to answer within the scope of a single study.

Examples of different versions might include:

- "What is the impact of social media on adolescent mental health?"
- "How does daily social media usage affect anxiety levels among high school students?"
- "What are the effects of social media interaction on anxiety and self-esteem in adolescents aged 13–17?"

**Criteria Check**

After drafting multiple versions, evaluate each against the criteria for a good research question: Is the question specific and precise, avoiding ambiguity? Can it be answered through empirical investigation and data collection? Does it address a gap in the existing literature or have practical implications for the field? Is it realistic in terms of time, resources, and access to data? Through this process, you might refine your question to "How does daily social media usage affect anxiety levels among high school students?" because it meets these criteria effectively.

## STEP 4: REFINE YOUR QUESTION

We are now at the bottom of the funnel. This is the final step that involves refining your question through feedback and iteration.

**Feedback**

Seeking input from others helps with refining your research question. As emphasized by Ravitch and Carl (2016), "Peer debriefing is an important strategy for enhancing the quality and credibility of qualitative research" (p. 189). For quantitative research, the same is also true. Seeking feedback is immensely helpful in making sense of your research question and whether the analysis is appropriate for the type of data. Discuss your research question with peers, mentors, and instructors. Share your rationale and listen to their feedback and suggestions. They may offer perspectives or insights you had not considered. Use the feedback to refine your question, making it clearer and more focused. Be open to constructive criticism, in fact, welcome it with open arms. Feedback and criticism are opportunities for growth and development of your question. Even if the feedback is invalid, it still gives you the chance to know the strengths of your question. But, all the best feedback in the world would not help you unless you are willing to make changes to your question, so be open and flexible. For example, after discussing with a mentor, you might adjust your question to "How does daily social media usage impact anxiety levels among high school students in urban areas?" to add more specificity to your study's context.

**Iterative Process**

Developing a research question is an iterative process that may continue even as you begin your research. As noted by Maxwell (2013), "The research question… should remain open and flexible to modification throughout the study" (p. 73). Be prepared to revisit and revise your question as you look deeper into the topic and gather more information. Your understanding of the subject matter will evolve, potentially leading to refinements in your question. As I said before, stay flexible and open to modifying your question based on new insights and information. Your adaptability will only lead to more meaningful and impactful research questions. To help with learning how to craft a research question, see Table 3 for a useful exercise.

## TABLE 3.

### Interactive Exercise: The 5 Whys

To help you dig deeper into your research interest and refine your question, let us engage in the "5 Whys" exercise. This technique, originally developed by Sakichi Toyoda for the Toyota Motor Corporation, is a tool for identifying the cause of an issue or the core of a research interest (Serrat, 2017).

Instructions:

1. Start with your initial research question or topic.
2. Ask "Why?" in relation to this question. Write down the answer.
3. Take that answer and ask "Why?" again. Repeat this process five times.
4. Review your answers to uncover the underlying motivations and refine your focus.

Example: Initial Question: "How does social media affect mental health?"

1. Why does social media affect mental health?
   - It influences how people interact and perceive themselves.
2. Why do interaction and self-perception matter?
   - They are critical components of an individual's self-esteem and anxiety levels.
3. Why are self-esteem and anxiety levels important?
   - They directly impact an individual's overall mental health and well-being.
4. Why focus on mental health and well-being?
   - Mental health issues, such as anxiety, are prevalent among adolescents and can have long-term effects.
5. Why is this prevalent among adolescents?
   - Adolescents are in a critical developmental stage and are highly influenced by their social environments, including social media.

Refined Question: "How does daily social media usage impact self-esteem and anxiety levels among adolescents?"

Now it is your turn. Start with an initial research question and work through the 5 Whys.

## INTEGRATING CLINICAL EXPERIENCE INTO RESEARCH QUESTIONS

Clinical work serves as a fertile ground for generating valuable research questions in counseling. The direct interaction with clients provides counselors with unique insights into the complexities of mental health issues and the effectiveness of various therapeutic approaches. This experiential knowledge can lead to research questions that are not only rigorous academically, but possessing the properties of practical relevance and clinical utility (Sim & Kaluge, 2023).

Reflective practice, as described by Schön (1983), helps counselors critically examine their clinical experiences, allowing for the identification of gaps between theory and practice, recognize patterns in client outcomes, and uncover areas where current research falls short. For instance, a counselor working with clients struggling with social anxiety exacerbated by social media use might recognize the need for research on adapting cognitive-behavioral interventions to address this modern manifestation of anxiety.

Or, take the concept of practice-based evidence, as discussed by Barkham and Mellor-Clark (2003), where they describe an approach that emphasizes the importance of systematically collecting data from routine clinical practice to inform research and improve therapeutic outcomes. By paying attention to patterns in client outcomes and feedback, counselors can formulate research questions that directly address practical challenges in therapy. In fact, many counselor journals are actively accepting journal submissions that focus more on case studies and data from clinical sites.

Moreover, the scientist–practitioner model, a cornerstone of counseling psychology and counseling training (Stoltenberg et al., 2000), encourages counselors to integrate research and practice continually. This model posits that clinical work should inform research questions, and research findings should, in turn, enhance clinical practice. For example, a counselor might observe that mindfulness techniques seem more effective for some clients than others, leading to a research question about the client characteristics that predict the effectiveness of mindfulness-based interventions. Interdisciplinary connections can also spark valuable research questions. As Norcross and Lambert (2011) argue, integrating insights from related fields can lead to innovative approaches in counseling. A counselor with an interest in technology, for instance, might explore how virtual reality exposure therapy compares to in vivo exposure in treating specific phobias.

## Exercise: From Clinical Observation to Research Question

Instructions:

1. Reflect on your recent clinical experiences or observations.
2. Identify a recurring theme, challenge, or pattern that intrigues you.
3. Formulate an initial research question based on this observation.
4. Apply the criteria we have discussed to refine your question.
5. Share your question with a peer and get feedback.

**Example**

*Clinical Observation*: Many clients report using their smartphones in bed and having trouble sleeping.

*Initial Question*: "How does nighttime smartphone use affect sleep quality?"

*Refined Question*: "What is the relationship between pre-sleep smartphone use and sleep quality among young adults (18–25) with diagnosed insomnia?" (Priya & De Guzman, 2023)

Grounding your research questions in clinical experience, you ensure that your research remains relevant to practice and contributes meaningfully to the field of counseling.

Summary of Key Points

1 A well-crafted research question is fundamental to successful research, providing clarity, focus, and direction.
2 The process of developing a research question involves identifying areas of interest, narrowing focus, formulating initial questions, and refining through feedback and iteration.
3 Effective research questions are specific, researchable, significant, and feasible.
4 Tools like the "5 Whys" technique and structured worksheets can aid in developing and refining research questions.
5 Peer review and discussion are valuable for gaining diverse perspectives and improving your research question.
6 Evaluating your research question against key criteria ensures its quality and effectiveness.
7 Integrating clinical experiences into research questions enhances the relevance and practicality of your research.

## CONCLUSION

The ability to craft a well-defined, precise, and relevant research question is an invaluable skill. Developing a robust research question is the foundation of the research project. Hopefully, this chapter has equipped you with the skills to develop research questions, from initial, broad curiosity to a refined, precise question. We have looked at examples, in this chapter, of carefully constructed research questions that provide clarity, focus, and direction, serving as a compass for your entire research journey.

We began by emphasizing the importance of research questions in bridging the gap between academic inquiry and practical application in counseling. Through various exercises and examples, we have illustrated how to transform broad areas of interest into specific, researchable questions that contribute meaningfully to the field. Hopefully, you see the necessity for aligning research questions with both rigor and practical relevance to counseling. Yet, this is hard to accomplish without a systematic approach. So please revisit the "5 Whys" exercise if your research question needs some more refining. As counselors in training, your unique perspectives and experiences provide fertile ground for meaningful research. By crafting research questions that resonate with your clinical observations and professional interests, you contribute not only to the academic discourse but also to the advancement of counseling practice. Remember, the process of developing a research question is often iterative and may evolve as you explore your topic. Embrace this evolution as part of your growth as a researcher. Stay curious, remain open to new insights, and continually reflect on how your research can best serve the field of counseling and the clients we aim to help. Let the skills and strategies learned in this chapter guide you whether you are exploring the impact of new therapeutic techniques, investigating the nuances of multicultural counseling, or examining the intersection of technology and mental health; your well-crafted research questions will light the way to discoveries that can enhance our understanding and improve our practice.

# 7

# Literature Review: Decoding the Language of Research

The knowledge that informs counseling practice and research does not materialize out of thin air. It is the product of years of dedicated searching, rigorous study, and thoughtful reflection on the works of other scholars. In the words of Sir Isaac Newton, "If I have seen further, it is by standing on the shoulders of giants." We counselors stand on the shoulders of giants. Your work in the present and future is informed and shaped by the collective wisdom of generations of counselors, psychologists, and mental health researchers. Our understanding of human behavior, mental health, and therapeutic interventions has been built incrementally, study by study, theory by theory. Each piece of research, no matter how small, contributes to this grand mosaic of knowledge, pushing the boundaries of our understanding and refining our practices.

As counselors-in-training and budding researchers, our goal is to make our own small but meaningful contribution to the corpus of knowledge generated by our field. We seek to add our voices to the ongoing discourse, to fill gaps in knowledge or practice, and to push the field forward in new and exciting ways. But to do so effectively, we must first understand and appreciate the work that has come before us. This is where the literature review comes into play. A thorough review of the literature is the first step of engaging with the rich history of our field and decoding the language of research that has shaped counseling as we know it today. It allows us to trace the evolution of ideas, to identify current trends and patterns, and to recognize, for example, ways that marginalized populations have been underserved and forgotten.

As we discussed in the last chapter, reviewing the literature precedes and follows the development of research questions. The reason being, more often than not, someone has already investigated your research interest/question. Do not lose heart! This does not mean you should abandon your research inquiry; it only means you need to refine, refocus, and/or nuance your question in light of the current evidence.

The literature review gives you a sense of what is going on in the field. It informs your research questions and enhances your clinical practice. But if you have never been taught how and where to examine the literature, how would you know? It is a skill you are assumed to have, but rarely are we ever actually taught. Navigating the vast sea of academic literature effectively can be absolutely overwhelming. It can be like searching for a needle in the haystack and after hours, days, and even weeks without finding the needle, you may be liable to give up. That is where this chapter comes in. In this chapter, we will cover the skills to critically evaluate evidence, synthesize complex ideas, and identify gaps in current knowledge—skills that are invaluable both in research and in clinical settings.

We will explore the literature review process and cover strategies to make this often-daunting task more manageable and, dare I say, even enjoyable. We will cover everything from defining your research question to utilizing technology in your literature search and analysis. Along the way, you will get practical tips, real-world scenarios, and interactive activities to help you develop your skills as a critical consumer and producer of research.

## THE IMPORTANCE OF LITERATURE REVIEWS IN COUNSELING RESEARCH

Primarily, a literature review provides the backdrop against which your research question emerges, helping you understand where your study fits within the broader landscape of counseling research and practice (Booth et al., 2016). As I said in the introduction, good research does not drop out of the sky. Good research and research questions not only reference what has already been done, it also critically understands and evaluates, and builds on, the existing evidence. Once you have a strong grasp of the literature then, and only then, will you be able to formulate research questions, hypotheses, theoretical developments, or critiques that *actually* advance the body of knowledge, instead of ignorantly repeating what has already been done.

But make sure to avoid the recency bias when looking at the literature, where the latest studies are given privilege and expected to be cited. Although citing recent studies is preferable for several good reasons (typically the standard is to cite studies published in the last 5 to 10 years), I would also encourage you to read the literature with a sense of history. See how your topic has progressed, morphed, and evolved over the last 30-40 years. What have been the major trend lines and patterns? Where is the literature and why? Why that direction and not others? What questions have been answered and what remains unanswered? What answers are based on faulty evidence? And what questions have not been imagined yet? There is a place for dreaming when doing research, and then enters into the process at the literature review phase.

Putting a finer point on it, a thorough literature review is instrumental in identifying specific areas where knowledge is lacking and/or where findings are contradictory. These are what have been conventionally termed as *gaps in the literature*. And it is the addressing of these gaps that often forms the basis for new research questions (Hart, 2018). By critically analyzing existing research, you can spot understudied populations or contexts, identify methodological limitations in previous studies, and uncover conflicting findings that need resolution through additional research.

## DEFINING A RATIONALE

Your comprehensive review of the literature should enable you to demonstrate the need for your research (Galvan & Galvan, 2017). By examining what has been done (and what has yet to be done), along with describing the problem and its significance, you provide a powerful rationale for your study. This justification is imperative for establishing the relevance and significance of your research question, articulating the potential contributions of your study to the field, and providing reasoning to funding bodies, or ethics committees, and other stakeholders who may need to approve your research. Conducting research is quite costly and time-consuming, so if there is not a good reason/rationale for your study, why do it? Why fund it? Why publish it?

## JUSTIFYING YOUR METHODOLOGY

As you have read in this textbook, and I am sure in your other textbooks, research methodologies and designs are plentiful. So, why choose your design and strategy? There are so many to choose from, you might as well pick one out of a hat? Well, it is not that easy. Your decision of a methodology/design could have serious implications.

Suppose you have a great research question, but you are not sure about what design you should use. You are considering two designs that seem to have equal usefulness; so to not waste anymore time, you choose one. The choice of one design over the other may either reveal information or obscure it. And what a terrible waste it would be if a great research question goes to waste because the design did not produce evidence that could properly address the question.

Why leave design to chance? Why invest your time and resources into a design that you aren't confident in when the research literature is replete with other studies offering ideas into research methods you may not have considered. These studies will also help you identify pitfalls to avoid in your own study design (Ridley, 2012). By examining the methodologies used by other researchers, you can also get a sense of the measures and instruments commonly used, understand the strengths and weaknesses of different data analytic strategies, and learn from the limitations noted in previous studies to improve your own methodology. You may not realize it yet, but another researcher may have already done a lot of work for you. And learning from their mistakes or suggestions could save you a great deal of time. You just have to find it in the literature.

### DEVELOPING CRITICAL THINKING SKILLS

Perhaps the most important part of the process of analyzing and synthesizing literature is the development of critical thinking skills, which are essential for both research and clinical practice (Machi & McEvoy, 2016). As you engage with the literature, you will learn to evaluate the quality and credibility of research evidence, recognize potential biases in study designs and interpretations, and synthesize information from diverse sources to form cohesive arguments. These skills are not only vital for conducting research but also for engaging in evidence-based practice as a counselor, enabling you to make informed decisions about which interventions to use with your clients based on the most current and robust evidence available.

## UNDERSTANDING THE LITERATURE REVIEW PROCESS

Now that we have a sense of *why* the literature review is important, let us talk about *how* to conduct a literature review. The literature review process can be distilled into several key steps, each needed for developing a comprehensive and insightful review. The foundation of any effective literature review is a well-defined research question (although, like we discussed before, a preliminary literature review may be needed to define the initial research question).

A clear, focused question helps narrow the scope of your review and secures the relevance in sourcing literature (Booth et al., 2016). Without a research question, you could be pursuing endless avenues. The research question tells you about where to look as well as where *not* to look. Yes, you may have stumbled upon an interesting line of research findings, but are they relevant? If it is not relevant, then it is got to go. You have got to develop a ruthless cutting board. Every piece of information needs to be ruthlessly assessed by its relevance to the research question/topic.

Once you have a well-defined question, where do you start gathering information? Consider utilizing various sources to secure a comprehensive review, including academic journals, books, conference proceedings, and online databases. Develop a search strategy using keywords related to your research question, and use Boolean operators to refine your search. Fink (2019) emphasizes the importance of using databases like PsycINFO, ERIC, and PubMed, which are invaluable resources for counseling research. It is important to keep a record of your search strategies, including the databases searched, keywords used, and any filters applied. You are leaving yourself a bread crumb trail so you can retrace your steps later. There is only so much information your working memory can hold onto; this step saves you a headache down the road by avoiding duplicating efforts but also allows you to replicate your search later, if needed.

## GOOGLE SCHOLAR

Yet, these research search tools may be a bit cumbersome to use; that is why I typically start with Google Scholar. There is much to be said about Google Scholar, first of all, it is free. Secondly, it shows you information, for example, about a research article in terms of how often it has been cited, what studies have cited, the different websites that host the article, author profiles, etc.... Google Scholar provides a great deal of information with very little effort put into the initial search. I recommend Google Scholar as a starting point and then moving onto the academic search tools when you run into limitations or paywalls.

## RELEVANCE, CREDIBILITY, AND QUALITY

As you gather literature, evaluate the relevance, credibility, and quality of each source. Some articles may be quite interesting, but irrelevant. These are the hardest to cut, but in the final analysis, they are not adding to your research article, but detracting. Furthermore, consider not only the source's direct relevance to your research question, as we discussed before, but also if the article is from a reputable journal or by a recognized expert in the field. Also, evaluate the soundness of its methodology and the support for its conclusions. Studies with novel findings may be just that, novel findings that can never be replicated again because the methodology was poor and the analysis was filled with errors. Ridley (2012) advises prioritizing peer-reviewed journal articles, as they have undergone rigorous evaluation. However, do not overlook influential books or seminal works that have shaped the field.

## ORGANIZATION IS KEY

But let us say you hit pay dirt on your first search and you find several perfect articles. How do you organize the information you are gathering in a way that is helpful to you later on? Group the literature into themes or categories that align with your research question. This helps structure your review and identify key areas of focus. Machi and McEvoy (2016) recommend using reference management software like EndNote, Zotero, or Mendeley to organize your sources efficiently, allowing you to store citations, full-text articles, and your notes in one place.

The heart of a literature review lies in the synthesis and analysis of the gathered information. This step involves identifying patterns, trends, gaps, and contradictions in the literature. As Hart (2018) notes, synthesis involves combining information from different sources to create a coherent understanding of the topic. Look for common findings across multiple studies, emerging areas of research in your field, areas where more research is needed, and conflicting findings that warrant further investigation.

Finally, develop a structured narrative that integrates your findings and sets the stage for your research. Your literature review should include an introduction to the topic; a presentation of the synthesized findings organized by themes or categories; and a conclusion that summarizes key findings, identifies gaps in current knowledge, and justifies the need for your research. Throughout the writing process, maintain a critical stance. As Galvan and Galvan (2017) emphasize, do not simply describe what others have found; evaluate the strengths and limitations of existing research and contextualize the findings to your study, showing how your study will contribute to the field.

## CREATIVE STRATEGIES FOR MANAGING LITERATURE

So, you have got a strong research question, you have found some databases with promising articles, leading to the identification of articles that are highly relevant to your research question. Now what? How do you manage the literature as you proceed with writing? Managing articles can be daunting, especially when dealing with a large volume of sources. Typically, research papers cite between 20 and 30 sources, with some papers citing up to 50 sources. In order to effectively manage this volume of information, you will need some creative strategies that can make it more manageable and even enjoyable.

Creating an annotated bibliography as you read is a powerful way to engage critically with each source and facilitate easier synthesis later. Machi and McEvoy (2016) recommend including the full citation in APA format, a brief summary of key points, an evaluation of the source's strengths and weaknesses, and its relevance to your research question. Consider using a digital tool like Notion or Evernote to create your annotated bibliography, allowing for easy organization, tagging, and searching of your annotations. Please see an example of an annotated bibliography in Table 1.

**TABLE 1.**

| |
|---|
| Lomas, T., Edginton, T., Cartwright, T., & Ridge, D. (2014). Men developing emotional intelligence through meditation? Integrating narrative, cognitive and electroencephalography (EEG) evidence. *Psychology of Men & Masculinity*, *15*(2), 213–224. https://doi-org/10.1037/a0032191.supp (Supplemental) |
| Men's adherence to traditional masculine norms has been correlated with negative mental and physical health outcomes, specifically emotional restriction, suicide, depression, substance abuse, externalization- maladaptive coping strategies. In an effort to remediate the negative effect of emotional numbing, suppression and dysregulation engendered by traditional masculine norms, authors conducted a longitudinal, mixed-methods study to explore how meditation may increase study participants' emotional intelligence and thereby improve mental health outcomes. They discovered that training attention tended to precede EI development, which in turn preceded ability to better manage well-being. Due to the design, researchers could not establish a sequential or temporal relatedness between attention, EI, and well-being. The study participants' improved performance could have been due to practice effects, however, this concern is minimal since the pretest and posttest were one year apart. Additionally, the reported increase of EI among study participants could have been performative signaling since men, who strongly identify with traditional masculine norms, are motivated by status and recognition, thus creating some doubt about the findings. |

Concept mapping is another visual technique that can help you organize and connect key themes and concepts from the literature. Ridley (2012) suggests that this visual representation can reveal relationships between ideas and highlight gaps in the literature. To create a concept map, start with your main research question or topic in the center, add major themes or concepts as branches, connect related ideas with lines or arrows, and add notes or brief summaries to each concept. Tools like MindMeister, XMind, or even simple drawing software can help you create digital concept maps.

Journaling your own personal thoughts and reflections can help you develop your ideas over time and track the evolution of your understanding. This tip fits in nicely with the reflective practices we have discussed at length in previous chapters. Booth et al. (2016) emphasized the value of documenting your thoughts, questions, and insights as you review the literature. Your research journal might include initial reactions to articles or books you have read, questions that arise as you engage with the literature, connections you notice between different sources or ideas, potential gaps or contradictions you identify in the existing research, and ideas for your own research design or methodology.

Utilizing collaborative platforms can provide diverse perspectives and help you catch blind spots in your analysis. Fink (2019) suggests that discussing literature with peers or research groups can enhance your understanding and interpretation of the material. Consider using tools like Google Docs for collaborative writing and commenting, Slack or Microsoft Teams for ongoing discussions about literature, or Zotero groups for sharing and annotating sources. I often approach others with an idea to gauge their interest. If they give me a positive response, I will quickly share a Google Document with them and start hashing out an outline. That outline is the true test of whether you will work well together and you can agree upon a shared vision for the project. The fact that the document is shared and both parties can see the real-time changes facilitates this process.

And for those who are visually oriented, sketch-noting or visual note-taking can be an effective way to summarize and remember key points from the literature. This technique involves combining text with simple drawings or diagrams to represent ideas. While this method may take some practice, it can be a powerful way to engage with the material and create memorable summaries of complex ideas. I like putting my ideas down on a whiteboard and giving myself the space for free association either by myself or with a research partner. But you do not need to be limited by physical space; there are several virtual whiteboards you can use online. I typically use Microsoft Whiteboard, Witeboard, or the whiteboard feature in Zoom.

Final note, employing these creative strategies can help transform the potentially overwhelming task of managing literature into an engaging and insightful process. Remember, the goal is not just to collect information, but to actively engage with it, make connections, and develop your own understanding of the field.

## INTEGRATING THEORETICAL FRAMEWORKS

Hopefully you have gotten the impression that the research question is a high priority in the research project and literature review process. However, there is one other essential component to consider, and that is using a theoretical framework, which exists more so in the background, whereas the research question is more in the forefront, but it is nonetheless critical. Theoretical frameworks are key aspects of conducting a broad and thorough literature review and developing a grounded research project. Anfara and Mertz (2014) posit that theoretical frameworks provide a structured lens through which to view your research topic, helping to clarify relationships between concepts and variables, and situating your study within the broader context of existing knowledge. Without a theoretical framework, your research project is a bit like a rudderless boat: you do not know where you are going and where you came from. A theoretical paradigm gives you direction, helps formulate research questions and hypotheses, points to certain methodologies, helps with data analysis and interpretation and understanding their implications, and help provide suggestions for future research projects. Theories help you organize your literature review by providing a structure for categorizing and analyzing existing research.

In order to integrate theoretical frameworks into your literature review and research, begin by identifying relevant theories in your field that provide an explanation for the problem facing the population of interest and possible solutions. For instance, if you are studying social media's impact on adolescent anxiety, you might consider theories such as Social Comparison Theory (Festinger, 1954) Uses and Gratifications Theory (Katz et al., 1973), and the Cognitive Model of Anxiety (Beck et al., 1985). Theories allow you to go beyond description of the problem; they get at why the problem is there in the first place.

Next, evaluate how well each theory explains the phenomena you are studying. Consider how the theory defines key concepts related to your research, what assumptions it makes, and how it has been applied in previous research similar to yours. Some theories may only offer partial explanations of the problem, whereas some theories are from another field, but perfectly explain the phenomenon you are studying. To illustrate, *Social Comparison Theory* might be relevant in explaining how exposure to idealized images on social media could lead to increased anxiety in adolescents. The hallmark of a theory is that it provides a degree of *explanatory power* to the phenomenon you are interested in exploring. A theory helps you understand the causes and consequences of the phenomenon, with tangible solutions. A theory that lacks explanatory power is merely just a description. Descriptions do not help generate research questions and hypotheses, and they do not help with data analysis and interpretations.

But, I would not dismiss a theory too quickly. Many researchers will adapt, refine, or blend two theoretical perspectives together to increase its explanatory power. Consider how different theories might complement or contradict each other in explaining your research topic. This synthesis can provide a more comprehensive understanding of your subject. For instance, while *Social Comparison Theory* might explain the mechanism by which social media affects anxiety, *Uses and Gratifications Theory* could shed light on why adolescents engage with social media despite potential negative effects. The Cognitive Model of Anxiety might help explain individual differences in how adolescents respond to social media use.

Use your chosen theoretical framework(s) to structure your literature review and guide your analysis of existing research. This might involve organizing your review around key concepts from the theories, analyzing how previous studies have applied these theories, and identifying gaps in how theories have been applied to your specific research question.

Your goal is not to force your research to fit into a particular theory, but to use theoretical frameworks as tools to deepen your analysis and situate your work within the broader scholarly conversation in your field. Theories are not a mold, but a window. They open up possibilities and options. As you develop your literature review, continually reflect on how these theories inform your understanding of the literature and guide your own research questions and design.

## ETHICAL CONSIDERATIONS IN LITERATURE REVIEWS

While literature reviews may seem less ethically fraught than primary research involving human subjects, they still need to be thought through ethically. One of the most fundamental ethical principles in academic writing is giving credit where it is due. This involves citing all sources properly and using appropriate citation styles. In counseling research, the American Psychological Association (APA) style is most commonly used. Make sure you are using the most recent edition of the APA manual (APA, 2020). As noted by Mertens (2015), proper attribution not only avoids plagiarism but also allows readers to trace the development of ideas and verify information if needed.

Plagiarism, whether intentional or unintentional, is a serious ethical breach. To avoid plagiarism, paraphrase ideas in your own words, making sure to still cite the original source. Use direct quotes sparingly, and always with proper citation and quotation marks. A paper may be so heavily quoted, even though you have proper attributions, there is no originality present. Be careful when taking notes to clearly distinguish between direct quotes, paraphrases, and your own ideas. Roig (2015) pointed out, self-plagiarism (reusing your own previously published work without citation) is also considered unethical in academic writing.

It is important and ethical to represent the findings of studies you review accurately and in context. That means you have to actually read them and understand them. Without full comprehension and critical analysis of the study's findings, you run the risk of misrepresenting the work. And, or, you represent the author's misguided conclusions. So, make sure to provide an accurate report of the finding with critical analysis, sharing context, and resisting the temptation to cherry-pick. Do not overstate or understate the conclusions of studies you review for the sake of drawing more eyes to your paper. Include relevant information about the study's limitations or conflicting findings. Do not selectively report only findings that support your argument, while ignoring contradictory evidence. As emphasized by Cooper (2016), misrepresentation of findings, even if unintentional, can lead to the propagation of misinformation and flawed conclusions.

Be aware of your own biases and strive for objectivity in your analysis and synthesis of the literature. This includes acknowledging your own perspective, including diverse viewpoints, and critically evaluating all studies. Be transparent about your theoretical orientation or any potential conflicts of interest. Make an effort to include studies that represent a range of perspectives on your topic. Apply the same level of critical analysis to studies regardless of whether they support or contradict your expectations. Pannucci and Wilkins (2010) note that while complete elimination of bias may be impossible, awareness and transparency can help mitigate its effects.

If you have access to unpublished studies or confidential information, obtain permission before citing unpublished work, respect embargoes on data or findings that are not yet publicly available, and be cautious about citing personal communications, ensuring you have the communicator's permission.

When reviewing literature from diverse cultural contexts, be aware of cultural biases in research methodologies and interpretations. Avoid making broad generalizations based on studies conducted in specific cultural contexts and use culturally sensitive language in your writing.

By adhering to these ethical principles, you not only maintain the integrity of your work but also contribute to a culture of ethical research in the field of counseling. Bear ethical considerations in mind to inform every stage of your literature review process, from selecting sources to synthesizing findings and drawing conclusions.

## APPLYING YOUR LITERATURE REVIEW TO PRACTICE

A thorough literature review is not just for personal gain and enrichment, or an academic exercise; it has the potential to inform and enhance your counseling practice. As you synthesize and analyze the existing research, you are building a foundation of evidence-based knowledge that can directly impact your work with clients. Melchert (2015) argued that evidence-based practice in counseling involves incorporating the best research evidence available in conjunction with clinical expertise, and wisdom, along with client interests. Your literature review can help you identify effective interventions for specific issues or populations, understand the theoretical foundations of various counseling approaches, and recognize potential limitations or contraindications of certain techniques.

The process of conducting a literature review sharpens your critical thinking skills. As you evaluate research studies, you develop the ability to assess the quality and relevance of evidence, recognize potential biases or limitations in research findings, and synthesize information from multiple sources to inform clinical decisions. These skills can help you become a more discerning consumer of research, enabling you to continually update your practice based on the latest evidence, or avoid faddish treatment approaches based on faulty or weak findings.

Your literature review may reveal gaps between current research and common clinical practices. As noted by Beutler et al. (2016), identifying these gaps can highlight areas where current practices may not be supported by evidence, inspire you to innovate in your clinical work, and motivate you to conduct your own research to address these gaps. A comprehensive understanding of the literature can enhance your ability to educate clients about their concerns and treatment options. You can provide clients with accurate, research-based information about their issues, explain the rationale behind your chosen interventions, and offer realistic expectations about treatment outcomes based on research findings. Your literature review can also be a valuable resource in supervision and consultation. You can discuss research findings with supervisors or colleagues to gain new perspectives, use the literature to support or challenge clinical decisions, and contribute to case conceptualizations by bringing relevant research insights.

## CONCLUSION

Conducting a thorough literature review is a fundamental skill for counselors-in-training and an ongoing practice for experienced professionals. It forms the backbone of evidence-based practice, informs clinical decision-making, and contributes to the advancement of the counseling field. Throughout this chapter, we have explored the process of conducting a literature review, from defining your research question to synthesizing findings and applying them to practice. We have discussed creative strategies for managing literature, the importance of integrating theoretical frameworks, and the ethical considerations that should guide your work.

Randolph (2019) emphasized that a well-conducted literature review is more than a summary of existing research; it is a critical analysis that demonstrates your understanding of the field and your ability to synthesize complex information. This process not only enhances your research skills but also directly impacts your clinical practice. By engaging deeply with the literature, you are better equipped to provide evidence-based interventions and to educate your clients about their concerns and treatment options. The integration of theoretical frameworks, as discussed by Anfara and Mertz (2014), provides a structured lens through which to view your research topic and situate your study within the broader context of existing knowledge. This theoretical grounding enhances the depth and rigor of your literature review and subsequent research. Ethical considerations, as highlighted by Mertens (2015) and Roig (2015), should be at the forefront of your mind throughout the literature review process. Proper attribution, accurate representation of findings, and awareness of potential biases maintain the integrity of your work and ensure contributing responsibly to the field.

The use of technology and digital tools can significantly enhance the efficiency and effectiveness of your literature review process (van Eck & Waltman, 2010). However, it is important to remember that these tools are aids to, not substitutes for, critical thinking and analysis. As you apply your literature review findings to practice, remember that this process, Melchert (2015) argues, is about integrating the best available research evidence with clinical expertise and client values. This integration is at the heart of evidence-based practice in counseling. Remember that a literature review is not a one-time task, but an ongoing process of engagement with the evolving body of knowledge in our field. As Booth et al. (2016) suggest, make it a habit to regularly review and critically engage with new research in your areas of interest.

By mastering the art and science of literature review, you are not only enhancing your own practice but also positioning yourself to contribute meaningfully to the field of counseling. Whether you go on to conduct original research, develop new interventions, or simply provide the best possible care to your clients, the skills you have developed in conducting literature reviews will serve as a strong foundation for your career. As you move forward, continue to approach the literature with curiosity, critical thinking, and an eye toward practical application. Remember that every study you read, every connection you make, and every insight you gain adds one more piece of knowledge that directly impacts the quality of care you provide to your clients. In the words of Hart (2018), "A researcher cannot perform significant research without first understanding the literature in the field" (p. 1). Here is my enhanced version of Hart's statement—A clinician cannot provide meaningful counseling without first understanding the literature in the field.

8

# Where to Find Data and How to Gather It

Effective data collection and analysis form the foundation of evidence-based practice and contribute to the advancement of counseling theory and techniques (Heppner et al., 2016). As counselors, we often encounter situations in our practice that leave us feeling stuck, uncertain, or concerned about client outcomes. You may find yourself hitting a plateau in your clinical skills, unable to pinpoint why a particular client is not making progress, or working in an agency that consistently falls short of its treatment goals. These scenarios can be frustrating and disheartening, but they also present an opportunity for growth and improvement through the application of research skills.

This chapter focuses on how to leverage research competencies to address common clinical challenges and enhance your practice. We will explore the critical process of identifying the proper type of data to collect when faced with unclear problems, such as a declining client or stagnant therapeutic progress. You will learn strategies for gathering relevant information efficiently and effectively, as well as techniques for analyzing and interpreting that data to derive meaningful insights.

By developing these research-oriented problem-solving skills, you will be better equipped to identify the root causes of clinical plateaus or setbacks, develop targeted interventions based on evidence, evaluate the effectiveness of your therapeutic approaches, contribute to quality-improvement efforts in your agency or private practice, and enhance overall client outcomes through data-informed decision-making.

## POPULATIONS AND SAMPLES

So, let us start with some basics. What is a population, a sample, sampling, and why is it important? For quantitative research (and for qualitative research as well, but with some qualifications), the goal is to learn something about populations, or subpopulations. In research, the aim is to understand or draw conclusions about large groups of individuals, known as populations. However, studying entire populations is usually impractical or impossible due to constraints of time, resources, and accessibility. This is where sampling comes into play. A sample is a subset of a population that researchers study to make inferences about the larger group (Creswell & Creswell, 2018). The process of selecting a sample from a population is called *sampling*; more on this in the next section.

For example, I may be interested in developing a reading program for elementary school children who live in rural areas. I would like to know if my reading program will help increase reading skills among this group, but how could I ever feasibly access the whole group? The money, time, energy, and number of researchers I would need in order to test my reading program with all elementary school children living in rural areas would be impossible. In light of this reality, where does that leave research? Are the questions I want answered unanswerable? Thankfully, no.

This is where sampling and data collection come into play. Even though we cannot access the totality of the population we want to study, we can draw a sample from the population. And that sample, even though a fraction of the size of the population, within a degree of certainty represents the struggles of the population and, if given my reading program, will also show the effectiveness that my reading program might have on the whole group. So, if I can determine that my reading program was helpful for my sample, then I can reasonably assume my reading program will be useful for others in the population. But I am making an assumption. Can you tell what it is? I am assuming my sample represents the population. According to the National Center for Education Statistics (2019), there are about 9.8 million rural elementary school children living in the United States. So, if I sample 200 of them from a school in Ohio, for example, what is the likelihood that my sample is similar to the whole group? Well, it is quite possible that my sample may not accurately represent the diversity of rural elementary students across the country. Therefore, I would have to either keep recruiting until my sample does represent the population, or I would have to narrow down my population down to something like rural elementary school children in the Midwestern United States between ages 8 and 10.

It is also important to draw a distinction between the population and the *accessible population*. The accessible population is the portion of the target population that the researcher can realistically access. This might be rural elementary school children in three specific counties in Ohio. The sample, yes, is a subset of the population, but it is also the group of individuals I draw from the accessible population (researchers' access may vary depending on their location and the funding of their research). Understanding these distinctions helps the researcher only make claims about effects observed among the sample and then making accurate generalizations to populations. In other words, researchers need to be aware of the limitations of their studies and the extent to which their findings can be generalized (Banerjee & Chaudhury, 2010).

## SAMPLING STRATEGIES

There are different ways participants are selected for a study that can alter the validity and generalizability of the results. Broadly, sampling strategies can be categorized into *probability* and *non-probability methods*, each with its own strengths and limitations. Probability sampling methods, commonly used in quantitative research, increase the probability, in theory, that every member of the population has a chance of being selected greater than zero. As Martínez-Mesa et al. (2016) explain, these methods enhance the representativeness of the sample and the generalizability of the findings. Simple random sampling, where each individual has an equal chance of selection, is the most straightforward probability method.

Not to confuse or overcomplicate things, but what if your population of interest has meaningful and important subgroups within the larger group? *Stratified sampling* allows you to identify those subgroups (strata) based on specific characteristics before random selection within each stratum. This method is particularly useful when researchers want to secure representation from all subgroups within the population. Please see Table 1 for three examples of stratified sampling.

**TABLE 1.** Stratified Sampling

Educational Research: Suppose you are studying the effects of a new teaching method across a school district. Your population includes students from various socioeconomic backgrounds, ethnicities, and academic performance levels. You might use stratified sampling to ensure representation from each of these subgroups:

- Strata: Low, middle, and high socioeconomic status
- Strata: Different ethnic groups
- Strata: Low, average, and high academic performers

Mental Health Study: If you are researching depression in adults, you might want to ensure representation across different age groups and genders:

- Strata: Young adults (18-30), middle-aged (31-50), older adults (51+)
- Strata: Male, female, non-binary

Counseling Effectiveness Research: When studying the effectiveness of a new counseling technique, you might stratify based on:

- Strata: Type of presenting problem (anxiety, depression, relationship issues)
- Strata: Previous counseling experience (none, some, extensive)

*Cluster sampling*, on the other hand, involves randomly selecting groups (clusters) rather than individuals, which can be efficient for geographically dispersed populations. Please see Table 2 for three examples.

**TABLE 2.** Cluster Sampling

National Education Survey: If you are conducting a nationwide study on high school students' career aspirations, you might:

- First, randomly select school districts (clusters) from different regions of the country
- Then, survey all students within the selected districts

Community Mental Health Assessment: For a statewide mental health needs assessment:

- Randomly select counties (clusters) within the state
- Survey all residents or a random sample within each selected county

Counselor Training Evaluation: To evaluate the effectiveness of a new counselor training program across a large counseling organization:

- Randomly select branch offices (clusters) of the organization
- Assess all counselors within the selected branches

Nonprobability sampling methods, more commonly used in qualitative research but also used in quantitative research, while not allowing for statistical generalization, can be valuable in certain research contexts. Etikan et al. (2016) argue that these methods are particularly useful in exploratory research, pilot studies, or when probability sampling is not feasible due to practical or ethical constraints.

*Convenience sampling* involves selecting participants based on their availability and willingness to participate. While this method is often criticized for its potential to introduce bias, it can be useful in preliminary studies or when resources are limited. *Purposive sampling* involves selecting participants who meet specific criteria relevant to the research question. This method is particularly useful when the research aims to study a specific subset of the population. Snowball sampling, where initial participants recruit additional participants from their networks, can be effective for reaching hidden or hard-to-access populations.

As Elfil and Negida (2017) point out, each sampling method has its strengths and weaknesses. Probability sampling methods generally provide more generalizable results but can be more resource-intensive and may not be feasible in all research contexts. Nonprobability methods, while potentially limiting generalizability, can provide rich, in-depth data and may be more practical in certain situations. The choice of sampling strategy should be guided by the research question, the characteristics of the population being studied, and practical considerations such as time and resources.

# QUANTITATIVE DATA COLLECTION

So, now that we have got the very important topics of population, sample, and how to access those sample groups, let us talk about getting data from those groups. For quantitative data collection in counseling research, the aim is to gather numerical data that can be statistically analyzed to test hypotheses and draw generalizable conclusions. One of the most common methods is the use of surveys and questionnaires. As Fowler (2014) notes, well-designed surveys can provide standardized data from large samples, allowing researchers to examine trends, attitudes, and behaviors across populations. However, the effectiveness of surveys largely depends on the quality of the questions and the representativeness of the sample.

Standardized assessments are another important tool in quantitative data collection. These instruments, which have been validated through rigorous psychometric testing, provide a consistent means of measuring psychological constructs. Hunsley and Mash (2008) emphasize the importance of using standardized assessments in both research and clinical practice, as they offer a reliable way to measure change over time and compare individuals or groups to established norms. Examples include the Beck Depression Inventory (BDI) for measuring depression severity or the Generalized Anxiety Disorder 7-item (GAD-7) scale for assessing anxiety symptoms.

Experimental and quasi-experimental designs represent more complex approaches to quantitative data collection. As described by Shadish et al. (2002), these designs allow researchers to examine causal relationships between variables. In true experimental designs, participants are randomly assigned to different conditions, allowing researchers to control for confounding variables. Quasi-experimental designs, while lacking random assignment, still attempt to establish causal relationships and can be valuable when randomization is not feasible or ethical. For instance, a researcher might compare outcomes for clients who choose different types of therapy, controlling for other factors that might influence results.

**TABLE 3.**

| DATA GATHERING STRATEGY | DESCRIPTION | ADVANTAGES | LIMITATIONS | BEST USED FOR |
|---|---|---|---|---|
| Surveys | Self-reported information collected via questionnaires | Large sample sizes, cost-effective, easily quantifiable | Potential for response bias, limited depth | Gathering data on attitudes, behaviors, or characteristics from large populations |
| Structured Interviews | Structured questions asked by an interviewer | Consistent data collection, high response rates | Time-consuming, potential for interviewer bias | Collecting standardized responses from a specific sample |
| Standardized Assessments | Validated instruments measuring specific constructs | Reliable, validated measures, comparable across studies | May not capture individual nuances or context | Measuring psychological constructs or symptoms |
| Experimental Methods | Controlled manipulation of variables to test hypotheses | Allows for causal inferences, high internal validity | Artificial settings may limit external validity | Testing causal relationships between variables |
| Secondary Data Analysis | Analysis of existing datasets or records | Time and cost-efficient, access to large datasets | Limited control over data quality, may lack specific variables | Analyzing trends over time or large-scale patterns |
| Physiological Measurements | Collection of physical or biological data | Objective measures, not subject to self-report biases | Often requires specialized equipment, limited to certain variables | Collecting physiological data related to psychological states |

## QUALITATIVE DATA COLLECTION

Qualitative data-collection methods focus on gathering rich, descriptive data that can provide in-depth insights into individuals' experiences, perceptions, and behaviors. Interviews are a cornerstone of qualitative research in counseling. Brinkmann and Kvale (2015) describe various types of interviews, including structured interviews with predetermined questions, semistructured interviews that allow for some flexibility, and unstructured interviews that are more conversational in nature. The choice of interview type depends on the research question and the depth of information sought.

Focus groups, as outlined by Krueger and Casey (2015), involve facilitated discussions with small groups of participants. This method can be particularly useful for exploring shared experiences or generating ideas for interventions. Focus groups allow researchers to observe group dynamics and gather a range of perspectives in a relatively short time. However, they require skilled facilitation to ensure all participants have the opportunity to contribute and to manage potential group effects.

Observation techniques, whether participant or nonparticipant, can provide valuable data about behaviors and interactions in natural settings. Creswell and Poth (2018) highlight the importance of systematic observation protocols to maintain consistency and reduce bias in data collection. In counseling research, observation might be used to study counselor–client interactions or group therapy processes.

**TABLE 4.**

| DATA GATHERING STRATEGY | DESCRIPTION | ADVANTAGES | LIMITATIONS | BEST USED FOR |
|---|---|---|---|---|
| Semistructured Interviews | One-on-one conversations with flexible questioning | In-depth individual perspectives, flexibility | Time-intensive, potential for interviewer influence | Exploring individual experiences and perspectives |
| Focus Groups | Facilitated group discussions on specific topics | Group dynamics, efficient for multiple viewpoints | Dominant voices may skew discussion | Generating ideas, exploring shared experiences |
| Participant Observation | Researcher participates in and observes the setting | Rich contextual data, natural behavior observation | Time-consuming, potential observer effect | Studying behaviors and interactions in natural settings |
| Document Analysis | Systematic review of existing documents or artifacts | Nonintrusive, provides historical/contextual data | Limited to available documents, potential bias in selection | Understanding organizational culture or historical contexts |
| Open-ended Surveys | Questionnaires with open-ended response options | Allows for larger sample sizes in qualitative research | Lacks opportunity for probing or clarification | Gathering qualitative data from a larger sample |
| Photo-elicitation | Using images to stimulate discussion or reflection | Visual stimuli can evoke deeper responses | Interpretation of visual data can be subjective | Exploring topics that are difficult to articulate verbally |
| Narrative Inquiry | Collection and analysis of personal stories | Captures personal experiences and meanings | Relies on participants' ability to articulate experiences | Understanding personal life stories and experiences |
| Ethnography | Immersive study of a culture or community | Comprehensive understanding of cultural contexts | Time-intensive, potential for researcher bias | Studying cultural practices and social phenomena |

## MIXED METHODS APPROACHES

Increasingly, researchers are recognizing the value of combining quantitative and qualitative approaches in what is known as mixed methods research. Creswell and Plano Clark (2018) argue that mixed methods can provide a more comprehensive understanding of complex phenomena than either approach alone. For instance, a study on the effectiveness of a new counseling intervention might use quantitative measures to assess symptom reduction, while qualitative interviews explore clients' experiences of the intervention and the perceived mechanisms of change. This integration of methods can lead to more nuanced and practically applicable findings.

**TABLE 5.** Comparison of Quantitative and Qualitative Data-Collection Methods

| DATA GATHERING STRATEGY | DESCRIPTION | ADVANTAGES | LIMITATIONS | BEST USED FOR | QUANTITATIVE COMPONENT | QUALITATIVE COMPONENT |
|---|---|---|---|---|---|---|
| Convergent Parallel Design | Concurrent collection of quantitative and qualitative data | Comprehensive understanding, triangulation of findings | Challenging to integrate different types of data | Comparing different perspectives on a topic | Surveys, experiments, standardized assessments | Interviews, focus groups, open-ended questions |
| Explanatory Sequential Design | Quantitative data collection followed by qualitative | Qualitative data explains quantitative results | Time-consuming, may require larger sample for qualitative phase | Explaining quantitative results in more depth | Large-scale surveys or experiments | Follow-up interviews or focus groups |
| Exploratory Sequential Design | Qualitative data collection followed by quantitative | Quantitative data tests or generalizes qualitative findings | May be difficult to specify quantitative phase based on qualitative results | Developing and testing new instruments or theories | Testing hypotheses generated from qualitative phase | Exploratory interviews or focus groups |
| Embedded Design | One data type embedded within a larger design of the other type | Efficient use of resources, enhances a primary method | Secondary method may not be given enough priority | Adding qualitative context to experimental studies | Experimental design with qualitative component | Qualitative exploration within experimental design |
| Transformative Design | Framed within a transformative theoretical perspective | Addresses issues of social justice and inequality | Requires expertise in both transformative methods and mixed methods | Studying marginalized populations or sensitive topics | Quantitative measures of inequality or discrimination | In-depth study of marginalized group experiences |
| Multiphase Design | Multiple phases of quantitative and qualitative data collection | Allows for long-term, complex project development | Complex, time-consuming, requires significant resources | Evaluating complex interventions or programs over time | Multiple quantitative phases (e.g., surveys, assessments) | Multiple qualitative phases (e.g., interviews, observation) |

# DATA COLLECTION AND ANALYSIS FOR CLINICIANS

Data collection and analysis are vital skills for practicing clinicians. Implementing standardized assessments in clinical practice, as advocated by Hunsley and Mash (2008), can provide valuable information about client symptoms and progress. These assessments can be used at intake to inform diagnosis and treatment planning, and then administered regularly to track changes over time. Lambert (2013) emphasizes the importance of systematic progress monitoring in therapy. This involves regularly collecting data on client outcomes and using this information to guide treatment. Such practices have been shown to improve therapy outcomes, particularly for clients who are not responding well to treatment. Bickman (2008) argues that using data to inform treatment decisions is a key component of evidence-based practice. This might involve adjusting treatment approaches based on client progress data, or using research findings to select interventions that have shown effectiveness for specific problems or populations.

## INTERPRETING AND IMPLEMENTING DATA IN CLINICAL PRACTICE

The ability to interpret and implement data effectively empowers clinicians striving to provide evidence-based care. The APA Presidential Task Force on Evidence-Based Practice (2006) defines evidence-based practice in psychology as the integration of the best available research with clinical expertise in the context of patient characteristics, culture, and preferences. This definition underscores the importance of not only being aware of research findings but also knowing how to apply them judiciously in clinical settings.

Using research findings to guide interventions requires a nuanced understanding of both the research literature and the unique needs of individual clients. For instance, a meta-analysis might suggest that cognitive-behavioral therapy (CBT) is effective for treating generalized anxiety disorder, but the clinician must consider how to adapt these techniques to suit the specific circumstances, cultural background, and preferences of each client.

The concept of practice-based evidence, as described by Barkham et al. (2010), complements traditional evidence-based practice by emphasizing the importance of data collected in real-world clinical settings. This approach involves systematically collecting outcome data from one's own practice and using this information to refine and improve interventions. Practice-based evidence can be particularly valuable for understanding how established interventions perform in specific clinical contexts or with particular client populations.

Continuous quality improvement in clinical settings, as outlined by Boswell et al. (2015), involves ongoing efforts to enhance the effectiveness and efficiency of care. This might involve regular review of client outcome data, solicitation of client feedback, and adjustment of treatment approaches based on this information. Such practices can help clinicians identify areas for improvement in their own work and contribute to the overall advancement of clinical practice.

## ETHICAL CONSIDERATIONS IN DATA COLLECTION AND USE

Ethical considerations are paramount in both research and clinical applications of data collection and analysis. Fisher (2013) emphasizes the critical importance of informed consent in research contexts. Participants must be fully informed about the nature of the study, potential risks and benefits, and their rights as participants. In clinical settings, clients should be informed about the purpose and use of any assessments or data-collection procedures.

Data privacy and security have become increasingly important concerns in the digital age. Lustgarten et al. (2020) discuss the ethical implications of digital record-keeping and data sharing in mental health contexts. Clinicians and researchers must be vigilant about protecting client/participant confidentiality, ensuring secure storage of data, and being transparent about how data will be used.

Cultural sensitivity in data collection and interpretation is another very important ethical consideration. Sue et al. (2019) argue that cultural competence is essential in all aspects of psychological practice, including research and assessment. This involves considering how cultural factors might influence the validity of assessment tools, the interpretation of data, and the applicability of research findings to diverse populations.

**TABLE 6.** Ethical Checklist for Data Collection in Counseling

- Informed consent obtained from all participants/clients
- Clear explanation of data use and storage provided
- Confidentiality and anonymity measures in place
- Cultural sensitivity considered in method and content
- Potential risks to participants/clients identified and minimized
- Plan for secure data storage and disposal in place
- Procedure for participant/client withdrawal established
- Potential conflicts of interest disclosed
- Approval from relevant ethical review board obtained (for research)
- Plan for sharing results with participants/clients (if applicable)

# IMPLEMENTATION STRATEGIES FOR DATA-DRIVEN PRACTICE

Implementing a data-driven approach in counseling practice requires careful planning. The last thing you want to do is to gather data in a haphazard manner. In a practical sense, this will be off putting to clients, but most importantly, it will compromise the veracity of your findings. Proctor et al. (2009) outline several strategies for implementing evidence-based practices in mental health settings. These include providing training and ongoing support for clinicians, adapting interventions to fit the local context, and addressing organizational barriers to change.

One effective strategy is the use of measurement-based care (MBC), as described by Lewis et al. (2019). MBC involves the systematic administration of symptom rating scales to monitor client progress and inform treatment decisions. This approach can help clinicians identify clients who are not responding well to treatment and make timely adjustments to their interventions.

Another important aspect of implementation is the development of a culture that values data and continuous improvement. Aarons et al. (2011) discuss the role of leadership in fostering such a culture. Leaders in counseling organizations can promote data-driven practice by providing resources for data collection and analysis, recognizing and rewarding evidence-based practice, and modelling the use of data in their own decision-making processes.

## CHALLENGES AND LIMITATIONS

While the benefits of data-driven approaches in counseling are clear, it is important to acknowledge the challenges and limitations. Lilienfeld et al. (2013) discuss several barriers to the adoption of evidence-based practices in clinical psychology, including skepticism about research findings, concerns about the applicability of group-level data to individual clients, and the time and resource constraints faced by many practitioners.

There is also the risk of over-relying on quantitative data at the expense of clinical judgment and the therapeutic relationship. Wampold (2015) argues that common factors, such as the therapeutic alliance and therapist effects, play a role in therapy outcomes. A balanced approach that integrates empirical data with clinical expertise and client preferences is necessary for effective practice.

## FUTURE DIRECTIONS

Looking to the future, several trends are likely to shape the landscape of data collection and use in counseling. The growing field of precision mental health, as described by Bickman et al. (2016), aims to tailor interventions to individual clients based on their unique characteristics and circumstances. This approach relies heavily on sophisticated data-analysis techniques to identify patterns and predict treatment outcomes.

Technological advancements are also opening up new possibilities for data collection and analysis. Torous and Roberts (2017) discuss the potential of digital phenotyping—using data from smartphones and other devices to gain insights into mental health symptoms and behaviors. While such approaches offer exciting possibilities, they also raise important ethical questions about privacy and the boundaries of the therapeutic relationship.

Finally, there is a growing recognition of the need for more diverse and representative data in counseling research. Arnett (2008) critiques the overreliance on WEIRD (Western, Educated, Industrialized, Rich, and Democratic) samples in psychological research. Future research efforts will need to prioritize the inclusion of diverse populations to maintain that findings are applicable across different cultural contexts.

## CONCLUSION

The integration of data collection, analysis, and interpretation into counseling practice represents a significant opportunity to enhance the effectiveness and accountability of our field. As we have explored in this chapter, data can inform every aspect of counseling, from selecting interventions to monitoring client progress and evaluating overall program effectiveness.

However, as Norcross and Wampold (2011) remind us, the ultimate goal of data-driven practice is not just to accumulate knowledge, but to improve client outcomes. As counselors, our challenge is to harness the power of data while maintaining the empathy, creativity, and human connection that are at the heart of effective therapy.

By embracing a thoughtful, ethical approach to data use, we can contribute to the advancement of our field, provide more effective care for our clients, and ultimately fulfill our professional commitment to evidence-based practice. As we move forward, ongoing dialog, critical reflection, and a commitment to lifelong learning will be essential in navigating the evolving landscape of data-driven counseling practice.

9

# Research in Practice: Conducting Studies in Clinical Settings

The field of counseling and psychotherapy has long grappled with the challenge of bridging the gap between research and practice. While laboratory studies and randomized controlled trials conducted in highly controlled settings have been instrumental in establishing the efficacy of various therapeutic approaches, they often fall short in terms of real-world applicability.

Laboratory settings excel at establishing internal validity—the extent to which we can confidently attribute observed effects to the manipulated variables. These tightly controlled environments allow researchers to minimize confounding factors and isolate specific variables of interest. However, this strength often comes at the cost of external validity or the degree to which findings can be generalized to real-world clinical settings and diverse patient populations. In contrast, research conducted in clinical practice settings offers a unique opportunity to enhance the external validity and generalizability of findings. By studying therapeutic processes and outcomes in the context of actual clinical practice, researchers can capture the complexity and variability that characterize real-world therapeutic encounters. This approach allows for the examination of how interventions perform under typical practice conditions, with diverse client populations, and in the face of real-world constraints and challenges.

Practice-based research can provide insights into the effectiveness of treatments when applied in naturalistic settings, accounting for factors such as comorbidities, client preferences, and therapist effects—elements often controlled for or excluded in laboratory studies. Moreover, this type of research can shed light on the process of therapy itself, uncovering nuances in therapeutic relationships and change mechanisms that may be difficult to capture in more artificial settings.

However, conducting research in clinical practice is not without its challenges. Practitioners must navigate ethical considerations, time constraints, and methodological complexities while maintaining the primacy of client care. Despite these challenges, the potential benefits of practice-based research are substantial, offering a path to more relevant, applicable, and impactful findings that can directly inform and improve clinical practice.

This chapter explores the unique aspects of conducting research in clinical practice settings, drawing on insights from practitioners who have successfully integrated research into their clinical work. We will examine models for simultaneous practice and research, different designs, strategies for planning and executing clinical studies, and approaches to overcoming common challenges. Research conducted in clinical settings offers one of the best representations of the practitioner–researcher model, where counselors can contribute to the advancement of the field while enhancing the quality and effectiveness of their clinical work. So, let's start with discussing a model for how to do practice and research together and then discuss establishing a strong foundation in design.

## PRACTICE AND RESEARCH MODELS

Persons (2018) proposed a model for conducting research in clinical practice that she calls "Simultaneous Practice and Research." The Person's model describes how research activities can be integrated into clinical practice. This model is based on the principle that many research and practice activities can occur concurrently. In this approach, research is based on hypotheses that clinicians develop and data they collect as part of their daily clinical work. The *simultaneous practice and research model* has a strong intuitive logic behind it because good clinical work already relies on hypothesis-testing, especially about the mechanisms that maintain a patient's symptoms and underpin the change process. These hypotheses are born out of genuine interest in helping clients get better, but they also are relevant for others in the field. Therefore, the data clinicians collect may be highly relevant for other practitioners who are working with clients with similar presentations (Persons, 2018).

Persons' model is great; however, the simultaneous practice and research model is one of many that have been developed in the last 30 years. For example, the *practice-based evidence* (PBE) model, developed by Barkham and Mellor-Clark (2003), emphasizes the systematic collection of data in routine clinical practice to evaluate treatment effectiveness in real-world settings. This model involves implementing standardized outcome measures across a practice or clinic, allowing for the comparison of different therapeutic approaches and practitioner effectiveness. There is also the *patient-focused research model*, proposed by Howard et al. (1996), which focuses on monitoring individual patient progress throughout treatment. This approach uses frequent assessments to track client change and provide feedback to clinicians, allowing for real-time adjustments to treatment plans.

The *practice research network* model, described by Castonguay et al. (2013), involves creating collaborative networks of practitioners and researchers. These networks work together to identify clinically relevant research questions and conduct studies across multiple practice settings, combining the strengths of academic research with the realities of clinical practice. The *evidence-based practice in psychology* model, endorsed by the American Psychological Association (APA, 2006), integrates the best available research evidence with clinical expertise and patient values/preferences. This model encourages clinicians to stay current with research literature and apply findings in a way that considers the unique characteristics of each client. The *collaborative practice improvement model*, developed by Duncan et al. (2010), emphasizes ongoing client feedback and outcome monitoring as a way to continuously improve clinical practice. This approach involves clients as active collaborators in the research process.

The scientist–practitioner model, long established in clinical psychology training programs (Baker & Benjamin, 2000), encourages clinicians to approach their work with a scientific mindset, continuously evaluating their practices and contributing to the knowledge base of the field.

Each of these models offers unique strengths in bridging the gap between research and practice. They share common themes of systematic data collection, ongoing evaluation of clinical outcomes, and a commitment to using empirical evidence to inform and improve practice. Counselors might choose to adopt elements from multiple models, tailoring their approach to fit their specific practice setting and research interests.

Importantly, all these models emphasize that research integration is not a one-time event, but an ongoing process. They encourage clinicians to cultivate a mindset of curiosity and inquiry, continuously seeking to understand and improve their clinical work through systematic observation and analysis. This approach not only enhances individual practice but also contributes to the collective knowledge of the counseling field, fostering a culture of evidence-based, reflective practice.

## PROGRAM EVALUATION IN CLINICAL RESEARCH

Program evaluation is a systematic method for collecting, analyzing, and using information to answer questions about projects, policies, and programs, particularly about their effectiveness and efficiency. In the context of counseling and clinical research, program evaluation facilitates assessing the impact of interventions, improving service delivery, and demonstrating the value of counseling services.

Rossi et al. (2019) defined program evaluation as "the use of social research procedures to systematically investigate the effectiveness of social intervention programs" (p. 3). In clinical settings, this process can be applied to evaluate individual therapeutic approaches, group interventions, or entire counseling programs.

## TYPES OF PROGRAM EVALUATION

There are several types of program evaluation that counselors might employ in clinical settings. Needs assessment, as described by Altschuld and Kumar (2010), helps identify the needs of a target population and informs program planning. Process evaluation focuses on program implementation and delivery, assessing whether a program is being carried out as intended (Saunders et al., 2005). Outcome evaluation measures the extent to which a program achieves its intended outcomes or effects (Newcomer et al., 2015). Impact evaluation assesses the long-term and broader effects of a program, including unintended consequences (White, 2010). Cost-effectiveness evaluation examines the balance between a program's costs and its outcomes (Levin & McEwan, 2001).

## INTEGRATING PROGRAM EVALUATION INTO CLINICAL RESEARCH

Program evaluation can be seamlessly integrated into the research activities of clinical practitioners. For example, a counselor implementing a new group therapy program for anxiety might conduct a needs assessment to understand the specific anxiety-related challenges in their client population. They could then perform a process evaluation to make sure that the program is being delivered consistently and as designed. An outcome evaluation would measure changes in anxiety levels pre- and postintervention. An impact evaluation could assess long-term effects on clients' overall well-being and functioning. Finally, a cost-effectiveness evaluation would determine whether the program's benefits justify its costs.

Chen (2015) proposed a theory-driven approach to program evaluation, which emphasizes the importance of understanding the theoretical foundations of a program and how they relate to expected outcomes. This approach can be particularly useful in counseling settings, where interventions are often based on specific theoretical models.

## DATA COLLECTION AND ANALYSIS IN PROGRAM EVALUATION

Program evaluation typically involves a mix of quantitative and qualitative methods. Quantitative data might include standardized outcome measures, client satisfaction surveys, or service utilization statistics. Qualitative data could involve client interviews, focus groups, or case studies. The choice of methods should align with the evaluation questions and the nature of the program being evaluated (Patton, 2008).

Analysis in program evaluation often involves comparing actual program performance against established criteria or benchmarks. This might include comparing outcomes to those of a control group, to preintervention baselines, or to established standards in the field.

### CHALLENGES AND CONSIDERATIONS

Conducting program evaluation in clinical settings can present several challenges. Ethical considerations require evaluators to maintain client confidentiality and obtain appropriate consent. Resource constraints can limit the time and resources available for evaluation activities in clinical settings. Stakeholder engagement facilitates successful evaluation that often requires buy-in from various stakeholders, including clients, staff, and administrators. The complexity of clinical interventions, which often involve multiple components and occur in complex social contexts, can make it challenging to isolate program effects. Despite these challenges, program evaluation offers valuable benefits. It can provide evidence of program effectiveness, guide program improvement, inform resource allocation decisions, and contribute to the broader knowledge base in counseling and psychotherapy research.

## PRACTICE-BASED RESEARCH DESIGNS

When conducting research in clinical practice, counselors have several research designs at their disposal. Each design offers unique advantages and can be selected based on the research question, available resources, and practice constraints. Here are some of the most relevant designs for clinical settings:

*Single-Case Experimental Designs* (SCEDs), as described by Kazdin (2011), are particularly well suited to clinical practice settings. These designs involve intensive study of one or a small number of cases over time, with each participant serving as their own control. SCEDs typically involve establishing a baseline, introducing an intervention, and monitoring outcomes systematically. Key features of SCEDs include repeated measurements over time, flexibility to adjust interventions based on client response, and the ability to demonstrate causal relationships with small sample sizes. For example, a counselor might use an ABAB design (where A is baseline and B is intervention) to evaluate the effectiveness of a new anxiety management technique, measuring anxiety levels daily throughout baseline and intervention phases.

*Process research* focuses on understanding what happens during therapy sessions and how change occurs. This approach, advocated by researchers like Robert Elliott, can provide valuable insights into the mechanisms of therapeutic change. Process research might involve analyzing session transcripts or recordings, using moment-to-moment ratings of client experiences, and examining the relationship between in-session processes and treatment outcomes. For instance, a counselor might use the helpful aspects of therapy form after each session to identify critical incidents in therapy and link these to overall treatment outcomes.

*PBE* studies, as described by Barkham and Mellor-Clark (2003), involve systematically collecting data from routine clinical practice to evaluate treatment effectiveness in real-world settings. PBE studies often involve routine outcome monitoring, large sample sizes from naturalistic settings, and comparison of different therapeutic approaches as they occur in actual practice. A counseling center might implement a PBE approach by routinely administering standardized outcome measures to all clients and analyzing these data to compare the effectiveness of different therapists or treatment approaches.

*Qualitative case studies*, as outlined by McLeod (2010), offer an in-depth exploration of client experiences and therapeutic processes. These studies can provide rich, contextual information that may be missed in more structured quantitative approaches. Qualitative case studies might involve in-depth interviews with clients, analysis of therapist notes or reflections, and exploration of unique or exemplary cases. For example, a counselor might conduct a series of interviews with a client who experienced a significant positive change to understand the client's perspective on what contributed to their improvement.

*Mixed-methods designs* combine quantitative and qualitative approaches to provide a more comprehensive understanding of therapeutic processes and outcomes. These designs can be particularly valuable in clinical settings where both measurable outcomes and subjective experiences are important. A mixed-methods study might include quantitative outcome measures, qualitative interviews or open-ended questions, and integration of quantitative and qualitative findings. For instance, a counselor might track clients' depression scores using a standardized measure while also conducting periodic interviews to explore clients' subjective experiences of change.

*Action research*, as described by McNiff (2013), involves practitioners systematically investigating their own practice with the goal of improving it. This approach is particularly well suited to clinical settings as it directly links research to practice improvement. Action research typically involves cycles of planning, action, observation, and reflection. A counselor might use action research to develop and refine a new intake assessment process, iteratively implementing changes and evaluating their impact.

Each of these research designs offers unique advantages for conducting research in clinical settings. The choice of design should be guided by the research question, the constraints of the practice setting, and the counselor's expertise and resources. By selecting an appropriate design, counselors can contribute valuable insights to the field while enhancing their own clinical practice.

## BUILDING A RESEARCH DATABASE

Persons et al. (2021) provided practical strategies for creating a research database from clinical data. They emphasize the importance of collecting process and outcome data at every session, noting that patients benefit more when therapists regularly collect and review feedback about the patient's progress. Key recommendations from this paper include collecting data online for efficiency and ease of aggregation into a database, selecting assessment tools that allow data to be easily downloaded and exported for statistical analysis, and relying on measures widely used in the research community to facilitate comparison of results with other studies. Persons et al. also discussed the ethical and legal considerations of using clinical data for research purposes. They emphasize the importance of obtaining informed consent for research from patients and navigating the dual relationship of treatment provider and researcher carefully. They provide guidance on obtaining ethical review for research proposals and address legal issues such as Health Insurance Portability and Accountability Act (HIPAA) compliance.

## CHALLENGES OF CONDUCTING RESEARCH IN A PRACTICE SETTING

While practice-based research offers many benefits, it also presents unique challenges. Time constraints are a significant concern for many practitioners. Integrating research into clinical work requires careful planning and efficient data collection methods. One strategy is to incorporate research measures into routine clinical assessments, minimizing additional time demands. For example, counselors could use standardized outcome measures as part of their regular client check-ins, allowing for ongoing data collection without significantly disrupting clinical practice.

Financial considerations are also important. While large-scale studies may require external funding, many practice-based research projects can be conducted with minimal resources. Practitioners can leverage existing clinical data, use free or low-cost assessment tools, and collaborate with colleagues to share resources. Additionally, forming partnerships with local universities or research institutions can provide access to resources and expertise that may not be available within the practice.

Technology can greatly facilitate practice-based research. Electronic health records can be used for data collection and analysis, while online survey platforms can streamline the process of gathering client feedback. However, practitioners must maintain that any technology used complies with privacy regulations and ethical guidelines. It is helpful to select tools that are both user-friendly for clients and staff and secure enough to protect sensitive information.

## ETHICAL AND REGULATORY CONSIDERATIONS

Conducting research in practice settings requires careful attention to ethical issues. The dual role of practitioner–researcher can create potential conflicts of interest. It is critical to make sure that research activities do not compromise client care or therapeutic relationships. Clear communication with clients about the nature and purpose of research activities is essential. Practitioners should develop protocols for separating clinical and research activities, ensuring that clients understand their participation in research is voluntary and will not affect their treatment.

Informed consent is a critical ethical consideration. Clients must understand that their participation in research is voluntary and separate from their treatment. They should be informed about how their data will be used and any potential risks or benefits of participation. Consent forms should be written in clear, accessible language, and counselors should be prepared to discuss the research process with clients to maintain full understanding.

For practitioners affiliated with institutions, navigating Institutional Review Board (IRB) processes is an important step. While IRB requirements may seem daunting, they serve to protect both clients and researchers. Many IRBs have expedited review processes for low-risk studies, which can simplify the approval process for practice-based research. Practitioners should familiarize themselves with their institution's IRB procedures and seek guidance when needed.

Practitioners not affiliated with institutions may need to seek alternative forms of ethical oversight. This might involve consulting with colleagues, forming an advisory committee, or working with professional associations that offer research review services. Establishing a clear ethical framework for research activities, regardless of institutional affiliation, is key.

Data privacy and confidentiality are paramount in practice-based research. Researchers must make sure that client data are securely stored and that any published results do not include identifying information. The use of anonymized data and aggregate reporting can help protect client privacy. Practitioners should develop clear data management plans that outline how data will be collected, stored, and protected throughout the research process.

**TABLE 1** Ethical Considerations Checklist

- Informed consent process developed
- Data privacy and confidentiality measures in place
- Plan for separating clinical and research activities
- Potential conflicts of interest identified and addressed
- Ethical review process identified (IRB or alternative)
- HIPAA compliance ensured (if applicable)
- Plan for secure data storage and management
- Process for handling adverse events or unexpected findings
- Strategy for communicating research involvement to clients
- Plan for disseminating results while protecting client confidentiality

## INTERPRETATION STRATEGIES

In the context of clinical research, counselors approach data analysis and interpretation as an integral part of their practice-based research process. This process begins with thoughtful data collection, where counselors systematically gather information during their clinical work. They may use standardized measures, client feedback forms, or session notes to capture relevant data about client progress, intervention effectiveness, and therapeutic processes.

Once data are collected, counselors engage in analysis, which can involve both quantitative and qualitative methods. For quantitative data, they might calculate descriptive statistics to summarize trends or use inferential statistics to test hypotheses about treatment effectiveness. Qualitative data might be analyzed through thematic analysis, identifying patterns in client narratives or session transcripts. Many counselors use software tools to aid in this process, such as SPSS or R for quantitative analysis and NVivo or Atlas.ti for qualitative work.

Interpretation is a critical step where counselors make sense of their analytical findings. They consider not only statistical significance but also practical significance, asking themselves how the results translate to real-world clinical impact. Counselors contextualize their findings within existing literature and theory, reflecting on how their results confirm, challenge, or extend current understanding in the field. They also carefully consider the limitations of their study and the generalizability of their findings to other clinical contexts or client populations.

Based on their interpretations, counselors then make informed changes to their practice. This might involve modifying treatment approaches, adjusting assessment procedures, or implementing new interventions. The process is iterative, with counselors continuously collecting data on these changes to assess their impact, creating a feedback loop of practice improvement.

Throughout this process, counselors reflect on how their findings and experiences might be useful for the broader field of counseling. They consider how their observations from clinical practice-based research can contribute to the larger body of knowledge. This reflection might lead to presentations at professional conferences, publications in academic journals, or sharing insights with colleagues through professional networks.

By engaging in this cyclical process of data collection, analysis, interpretation, practice modification, and reflection, counselors not only enhance their own clinical work but also contribute to the advancement of the counseling profession as a whole. This approach bridges the gap between research and practice, ensuring that clinical insights are grounded in empirical evidence and that research findings are relevant to real-world counseling contexts.

**TABLE 2** Resource List

Statistical Software:

- R (www.r-project.org) (free)
- JASP (jasp-stats.org) (free)
- jamovi (free)
- SPSS (paid subscription)

Assessment Measures:

- PHQ-9 (Depression)
- GAD-7 (Anxiety)
- OQ-45 (General Functioning)

Data Collection Platforms:

- Google Forms
- SurveyMonkey
- REDCap
- Qualtrics

# APPLYING RESEARCH FINDINGS TO PRACTICE

The ultimate goal of practice-based research is to improve clinical practice and client outcomes. Counselors can use research findings to make evidence-based decisions about treatment approaches, modify interventions based on client feedback, and continuously improve their practice. For example, if data analysis shows a significant reduction in anxiety scores after implementing cognitive behavioral therapy (CBT), this suggests that CBT is effective for those clients and may inform decisions to continue or expand its use (Hofmann et al., 2012).

Continuous improvement involves using data to regularly assess the effectiveness of counseling interventions and make necessary adjustments (Lambert, 2010). This might involve regularly collecting data on client progress using standardized assessments, analyzing these data to identify trends, and adjusting interventions based on these insights. By implementing these data-driven practices, counselors can enhance the effectiveness of their interventions and improve client outcomes, ensuring that their approach remains dynamic, responsive, and aligned with the latest research and best practices in the field (Boswell et al., 2015).

**TABLE 3** Reflection Questions

| |
|---|
| How might conducting research influence your approach to clinical work? |
| What challenges do you anticipate in implementing practice-based research? |
| How could findings from your practice-based research contribute to the broader field? |
| What skills do you need to develop to effectively conduct practice-based research? |
| How might engaging in research affect your relationships with clients? |

## CONCLUSION

Practice-based research offers a powerful tool for improving clinical practice and contributing to the knowledge base of the counseling profession. By integrating research into their clinical work, practitioners can enhance their effectiveness, contribute to evidence-based practice, and bridge the gap between research and practice. While challenges exist, the potential benefits to clients, practitioners, and the field as a whole make practice-based research a worthwhile endeavor.

As the counseling profession continues to evolve, the integration of research and practice will become increasingly important. By embracing their role as practitioner–researchers, counselors can actively shape the future of their field, ensuring that clinical practice remains grounded in empirical evidence while addressing the real-world complexities of client care. Through thoughtful study design, ethical consideration, and rigorous interpretation of findings, counselors in clinical practice can make significant contributions to the advancement of the field.

# 10

# Writing and Presenting Research

The dissemination of counseling research findings plays an important role in our field. While traditional channels like the publication of a research paper in a peer-reviewed journal and conference presentations remain long-standing platforms of academic discourse and dissemination, the terrain of knowledge sharing has vastly expanded in our digital age. As counselors in training, licensed professionals, and educators, we have a wide range of avenues at our disposal for information-sharing. Research papers published in peer-reviewed journals and presentations at professional conferences play a vital role in building the evidence base for our profession and shaping best practices (Heppner et al., 2016). However, limiting ourselves to these traditional channels may inadvertently restrict the reach and impact of our work.

Presently, we have unprecedented opportunities to share knowledge through mediums that can reach broader audiences, including practitioners, clients, policymakers, and the general public (Barker, 2016). The counseling researcher has access to a plethora of dissemination methods from digital platforms such as podcasts, blogs, and social media that offer immediate and wide-reaching channels for sharing information. Interactive formats like webinars and community workshops provide opportunities for real-time engagement and knowledge exchange. Accessible publications, including e-books, open access journals, and popular press books, can translate complex research findings into digestible content for lay audiences. Policy-oriented channels, such as legislative testimonies and policy briefs, allow researchers to directly influence decision-makers. Technological innovations, including mobile apps and online forums, create new avenues for disseminating and applying research findings (Priem, 2013).

Each of these channels offers unique advantages in terms of accessibility, engagement, and reach. They allow us to get our message out to specific audiences, encourage dialogue, and translate complex research findings into practical information. As Brownson et al. (2018) noted, effective dissemination often requires going beyond traditional academic outlets to reach those who can apply the findings in practice.

This expansive view of research dissemination is not without controversy. Some in our field argue that broadening our focus beyond traditional academic outlets might dilute the rigor of our scholarship or blur the lines between evidence-based practice and popular psychology. These are valid concerns that we must address thoughtfully (Lilienfeld et al., 2013). However, I argue that embracing a more inclusive approach to dissemination does not diminish its value or credibility. Instead, it amplifies our collective voice, extends our influence, and ultimately enhances our ability to make an impact on our culture. As Funk et al. (2012) argued, bridging the gap between research and practice often requires innovative dissemination strategies that go beyond traditional academic publishing.

In this chapter, we will explore the various methods of writing and presenting research, from crafting research articles for publication in peer-reviewed journals to engaging audiences through innovative digital platforms. We'll discuss the strengths and limitations of each approach, ethical considerations in dissemination, and strategies for choosing the most effective channels for your work.

## THE RESEARCH PAPER

A well-structured and clearly written paper can effectively communicate your findings to the academic community, influencing practice and future research directions. Understanding the structure of a research paper is essential for both writing and evaluating academic work. Even if you don't intend on publishing, knowing how to write research helps you know how to critically read research. For many counselors in training, the language of research, the format of a research paper, can seem like hieroglyphs. I've taught many highly intelligent students who, despite their best efforts, can't make heads or tails of a research paper. So, let's start by breaking down a research paper into its key components and then discuss the ligaments that connect all the core parts together into a logical structure.

## TITLE PAGE AND ABSTRACT

A typical research paper in counseling follows a standard structure, with each section serving a specific purpose. The title should be clear, concise, and reflective of your research. The abstract, typically of 150–300 words, provides a brief summary of the entire study. As Bem (2003) noted, "The abstract is the most important paragraph in your article. It is the first thing that most people will read, and it is usually what is most accessed in electronic searches" (p. 3). Therefore, crafting a clear and an informative abstract is obviously quite important. It is humbling to say, but for many papers, the abstract might be the only part that readers actually look at.

## INTRODUCTION AND LITERATURE REVIEW

The introduction sets the stage for your research, providing background information and outlining aims/objectives. This is followed by a literature review that summarizes existing research and highlights gaps your study aims to fill. Machi and McEvoy's (2016) advise is that "The literature review is not a list describing or summarizing one piece of literature after another. Rather, it's a coherent argument that leads to the description of a proposed study" (p. 5). The most essential part of your introduction and literature review is providing the reader a clear rationale for why we need this study. The rationale, if articulated well, justifies your research question. And, as we discussed in Chapter 6, a clear, focused research question is the foundation of your study. Balkin and Kleist (2017) explained that "A good research question is clear, focused, concise, complex, and arguable" (p. 45). Without a focused research question and clear rationale, your study may get lost in the substantially increasing volume of research that has exploded over the last several years. This phenomenon has often been referred to as the "explosion of scientific literature" or "information explosion." Bornmann and Mutz (2015) found that scientific output doubles approximately every nine years, with this trend accelerating in the recent decades. This rapid increase is reflected not only in the number of articles published but also in the proliferation of academic journals. Ware and Mabe (2015) reported that, as of 2012, there were about 28,100 active scholarly peer-reviewed journals, collectively publishing around 1.8–1.9 million articles annually. With the massive increase in research output, it stands to reason that another researcher has considered what you've considered; they've entertained the same or similar research questions that you have. So, being well-versed in the research literature, having done the work of reviewing what others have done allows you to clearly state where there are gaps in the literature, and how your study will address that gap provides a clear rationale for why we need your study.

## METHODS SECTION

The methodology section is a key component of the research paper, providing a detailed roadmap of how the study was conducted. This section describes your research design, participants, and data collection methods, offering readers the necessary context to evaluate the validity and reliability of your findings. Young researchers often underestimate the importance of this section, but think back to Chapter 2 and the issues we discussed regarding the replication crisis. Writing a strong, clear, and comprehensive methods section allows for easier replication of your study. Nosek and Errington (2020) argued that replication allows other researchers to verify and build upon your findings, contributing to the cumulative nature of scientific knowledge. Creswell and Creswell (2018) emphasized that a well-described research design allows readers to understand the logic behind your methodological decisions. I think most researchers are very passionate about their research agenda. They would like to see other researchers also care about their research topic. So, by writing a clear methods section, with detailed information about your research design, participant selection, and data collection procedures, you enable other researchers to reproduce your study, test the robustness of your findings, and potentially extend your work to new contexts or populations.

## RESULTS SECTION

Results are then presented using appropriate tables, graphs, and statistics. This involves choosing the most suitable statistical tests for your data and research questions and reporting these results clearly and accurately. For quantitative studies, this includes providing relevant statistical information such as test statistics, degrees of freedom, $p$-values, and effect sizes (Cohen, 1988). For qualitative studies, results often involve the presentation of themes or categories derived from your analysis, supported by quotations or other raw data (Braun & Clarke, 2006). By communicating your results with clarity and accuracy, you not only strengthen your own paper but also, again, enable your work to be replicated by other researchers and who then will build upon what you started. Additionally, you may not realize it, but your results may also be helpful for a researcher investigating a different, but related set of research questions. Your thorough analysis and reporting of your results could help shed empirical light on a topic another researcher is studying. This broadens the degree of impact and helpfulness your work can have.

## DISCUSSION SECTION

The discussion section is where you discuss your results in a more straightforward, nontechnical language. This is a really important part of your paper where you can explore the meaning and implications of your findings within the broader scope of related research findings. In the discussion, you should start by briefly restating your main findings and then provide interpretation in light of theory or other research. This involves explaining how your results confirm or disconfirm your initial hypotheses or research questions. It is important to situate your findings within the existing literature, highlighting how they confirm, extend, or contradict previous research (Docherty & Smith, 1999).

Additionally, a key aspect of the discussion is addressing the implications of your findings. This could include theoretical implications that advance our understanding of certain phenomena, practical implications for counseling practice or policy, or suggestions for future research directions. Bansal and Corley (2012) emphasized the importance of clearly articulating the "so what?" of your study—why your findings matter and how they contribute to the field.

It is also really important to address the limitations of your study in the discussion section. This demonstrates scientific integrity and responsible research practices. It helps readers interpret your findings appropriately and helps other researchers have a clear sense of how they can work on future research projects that improve upon your study. Limitations might include methodological constraints, sample characteristics, or potential confounding variables. However, don't just list limitations—discuss how they might have impacted your results and suggest how future research could address these issues (Ioannidis, 2007).

The conclusion serves as a concise summary of your study's main findings and their significance. It should provide closure to your paper while also opening up new avenues for a thought or a research. Avoid simply restating your results; instead, synthesize your key points and emphasize the broader implications of your work. A strong conclusion leaves the reader with a clear understanding of your study's contribution to the field and its potential impact.

Finally, the reference list is a critical component that allows readers to verify your sources and explore topics of interest further. It should include all sources cited in your paper, formatted according to the appropriate style guide (e.g., American Psychological Association). Accuracy and completeness in your references not only demonstrate academic integrity but also situate your work within the broader scientific discourse (American Psychological Association, 2020).

## UNDERSTANDING AUTHORSHIP

Authorship in academic publishing is a critical aspect of research that carries both privileges and responsibilities. The International Committee of Medical Journal Editors (2019) provided widely accepted criteria for authorship. Fine and Kurdek (1993) emphasized that "Authorship credit should reflect the individual's contribution to the study" (p. 1141).

When determining the order of authorship, Winston (1985) suggested that "The order of authorship should be a joint decision of the coauthors. Authors should be prepared to explain the order in which authors are listed" (p. 255). It is important to have open discussions about authorship early in the research process to avoid potential conflicts later.

All authors share responsibility for the accuracy and integrity of the entire paper. As the Committee on Publication Ethics (2014) stated, "All authors should agree to be accountable for all aspects of the work and should be able to identify which co-authors are responsible for specific other parts of the work" (p. 3). This includes ensuring that the research was conducted ethically, the data are reported accurately, and the conclusions are supported by the evidence presented.

## SUBMITTING TO JOURNALS

Publishing in peer-reviewed journals contributes to the body of knowledge in counseling and advancing your academic career. When choosing a journal, consider its impact factor and reputation, but as Seglen (1997) cautioned, "Impact factors should not be used uncritically" (p. 498). Review the journal's aims and scope to make sure your work aligns with their focus. As Belcher (2019) advised, "Your chances of acceptance increase dramatically when you send your work to a journal that actually publishes your kind of article" (p. 130).

When preparing your manuscript for submission, meticulously follow the journal's formatting guidelines. Write a compelling cover letter to accompany your submission. As Gump (2004) stated, "A well-crafted cover letter can be your first step toward a successful publication" (p. 172).

Understanding the peer review process can help you navigate this critical stage of publication. When you receive reviewers' comments, approach them constructively. As Hyland and Jiang (2020) advised, "View reviewers' comments as an opportunity to improve your manuscript rather than as criticism" (p. 215). If invited to revise and resubmit, carefully revise your manuscript based on the reviewers' feedback. As Annesley (2011) suggested, "A thoughtful and comprehensive response to reviewers can significantly increase your chances of acceptance" (p. 2105).

**TABLE I** Checklist for Choosing the Right Journal

1. Scope and Focus
   [ ] Does the journal's scope align with your research topic?
   [ ] Have they published similar articles in recent issues?
   [ ] Is the journal's target audience appropriate for your work?

2. Journal Quality and Impact
   [ ] Check the journal's impact factor (if applicable).
   [ ] Review the journal's indexing in major databases.
   [ ] Assess the reputation of the editorial board.

3. Publication Model
   [ ] Determine whether it is open access or subscription-based.
   [ ] Consider any publication fees or article-processing charges.
   [ ] Check the journal's copyright and licensing policies.

4. Submission and Review Process
   [ ] Review the journal's submission guidelines.
   [ ] Check the average time from submission to first decision.
   [ ] Understand the peer review process (e.g., single-blind and double-blind).

5. Visibility and Reach
   [ ] Assess the journal's readership and circulation.
   [ ] Check if the journal offers options for promoting published articles.
   [ ] Consider the journal's policy on preprints and social media sharing.

6. Ethical Considerations
   [ ] Verify that the journal is not on predatory journal lists.
   [ ] Check the journal's policies on research ethics and integrity.
   [ ] Review the journal's stance on conflicts of interest.

7. Personal Fit
   [ ] Consider colleagues' experiences with the journal.
   [ ] Assess if publication in this journal will support your career goals.
   [ ] Ensure that you can meet any specific requirements (e.g., data sharing policies).

Remember, as Belcher (2019) advised, "Your chances of acceptance increase dramatically when you send your work to a journal that actually publishes your kind of article" (p. 130).

## COLLABORATING WITH OTHER RESEARCHERS

Collaboration is an increasingly important aspect of counseling research, allowing for the integration of diverse perspectives and expertise. To find potential collaborators, network at conferences and through professional organizations. Kienle and Kiene (2012) noted that "Informal interactions at conferences often spark collaborative research ideas" (p. 82). You can also leverage social media and academic networks. Côté and Darling (2018) observed that "Social media can serve as a powerful tool for identifying potential collaborators beyond your immediate professional circle" (p. 3).

When establishing collaborations, set clear expectations and goals. Bozeman and Youtie (2017) emphasized that "Clear communication about expectations is the foundation of successful research collaborations" (p. 128). Establish regular communication channels and practices, and have strategies in place for managing conflicts and ensuring equity. As noted by Bennett and Gadlin (2012), "Successful collaborations are characterized by mutual respect, trust, and a shared commitment to the research goals" (p. 11).

In collaborative research projects, clearly define roles and responsibilities. Cheruvelil et al. (2014) suggested that "Effective team science depends on a clear understanding of each member's role and how it contributes to the overall project goals" (p. 31). When coauthoring papers, remember that it "requires both individual effort and the ability to integrate diverse perspectives into a cohesive narrative" (Frassl et al., 2018, p. 5).

**TABLE 2** Checklist for Collaborating With Other Researchers

1. Identifying Potential Collaborators
   [ ] Attend conferences and networking events in your field.
   [ ] Engage with researchers on academic social media platforms.
   [ ] Review recent publications in your area of interest.
   [ ] Reach out to colleagues for introductions or recommendations.

2. Initiating Collaboration
   [ ] Clearly articulate your research interests and potential project ideas.
   [ ] Be open to others' ideas and perspectives.
   [ ] Discuss shared goals and potential outcomes of collaboration.
   [ ] Establish initial communication channels (e.g., email and video calls).

3. Setting Expectations
   [ ] Define roles and responsibilities for each collaborator.
   [ ] Agree on project timelines and milestones.
   [ ] Discuss authorship order and credit attribution early.
   [ ] Establish a process for decision-making and conflict resolution.

4. Communication Strategies
   [ ] Set up regular check-in meetings or calls.
   [ ] Choose collaborative tools for project management and file-sharing.
   [ ] Establish norms for response times and communication frequency.
   [ ] Create a shared document for tracking progress and action items.

5. Managing the Collaboration
   [ ] Regularly review and adjust project goals as needed.
   [ ] Address any issues or conflicts promptly and professionally.
   [ ] Celebrate milestones and successes together.
   [ ] Be flexible and understanding of others' commitments and constraints.

6. Ethical Considerations
   [ ] Discuss and agree on ethical standards for the research.
   [ ] Establish protocols for data-sharing and confidentiality.
   [ ] Address any potential conflicts of interest.
   [ ] Ensure compliance with institutional and funding agency requirements.

7. Concluding the Collaboration
   [ ] Plan for dissemination of results (e.g., publications and presentations).
   [ ] Discuss potential for future collaborations.
   [ ] Conduct a post-project review to identify lessons learned.
   [ ] Express appreciation for each collaborator's contributions.

Remember, as Bennett and Gadlin (2012) noted, "Successful collaborations are characterized by mutual respect, trust, and a shared commitment to the research goals" (p. 11).

# GRANT FUNDING AND WRITING

Securing funding is often critical for conducting impactful research in counseling. When identifying funding sources, consider government agencies, private foundations, and institutional grants. Coley and Scheinberg (2007) noted that "Understanding the priorities and review criteria of different funding agencies is crucial for targeting your grant applications effectively" (p. 45).

When writing a grant proposal, assess that whether each component aligns with and supports your central research question or hypothesis (Locke et al., 2014). Write a compelling narrative that convinces reviewers not just of the scientific merit of your work, but of its potential impact on clients or communities (Friedland & Folt, 2016). Develop a well-thought-out budget that demonstrates you have carefully planned your project and understand what resources are needed to complete it successfully (Browning, 2019).

If your grant is funded, remember that managing the project involves more than just conducting the research. Meet all reporting requirements thoroughly and on time. As Walterbusch et al. (2017) emphasized, "Thorough and timely reporting is crucial for maintaining good relationships with funding agencies and positioning yourself for future funding opportunities" (p. 87). Manage your budget effectively, demonstrating fiscal responsibility to your funders (Brewer & Walkenhorst, 2015). Maintain compliance with all grant conditions, as this is both an ethical obligation and critical for maintaining the integrity of the research process (Shamoo & Resnik, 2015).

## GRANT WRITING AND FUNDING FOR COUNSELORS

Securing funding facilitates conducting an impactful research in counseling but also for counselors working directly with clients, agencies, or communities. Whether you're a researcher, practitioner, or community advocate, grant writing skills can significantly enhance your ability to support your work and create positive change.

When identifying funding sources, consider government agencies, private foundations, and institutional grants. Coley and Scheinberg (2007) noted that "Understanding the priorities and review criteria of different funding agencies is crucial for targeting your grant applications effectively" (p. 45). For counselors working in agencies or community settings, local foundations and community organizations can be valuable sources of funding for client-focused programs or community initiatives.

When writing a grant proposal, evaluate that each component aligns with and supports your central question or project goal (Locke et al., 2014). Write a compelling narrative that convinces reviewers not just of the scientific merit of your work, but of its potential impact on clients or communities (Friedland & Folt, 2016). Develop a well-thought-out budget that demonstrates you have carefully planned your project and understand what resources are needed to complete it successfully (Browning, 2019).

For counselors seeking funding for client programs or community initiatives, it is critical to clearly articulate the need for the project, its potential impact, and how it aligns with the funding organization's goals. As Porter (2007) advised, "Private foundations often offer more flexibility in funding approaches compared to government agencies, but may have more specific focus areas" (p. 123). This flexibility can be particularly beneficial for innovative counseling programs or interventions.

If your grant is funded, remember that managing the project involves more than just conducting the research or implementing the program. Meet all reporting requirements thoroughly and on time. As Walterbusch et al. (2017) emphasized, "Thorough and timely reporting is crucial for maintaining good relationships with funding agencies and positioning yourself for future funding opportunities" (p. 87). Manage your budget effectively, demonstrating fiscal responsibility to your funders (Brewer & Walkenhorst, 2015). Maintain compliance with all grant conditions, as this is both an ethical obligation and important for maintaining the integrity of the project (Shamoo & Resnik, 2015).

**TABLE 3** Grant Writing Exercise for Counselors

Scenario:
You're a counselor working in a community mental health center. You've identified a need for a specialized support group for teenagers dealing with anxiety exacerbated by social media use. You want to secure funding to run this group for 1 year.

Exercise:

1. Identify Potential Funding Sources:
   - Research and list three potential funding sources (e.g., local foundations, government grants, and community organizations).

2. Draft a Brief Project Description (two to three sentences):
   - Clearly state the problem, your proposed solution, and the anticipated impact.

3. Outline Key Components of Your Grant Proposal:
   a. Need Statement:
      - What evidence supports the need for this program?
   b. Project Goals and Objectives:
      - List two to three specific, measurable goals.

c. Methods:
- Briefly describe how you will implement the support group.

d. Evaluation Plan:
- How will you measure the success of the program?

e. Budget:
- List major budget categories (e.g., staff time, materials, and facilities).

4. Anticipate Funder Questions:
- List two to three questions a funder might ask about your proposal and draft brief responses.

Reflection:
- What aspects of grant writing do you find most challenging?
- How might securing this grant impact your clients and community?

## PREPARING FOR PROFESSIONAL CONFERENCES

Professional conferences provide valuable opportunities to share your research, gain feedback, and network with other professionals in your field. Effective preparation can help you make the most of these events. When selecting a conference, consider the differences between national, regional, and specialized conferences. As Schwartz (2018) noted, "Choosing the right conference can significantly impact the visibility and reception of your research" (p. 87). Also, keep in mind that most conferences are hosted by professional organizations and typically require membership for presenters. Being an active member in the association helps you know your audience better. You might have amazing research findings, but if you don't know how to speak the language of your target audience, the impact of your findings will be reduced. Conferences also offer unique networking opportunities that can advance your career and research. Pearlman and Camarena (2018) noted that "Effective networking at conferences can lead to collaborations, mentorship opportunities, and even job prospects" (p. 209).

## CONFERENCE PRESENTATION PROPOSAL

Once you've selected a conference, the next step is to submit a conference presentation proposal. You'll need to craft a concise and an engaging proposal that captures the essence of your research, but make sure to carefully review and follow the conference's submission guidelines. Professional conferences typically employ a rigorous selection process for accepting submissions, often referred to as a peer review or juried review process. While these terms are sometimes used interchangeably, they can have subtle differences: *Peer review* generally implies that submissions are evaluated by experts in the field who are considered peers of the submitters. This process often involves blind or double-blind review, where the identities of the authors and reviewers are concealed from each other to maintain unbiased evaluation (Fyfe et al., 2020). *Juried review*, while similar, may suggest a more formal, competition-like process where a panel of experts (the jury) evaluates and selects submissions based on predetermined criteria. This term is often used in contexts where submissions are being judged for awards or special recognition in addition to acceptance (Harley et al., 2010). Both processes typically involve multiple reviewers assessing each submission based on criteria such as originality, methodological rigor, relevance to the conference theme, and potential impact on the field. The final decision for acceptance is usually made by a program committee that considers the reviewers' recommendations and balances the conference's overall composition (Marder, 2021).

So, what are the core components of the research proposal? The core components of a professional conference presentation proposal typically include several key elements, each serving a specific purpose in communicating the value and content of your proposed presentation. These components may vary slightly depending on the conference's specific requirements, but generally include the following:

1. Title: A concise, an informative, and an engaging title that accurately reflects the content of your presentation. Bem (2003) suggested that a good title should be both informative and catchy, capturing the essence of your work.
2. Abstract: A brief summary (usually of 150–300 words) that outlines the main points of your presentation. This should include the purpose, methods, results (if applicable), and conclusions of your work. Hutto (2009) emphasized that a well-crafted abstract is highly important as it is often the basis for acceptance decisions.
3. Learning objectives: Clear statements of what attendees will learn or gain from your presentation. These should be specific, measurable, and aligned with the conference's goals.
4. Relevance to the conference theme: An explanation of how your presentation fits within the conference's focus or theme, demonstrating its relevance to the intended audience.
5. Presentation format: Specification of your preferred presentation format (e.g., paper presentation, poster, and workshop), if the conference offers multiple options.
6. Methodology: For research presentations, a brief description of your research methods, including study design, data collection, and analysis techniques.
7. Presenter information: Biographical information about the presenter(s), including credentials and affiliations. This helps establish the credibility of the presenters.
8. References: A list of key references that support your work, demonstrating its grounding in current literature.

These elements provide an overview of your conference presentation proposal. Following this structure, with clear strong writing allows reviewers to assess its quality, relevance, and potential contribution to the conference. Haber and Lingard (2001) noted that a well-structured proposal not only increases your chances of acceptance but also sets the foundation for a clear and an impactful presentation.

## THE CONFERENCE PRESENTATION

As Duarte (2008) advised, "Think of your slides as billboards. When people drive, they only briefly take their eyes off their main focus—the road—to process a billboard. Similarly, your audience should focus on you more than your slides" (p. 145). Presenting at a conference requires careful preparation and skillful delivery. Building on Duarte and Reynolds' advice, several additional strategies can enhance your presentation's effectiveness. Knowing your audience is a must; Alley (2013) emphasized tailoring your content and delivery to their background and interests. Starting strong with a compelling hook or provocative question can immediately capture attention, as Heath and Heath (2007) noted that successful presenters grab the audience in the first 30 s. Structuring your presentation as a narrative can make it more engaging and memorable, with Gallo (2014) highlighting our innate responsiveness to stories. Effective use of visuals is key, but as Kosslyn (2007) advised, the goal is to illuminate, not to overwhelm. Active delivery, including vocal variety and gestures, is essential, with Berkun (2010) asserting that body language and tone matter twice as much as words. Time management is critical; Anderson (2016) recommended practicing with a timer to maintain comfortable delivery within the allotted time. Anticipating questions and preparing responses, as suggested by Burstein and Holman (2010), can boost your confidence during the question and answer session. Where appropriate, Weissman (2009) encouraged audience participation to transform listeners into active participants. Finally, Abela (2008) emphasized the importance of concluding with a strong summary or call to action, leaving your audience with a clear, memorable message. By focusing on these elements, you can create a presentation that not only informs but also inspires and engages your audience, making a lasting impact at the conference.

**TABLE 4** Case Study: Preparing an Effective Conference Presentation

Dr. Sarah Chen, a counselor specializing in adolescent mental health, was preparing to present her latest research on social media's impact on teen anxiety at the Annual Counseling and Mental Health Conference.

Preparation Steps:

1. Abstract Submission: Dr. Chen crafted a concise 250-word abstract highlighting her research question, methodology, key findings, and implications for practice.

2. Presentation Design:
   - Created a visually appealing slide deck with minimal text.
   - Used high-quality images and graphs to illustrate key points.
   - Included a QR code linking to additional resources.

3. Practice and Timing:
   - Rehearsed the presentation multiple times, refining content and delivery.
   - Timed each run-through to ensure it fit within the allotted 20 min.

4. Engagement Strategies:
   - Prepared thought-provoking questions for the audience.
   - Developed a brief interactive poll to gather audience perspectives.

5. Handouts and Resources:
   - Created a one-page summary of key findings for attendees.
   - Prepared a list of references and further reading.

Outcome: Dr. Chen's well-prepared presentation was well received, generating engaging discussions and potential collaboration opportunities with other researchers in the field.

## BEYOND TRADITIONAL CHANNELS: EMERGING PLATFORMS FOR RESEARCH DISSEMINATION

While research papers and conference presentations remain tried-and-true channels of research dissemination, the digital age has ushered in an embarrassment of riches when it comes to platforms for sharing scholarly work. These alternative dissemination methods offer unique advantages in terms of reach, accessibility, and engagement, engagement being possibly the most important innovation of the digital platforms. It is the grip of many academics that their work is only read by a handful of people. Yet, digital platforms offer a totally new way for researchers to communicate their findings. Podcasts, for instance, provide an auditory medium that can make complex research accessible to a broader audience by interviewing their findings with powerful, attention-grabbing narratives. Hew (2009) found that podcasts can enhance learning and engagement, particularly for auditory learners. Blogs offer a more informal, conversational approach to sharing research insights. Kjellberg (2010) observed that academic blogs can serve as a bridge between scholarly work and public discourse, allowing researchers to contextualize their findings for a general audience.

Social media platforms like Twitter (or X), Facebook, TikTok, and Instagram have become powerful tools for research dissemination. Côté and Darling (2018) demonstrated that scientists who use Twitter or X, for example, have a broader reach, particularly to nonscientific audiences. These platforms allow for real-time discussion and networking around research topics, fostering a more dynamic and interactive form of scholarly communication.

Interactive formats such as webinars and community workshops offer opportunities for direct engagement with audiences. Unlike traditional presentations, these formats allow for immediate feedback and discussion. Zoumenou et al. (2015) found that webinars can be an effective tool for disseminating research-based information to diverse, geographically dispersed audiences.

Accessible publications facilitate the translation of research from academic jargon to language designed for broader consumption. *Psychology Today*, *Counseling Today*, *Psychotherapy Networker Magazine*, and *Monitor on Psychology* are just a few examples of publications from professional organizations that are written for a broad audience, distilling research findings into a digestible format. There are also open access journals that have gained prominence, with Piwowar et al. (2018) reporting a significant increase in open access articles over the past two decades. This shift improves the accessibility of research findings to practitioners and the public alike. Popular press books and e-books offer another avenue for researchers to present their work in a more narrative, accessible format. Badke (2017) argued that such publications can significantly enhance the impact of research by making it comprehensible and relevant to nonacademic audiences.

Policy-oriented channels provide researchers with direct avenues to influence decision-making. Oliver and Cairney (2019) emphasized the importance of tailoring research communication to policymakers' needs, suggesting formats like policy briefs and legislative testimonies as effective means of translating research into actionable insights.

Technological innovations continue to create new possibilities for research dissemination. Mobile apps can make research findings interactive and personally relevant. For example, Boudreaux et al. (2014) described how mobile health apps can disseminate and apply research findings in real-world settings. Online forums and communities of practice offer spaces for ongoing discussion and application of research, fostering a collaborative approach to knowledge dissemination and implementation.

These various dissemination methods offer researchers unprecedented opportunities to extend the reach and impact of their work. By strategically employing these platforms alongside traditional academic channels, researchers can make sure their findings resonate with a wider audience, bridging the gap between scholarly inquiry and practical application.

## CONCLUSION

The ability to effectively communicate research findings, present at conferences, navigate authorship dynamics, submit to journals, collaborate with other researchers, and secure funding through grants, or share findings through a blog or podcast, are essential skills for counselors at all stages of their careers. The dissemination mindset and skill set not only advance your professional career, but also contribute to the broader field of counseling by disseminating knowledge, fostering innovation, and improving client outcomes. Throughout this chapter, we've explored the nuances of each of these areas, from crafting well-structured research papers to preparing engaging conference presentations, from understanding the intricacies of authorship to navigating the peer review process in journal submissions. We've also explored the importance of effective collaboration and the critical skill of grant writing, not just for researchers, but for counselors working directly with clients and communities.

As you apply these skills in your own professional journey, remember that mastery comes with practice and persistence. As Sword (2012) noted, "The best academic writing is cohesive, coherent, and clear" (p. 173). Each paper you write, presentation you give, or grant you apply for is an opportunity to refine your skills and contribute meaningfully to the field. The research and funding landscape in counseling is dynamic, with new challenges and opportunities emerging regularly. Stay curious, remain open to feedback, and continue to seek out opportunities to grow and learn. Silvia (2019) emphasized that "Clear writing reflects clear thinking" (p. 73).

Moreover, the skills discussed in this chapter have far-reaching implications beyond academia. They empower counselors to advocate for their clients, secure resources for underserved communities, and contribute to evidence-based practices that can improve mental health outcomes on a broader scale. By effectively communicating, through traditional or alternative channels, your work has the potential to create lasting positive change in the lives of individuals and communities.

As you move forward, consider how you can integrate these skills into your current role, whether you're a researcher, a practitioner, or both. Seek out mentors who excel in areas where you want to grow, and don't hesitate to collaborate with colleagues who have complementary strengths. Belcher (2019) suggested in the context of submitting a research paper that "Peer review before submission can significantly improve the quality of your manuscript and increase its chances of publication" (p. 282). The skills of writing, presenting, publishing, collaborating, and securing funding are not just academic exercises—they are the tools of dissemination. By continually honing these abilities, you position yourself to be a more effective advocate, practitioner, and contributor to the field of counseling. Embrace these challenges as opportunities for growth, and let your passion for helping others drive your efforts to communicate, collaborate, and innovate in your professional practice.

# 11

# Integrating Research Into Counseling Practice

Throughout this book, you've read different chapters attempting to cumulatively demystify research for counselors in training, with the ultimate aim of bridging the gap between research literacy and clinical practice. As a counselor, you have to wear many hats: helper, advocate, evaluator, and lifelong learner. Each of these roles is enhanced by a solid foundation in research literacy and the ability to critically evaluate and apply research findings. As Wampold and Imel (2015) asserted, "The integration of research and practice is essential for the continued development and improvement of psychotherapy" (p. 23). This integration is imperative for providing the highest quality care to your clients. Put simply, research literacy empowers you to stay at the forefront of evidence-based practices (EBPs), critically evaluating new approaches and making informed decisions about client care. It allows you to navigate the research explosion that is happening in the counseling field and many others. But, not every article you read has the same merit. Meltzoff and Cooper (2018) noted that "The ability to think critically about research is an essential skill for all mental health professionals" (p. 3).

At the heart of research competency is, as I said above, client care. A well-read counselor has a strong clinical intuition, allowing for the systematic observation and reflection on your own practice. It enables you to contribute to the field's knowledge base, whether through formal research or by conducting research as your clinical site as we discussed in Chapter 9. Being a counselor uniquely positions you to bridge the gap between research and practice, making sure that our field continues to evolve in ways that are both scientifically rigorous and clinically relevant.

This chapter aims to equip you with the tools to embody this integration in your daily practice. We'll explore practical applications of research literacy in assessment, treatment planning, and outcome evaluation. We'll discuss strategies for staying current with research findings and applying them judiciously in your clinical work. Finally, we'll consider how you can contribute to the field's knowledge base, even as a practicing clinician. Bear in mind that becoming a research-informed practitioner is a journey, not a destination. It requires ongoing curiosity, critical thinking, and a commitment to lifelong learning. But the rewards—for you, your clients, and the field of counseling—are immeasurable.

## WHY BRIDGING THE GAP?

Why is bridging the gap between research and practice so important for counselors? Consider the rapidly evolving nature of our field. New therapeutic approaches, assessment tools, and intervention strategies emerge regularly, each backed by varying degrees of empirical support. Without the ability to discern the quality and relevance of research, counselors risk either clinging to outdated practices or prematurely adopting unproven methods. As noted by Heppner et al. (2016), "Research competence allows practitioners to be discriminating consumers of new knowledge and to evaluate the applicability of research findings to their own practice" (p. 5).

Moreover, the ethical obligations of our profession demand that we provide the most effective care possible. The American Counseling Association (ACA)'s Code of Ethics (2014) stipulated that counselors have a responsibility to "keep current with the diverse populations and specific populations with whom they work" (C.2.f). This currency is maintained not just through experience, but through ongoing engagement with the latest research in our field.

Remember that the goal is not to transform counselors into full-time researchers, but to cultivate what Gelso (2006) termed the "scientist–practitioner attitude"—an openness to scientific thinking and a commitment to EBP that coexists comfortably with the art of counseling. Hopefully, by now, you are starting to feel empowered to engage with research not as a distant, academic exercise, but as a vital, ongoing part of your professional growth and clinical effectiveness.

## REVISITING RESEARCH LITERACY AND COMPETENCY

Research literacy and competency enable practitioners to stay current with evolving best practices, critically evaluate new approaches, and make informed decisions about client care. Research literacy in counseling encompasses several interconnected skills, including understanding various research designs and methodologies (Creswell & Creswell, 2018), basic statistical literacy (Norcross & Lambert, 2019), critical evaluation skills to assess the quality and applicability of research (Meltzoff & Cooper, 2018), ability to interpret results and their implications (Bornstein, 2017), and ethical awareness regarding research practices (ACA, 2014).

Developing these skills is an ongoing process. Counselors can enhance their research literacy through regular literature review of current research, participating in research-focused continuing education, joining professional organizations that provide research resources, engaging in collaborative learning with colleagues, taking online courses in relevant topics, and conducting small-scale action research projects in their own practice (Reason & Bradbury, 2008).

However, many counselors face challenges when engaging with research. Common obstacles include statistical anxiety, time constraints, difficulty seeing the relevance to practice, information overload, and lack of access to research. To overcome these challenges, counselors can start with basic statistical concepts and gradually build complexity, schedule dedicated "research time," focus on clinically oriented journals and case studies, use meta-analyses and systematic reviews as starting points, and utilize open-access resources and professional organization memberships for access to research.

By actively working to develop these skills and overcome common challenges, counselors can enhance their research literacy and competency. As Wampold (2015) noted, "The scientifically minded clinician is not bound by the specific treatments tested in trials but uses the research evidence to make decisions about how to best treat the patient" (p. 270). This approach not only improves individual practice but also contributes to the overall quality of the counseling profession.

## READING AND EVALUATING RESEARCH CRITICALLY

The ability to critically evaluate research is a cornerstone skill for counselors seeking to integrate evidence into their practice. This skill allows practitioners to discern which findings are most relevant and reliable for informing their work with clients. In this section, we'll explore the process of critically analyzing research articles, identifying strengths and weaknesses in research design, and assessing the applicability of research findings to clinical practice.

When approaching a research article, it is beneficial to follow a systematic process. Begin with the abstract, which provides an overview of the study's purpose, methods, and main findings. However, it is pivotal to remember that abstracts can be limited or biased, so they should serve as an introduction rather than a comprehensive summary (Greenhalgh, 2014).

After the abstract, examine the introduction carefully. This section should clearly state the research question or hypothesis and provide a comprehensive literature review that contextualizes the study within the existing body of knowledge. Pay attention to the theoretical framework presented, as it informs the study's approach and interpretation of results.

The methodology section is where your critical thinking skills become particularly important. Assess whether the research design is appropriate for the question being asked. Consider the sample size, selection process, and representativeness. Evaluate the measures or instruments used, focusing on their validity and reliability. The data collection and analysis procedures should be clearly described and justified.

When you reach the results section, look closely at how the data are presented. Are the statistical analyses appropriate for the data and research questions? Remember to pay attention to effect sizes, not just statistical significance (Sullivan & Feinn, 2012). Effect sizes can provide valuable information about the practical significance of the findings, which is often more relevant to clinical practice than statistical significance alone.

In the discussion section, assess how the authors interpret their findings. Look for a balanced interpretation that acknowledges both the strengths and limitations of the study. Consider how the findings relate to previous research and theory in the field. The conclusions should be justified based on the results presented and should offer clear implications for practice and future research.

Throughout this process, it is important to identify both strengths and weaknesses in the research design. A strong study might feature a large, representative sample with clear inclusion and exclusion criteria, while a weakness could be a small sample size or the use of convenience sampling. In terms of research design, randomized controlled trials (RCTs) are often considered the gold standard for intervention studies, but remember that other designs can be valuable depending on the research question.

The choice of measures is another critical aspect to evaluate. Studies that use validated, reliable instruments are generally more robust than those relying solely on self-report measures for objective outcomes. In data analysis, look for appropriate statistical tests and consideration of effect sizes. Be cautious of studies that make multiple comparisons without proper statistical correction, as this can increase the risk of false-positive results.

When it comes to assessing the relevance and applicability of research findings to your practice, several factors come into play. Consider how similar the study population is to your client base. As Sue et al. (2019) pointed out, research findings may not be generalized across different cultural or demographic groups. Evaluate whether the research setting matches your own practice environment and whether the interventions or outcome measures used in the study are feasible and appropriate for your work.

It is also important to look beyond statistical significance to consider whether the observed effects are meaningful in a practical sense (Kazdin, 2019). Consider how the findings fit with the established theories and other research in the field. Remember that even well-supported interventions need to align with client preferences and values (APA, 2006). Finally, consider the resource implications of implementing the findings in your practice.

To truly develop your skills in critical evaluation, regular practice is key. Choose recent research articles in your area of practice and work through them systematically. Ask yourself: What is the main research question? How might the sample limit the generalizability of the findings? What are the key strengths and weaknesses of the research design? Do you agree with the authors;' interpretation of their findings? How applicable are the findings to your practice, and what factors influence this applicability?

By engaging in this process regularly, you'll develop a nuanced understanding of research findings and their potential applications in your practice. As Norcross and Lambert (2018) aptly noted, "The thoughtful clinician neither uncritically accepts nor reflexively rejects research evidence, but instead engages in the vital process of adaptation and integration of the treatment to the individual patient" (p. 315). This process of critical evaluation is key to that adaptation and integration, allowing you to provide the most informed and effective care to your clients.

## UNDERSTANDING AND APPLYING RESEARCH DESIGNS IN COUNSELING

As we look deeper into the world of research in counseling, we need to understand the various research designs that form the backbone of our evidence base. Each design serves a unique purpose and comes with its own set of strengths and limitations. By familiarizing ourselves with these designs, we can better interpret research findings and even contribute to the field through our own studies.

Research designs in counseling broadly fall into three categories: quantitative, qualitative, and mixed methods. Quantitative designs seek to measure and analyze phenomena numerically, often testing specific hypotheses. Qualitative designs, on the other hand, explore experiences and meanings in depth, typically generating hypotheses rather than testing them. Mixed-methods designs combine elements of both, leveraging the strengths of each approach to provide a more comprehensive understanding of complex issues (Creswell & Creswell, 2018).

Within the realm of quantitative research, experimental designs are often considered the gold standard, particularly RCTs. In an RCT, participants are randomly assigned to either an intervention group or a control group, allowing researchers to make causal inferences about the effectiveness of a particular treatment. For instance, a landmark study by Seligman et al. (2006) used an RCT design to compare the effectiveness of cognitive therapy and antidepressant medication in treating depression, providing valuable insights that have shaped treatment approaches.

However, it is important to recognize that RCTs are not always feasible or ethical in counseling research. In such cases, quasi-experimental designs can be valuable alternatives. These designs lack random assignment but still attempt to establish causal relationships. For example, a counselor might compare outcomes for clients who choose to engage in group therapy versus individual therapy, controlling for other factors that might influence the results.

Correlational designs, while unable to establish causation, can reveal important relationships between variables. For instance, a study might explore the correlation between attachment styles and therapeutic alliance, providing insights that counselors can consider in their practice. Longitudinal designs, which involve repeated observations of the same variables over time, can offer a dynamic view of how therapeutic processes unfold. The Penn Psychotherapy Project, a landmark longitudinal study, has provided invaluable insights into the process of change in psychotherapy over extended periods (Luborsky et al., 1980).

Qualitative designs, while less focused on numerical data, offer rich, in-depth explorations of lived experiences. Phenomenological studies, for example, aim to describe and interpret the meanings of experiences from the perspective of those who have lived them. A counselor might use this approach to understand the experience of recovery from substance abuse, gaining insights that numbers alone couldn't capture. Grounded theory, another qualitative approach, aims to develop theories based on the systematic analysis of data. This can be particularly useful in areas where existing theories are inadequate or nonexistent.

Case studies, which can be either qualitative or quantitative, offer detailed examinations of individual cases. While their generalizability is limited, they can provide valuable insights into complex therapeutic processes and rare conditions. The famous case studies of Sigmund Freud, while controversial, have had a lasting impact on our understanding of psychotherapy.

Mixed-methods designs have gained popularity in the recent years, recognizing that complex phenomena often require multiple perspectives. For instance, a study might use quantitative measures to assess the effectiveness of a new counseling intervention, while also conducting qualitative interviews to understand clients' experiences of the intervention. This approach can provide a more holistic understanding than either method alone.

When selecting a research design for a particular question, counselors must consider various factors. The nature of the research question is paramount—some questions lend themselves to quantitative approaches, while others are better suited to qualitative exploration. Ethical considerations also play a pivotal role. For instance, withholding potentially beneficial treatment for the sake of a control group may not be ethically justifiable in some situations.

Practical constraints, such as time, resources, and access to participants, also influence design choices. A private practitioner interested in researching their own practice might opt for single-case designs or qualitative approaches that are feasible within their setting. Larger institutions or research teams might have the resources to conduct more extensive quantitative studies.

It is also important to consider the stage of knowledge in a particular area. In newer areas of inquiry, qualitative or exploratory quantitative designs might be more appropriate to generate hypotheses. In more established areas, confirmatory quantitative designs might be used to test specific hypotheses derived from existing theory and research.

As consumers of research, understanding these designs allows us to better evaluate the strengths and limitations of the studies we encounter. For instance, recognizing the potential for selection bias in nonrandomized studies, or the limitations of generalizability in qualitative research, can help us appropriately contextualize findings.

Moreover, this knowledge empowers us to contribute to the research base ourselves. Whether through formal research projects or systematic reflection on our own practice, understanding research designs allows us to structure our inquiries in ways that can meaningfully contribute to the field.

In the dynamic field of counseling, where each client presents a unique constellation of experiences and needs, no single research design can provide all the answers. Instead, we must draw on a diverse array of methodologies to build a comprehensive understanding of human experience and therapeutic change. By familiarizing ourselves with various research designs, we equip ourselves to navigate this complex landscape, continually refining our practice based on the best available evidence.

## APPLYING RESEARCH TO CLINICAL COUNSELING PRACTICE

The true value of research in counseling lies not just in its production or comprehension, but in its thoughtful application to clinical practice. As we bridge the gap between research and practice, we enter the realm of EBP, an approach that has gained significant traction in the recent years. However, applying research to practice is not a simple matter of following a recipe; it requires careful consideration, clinical judgment, and a nuanced understanding of both the research and the unique needs of each client.

EBP, as defined by the American Psychological Association (2006), involves the integration of the best available research with clinical expertise in the context of patient characteristics, culture, and preferences. This definition highlights that EBP is not about rigidly adhering to research findings, but rather about using research as one key step in a complex decision-making process.

When we talk about the "best available research," we're often referring to findings from well-designed studies, systematic reviews, and meta-analyses. For instance, the work of Wampold and Imel (2015) in their book "The Great Psychotherapy Debate" synthesized decades of research on psychotherapy effectiveness, providing valuable insights into what factors contribute to positive outcomes across different therapeutic approaches. Such comprehensive reviews can serve as a starting point for understanding what interventions might be most effective for particular issues.

However, it is critical to remember that even the most robust research findings are based on group averages and may not apply perfectly to any individual client. This is where clinical expertise comes into play. Experienced counselors develop a sense of how to adapt interventions to suit individual needs, when to persist with a particular approach, and when to change course. This expertise is not at odds with research evidence but rather complements it.

Integrating research into treatment planning often begins with a thorough assessment of the client's presenting issues, history, and goals. With this information in hand, a counselor can turn to the research literature to identify potentially effective interventions. For example, if a client presents with symptoms of post-traumatic stress disorder (PTSD), a counselor might consider cognitive processing therapy or prolonged exposure therapy, both of which have strong empirical support for treating PTSD (Watkins et al., 2018).

However, the choice of intervention isn't solely based on its empirical support. The counselor must also consider the client's preferences, cultural background, and individual circumstances. A client who is hesitant about exposure-based treatments, for instance, might be more amenable to a cognitive approach. Similarly, a client's cultural background might influence how they conceptualize their problems and what types of interventions they find acceptable.

Throughout the treatment process, counselors can use research to inform their decision-making. This might involve using standardized measures to track client progress, a practice supported by research on feedback-informed treatment (Lambert, 2017). By regularly assessing outcomes, counselors can determine whether the chosen intervention is having the desired effect and make adjustments as necessary.

Research can also guide counselors in addressing challenges that arise during therapy. For instance, if a client is struggling with homework compliance, a counselor might turn to research on strategies for enhancing engagement in between-session activities (Kazantzis et al., 2016). Similarly, research on the therapeutic alliance can inform strategies for addressing ruptures in the counseling relationship (Eubanks et al., 2018).

It is important to note that applying research to practice isn't just about using empirically supported treatments. It also involves staying current with research on common factors in therapy, such as the therapeutic alliance, which has been consistently linked to positive outcomes across various therapeutic approaches (Norcross & Lambert, 2018). Understanding this research can help counselors focus on cultivating strong therapeutic relationships alongside specific interventions.

Moreover, research application extends to understanding and addressing diverse client needs. For instance, research on multicultural counseling competencies (Sue et al., 2019) can inform how counselors work with clients from diverse backgrounds. Similarly, research on specific populations, such as LGBTQ+ clients or older adults, can provide valuable insights into the unique challenges and considerations for these groups.

As we apply research to practice, it is important to maintain a stance of critical reflection. This involves not only evaluating the quality and relevance of research but also reflecting on our own practice. Are we seeing the outcomes we would expect based on the research? If not, what factors might be contributing to this discrepancy? This reflective stance allows us to continually refine our practice and contribute to the field's understanding of how research translates into real-world settings.

It is also worth noting that the application of research to practice is not a one-way street. As practitioners, we are in a unique position to identify gaps in the research literature and generate questions that need further investigation. By maintaining a researcher's mindset in our clinical work, we can contribute to the development of practice-based evidence, complementing the EBP paradigm.

Applying research to clinical counseling practice is a complex, ongoing process that requires balancing multiple sources of information. It involves staying current with the latest research findings, critically evaluating their applicability to our specific clients, and integrating this knowledge with our clinical expertise and client preferences. While challenging, this integration of research and practice holds the promise of continually improving the quality of care we provide to our clients, ultimately leading to better outcomes and a stronger, more effective counseling profession.

## EVALUATING COUNSELING EFFECTIVENESS

Let's examine the integration of research and practice; we arrive at a critical juncture: How do we know if our counseling interventions are truly effective? Evaluating counseling effectiveness is not merely an academic exercise; it is a professional responsibility that allows us to evaluate whether we're providing the best possible care for our clients. Moreover, it is a powerful tool for professional growth, enabling us to refine our skills and adapt our approaches based on empirical evidence.

The process of evaluating counseling effectiveness begins with a fundamental shift in perspective. Rather than relying solely on our clinical intuition or client feedback, we must adopt a more systematic, data-driven approach. This doesn't mean abandoning our clinical judgment or disregarding client experiences; rather, it means supplementing these valuable sources of information with objective measures and structured evaluation methods.

One of the most widely used approaches to evaluating counseling effectiveness is outcome measurement. This involves assessing client progress using standardized measures at regular intervals throughout the counseling process. The Outcome Questionnaire-45, developed by Lambert et al. (2004), is a prime example of such a measure. It assesses symptoms, interpersonal relationships, and social role functioning, providing a comprehensive picture of client well-being.

However, it is critical to remember that no single measure can capture the full complexity of human experience and change. As such, many practitioners and researchers advocate for a multimethod approach to evaluation. This might involve combining standardized outcome measures with individualized goal attainment scaling, qualitative client feedback, and behavioral observations. For instance, Bordin's (1979) concept of working alliance, which encompasses agreement on goals, tasks, and the bond between the counselor and the client, can be assessed alongside symptom measures to provide a more holistic view of the therapeutic process.

The frequency of assessment is another important consideration. While traditional models often relied on pre–post measurement, contemporary approaches emphasize the value of continuous assessment. Routine outcome monitoring, as described by Boswell et al. (2015), involves regularly collecting outcome data throughout the course of therapy. This approach allows for the early detection of clients who are not responding well to treatment, enabling timely adjustments to the therapeutic approach.

When implementing outcome measurement in practice, it is all-important to consider the client's perspective. How do we introduce these measures in a way that enhances rather than detracts from the therapeutic process? Swift et al. (2015) suggested framing outcome measures as collaborative tools that can help both the counselor and the client track progress and identify areas for focus. This collaborative approach can actually enhance the therapeutic alliance and client engagement.

Of course, collecting data is only the first step; the real value lies in how we use this information. Analyzing and interpreting outcome data requires both statistical understanding and clinical acumen. For individual clients, we might look at clinically significant change and reliable change indices, which were introduced by Jacobson and Truax (1991). These statistical tools help us determine whether observed changes are meaningful and not just due to measurement error.

At a broader level, aggregating data across multiple clients can provide valuable insights into our overall effectiveness as practitioners. This kind of practice-based evidence can complement the EBP paradigm, allowing us to assess how well established interventions work in our specific practice context. It can also highlight areas where we might need additional training or supervision.

However, it is important to approach the interpretation of outcome data with nuance. A lack of improvement or even deterioration in scores doesn't necessarily indicate ineffective counseling. It might reflect an appropriate increase in distress as a client begins to confront difficult issues, or it could signal the need for a change in approach. This is where the integration of outcome data with clinical judgment becomes vital.

Moreover, we must be mindful of the limitations of our evaluation methods. Many standardized measures have been developed and normed on specific populations, which may limit their applicability to diverse client groups. As counselors, we have an ethical obligation to consider if our evaluation methods are culturally sensitive and appropriate for the clients we serve.

The process of evaluating counseling effectiveness extends beyond individual client outcomes. We must also consider the broader impact of our interventions. This might involve assessing changes in clients' interpersonal relationships, work functioning, or community engagement. A long-term follow-up can provide valuable insights into the durability of therapeutic gains and the real-world impact of our interventions.

Importantly, the evaluation of counseling effectiveness is not just about assessing client outcomes; it is also about evaluating and improving our own skills as counselors. Reflective practice, as described by Schön (1983), involves critically examining our own actions and decision-making processes. By combining this reflective approach with objective outcome data, we can continually refine our clinical skills and enhance our effectiveness.

In the recent years, technological advances have opened up new possibilities for evaluating counseling effectiveness. Electronic health records and practice management systems often include built-in outcome measurement tools. More sophisticated systems can provide real-time feedback and even use predictive analytics to identify clients at risk of negative outcomes. While these technologies offer exciting possibilities, they also raise important ethical considerations around data privacy and the potential for over-reliance on algorithmic decision-making.

As we engage in the process of evaluating counseling effectiveness, it is hard but necessary to maintain a balanced perspective. While outcome measurement provides valuable data, it doesn't capture the full richness of the therapeutic process or the myriad ways in which clients might experience growth and change. We must remain open to the unmeasurable aspects of human experience and the often subtle, qualitative shifts that can occur through the counseling process.

In conclusion, evaluating counseling effectiveness is a complex, multifaceted process that requires ongoing commitment and critical reflection. By embracing this challenge, we not only enhance our ability to serve our clients effectively but also contribute to the broader field of counseling research and practice. As we strive to bridge the gap between research and practice, the thoughtful evaluation of our work serves as a pivotal link, confirming that our interventions are not only grounded in empirical evidence but also demonstrably effective in the complex, real-world settings in which we practice.

## ENHANCING ASSESSMENT IN COUNSELING SESSIONS

Assessment is a cornerstone of effective counseling practice, serving as the foundation upon which we build our understanding of clients and formulate treatment plans. However, assessment is far more than a one-time event at the beginning of therapy; it is an ongoing process that informs and guides our work throughout the counseling relationship. In this section, we'll explore how research can enhance our assessment practices, making them more accurate, comprehensive, and beneficial to the therapeutic process.

The field of assessment in counseling has evolved significantly over the years, moving beyond simple symptom checklists to encompass a wide range of tools and techniques. This evolution has been driven by research that has deepened our understanding of human psychology, psychopathology, and the factors that contribute to well-being. As counselors, we have the opportunity—and indeed, the responsibility—to leverage this research to enhance our assessment practices.

One of the most significant developments in assessment research has been the move toward a more holistic, strengths-based approach. Traditional assessment often focused primarily on identifying problems and diagnosing disorders. While this remains an important aspect of assessment, research has highlighted the value of also identifying client strengths, resources, and resilience factors. The work of Martin Seligman and other positive psychology researchers has been instrumental in this shift. For instance, tools like the Values in Action Inventory of Strengths, developed by Peterson and Seligman (2004), allow us to assess character strengths alongside areas of difficulty.

This balanced approach to assessment aligns with the wellness model that underpins much of contemporary counseling practice. It allows us to develop a more complete picture of our clients, informing interventions that not only address problems but also build on existing strengths. Moreover, research by Scheel et al. (2012) suggested that strength-based assessments can enhance client engagement and foster hope, which are crucial factors in therapeutic success.

Another area where research has significantly impacted assessment is in our understanding of cultural factors. The work of scholars like Derald Wing Sue has highlighted the importance of cultural competence in all aspects of counseling, including assessment. This research reminds us that many traditional assessment tools were developed and normed on specific populations, often lacking diversity. As such, we must approach assessment with cultural humility, being aware of potential biases in our tools and interpretations.

The development of culturally adapted assessment tools is an ongoing area of research. For example, the Cultural Formulation Interview, included in the Diagnostic and Statistical Manual of Mental Disorders, Fifth Edition, provides a structured way to assess the impact of culture on a client's presenting problems. Similarly, researchers like Lillian Comas-Díaz have developed assessment approaches that are more appropriate for Latinx populations. As counselors, we need to stay abreast of these developments and select assessment tools that are appropriate for our diverse clientele.

Research has also enhanced our understanding of the assessment process itself. The work of Kirk Strosahl and others in the field of behavioral health consultation has highlighted the value of ongoing, collaborative assessment. This approach, often referred to as functional analysis, involves working with clients to identify the factors that maintain their problems in the here-and-now, rather than focusing solely on historical causes.

This functional approach to assessment aligns well with brief, solution-focused models of therapy. It allows us to quickly identify targets for intervention and track progress over time. Moreover, it engages clients as active participants in the assessment process, which can enhance their understanding of their own issues and increase their motivation for change.

The integration of technology into assessment practices is another area where research is driving innovation. Computer-adaptive testing, for instance, allows for more efficient and precise measurement of psychological constructs. The Patient-Reported Outcomes Measurement Information System, developed by the National Institutes of Health, is an excellent example of this approach. It uses item response theory to select the most informative questions for each individual, reducing assessment burden while maintaining accuracy.

Mobile technology is also opening up new possibilities for ecological momentary assessment (EMA), allowing us to gather real-time data about clients' experiences in their natural environments. Research by Shiffman et al. (2008) has shown that EMA can provide more accurate information about fluctuating states like moods or cravings compared to retrospective reports. While the use of such technologies in routine practice is still evolving, it represents an exciting frontier in enhancing our assessment capabilities.

However, as we embrace these technological advances, we must also be mindful of their limitations and ethical implications. Research on the digital divide reminds us that not all clients have equal access to or comfort with technology. Moreover, the use of digital tools in assessment raises important questions about data privacy and the potential for technology to interfere with the therapeutic relationship.

Another hugely important area of assessment research relates to risk assessment, particularly for issues like suicide and violence. The work of researchers like David Jobes on the Collaborative Assessment and Management of Suicidality has shown the value of engaging clients collaboratively in assessing and managing risk. This approach not only improves the accuracy of our risk assessments but also enhances the therapeutic alliance and client engagement in safety planning.

As we consider these various advances in assessment research, we need to remember that assessment in counseling is not just about gathering information—it is an intervention in itself. The questions we ask, the areas we choose to focus on, and the way we provide feedback all send powerful messages to our clients about what is important and what is possible in their journey of change.

Research by Finn and Tonsager (1997) on therapeutic assessment has shown that, when conducted collaboratively and with empathy, the assessment process can lead to significant therapeutic gains. Clients report feeling understood, gaining new insights into their problems, and experiencing increased hope and self-efficacy. As such, we should approach assessment not as a dry, technical process, but as an opportunity for therapeutic intervention and alliance building.

Enhancing assessment in counseling sessions involves staying current with research developments, critically evaluating new tools and approaches, and thoughtfully integrating them into our practice. It requires us to balance standardized measures with individualized, culturally sensitive approaches. Most importantly, it involves engaging our clients as active collaborators in the assessment process, leveraging it not just as a means of gathering information, but as a powerful intervention in its own right.

By embracing a research-informed approach to assessment, we can enhance the accuracy and comprehensiveness of our client conceptualizations, improve treatment planning, and ultimately provide more effective care. As we continue to bridge the gap between research and practice, our assessment methods serve as a necessary point of connection, where our interventions are tailored to the unique needs and contexts of each individual client.

## RESEARCH IN COUNSELOR SKILL DEVELOPMENT AND SUPERVISION

Research in counselor skill development and supervision has become increasingly sophisticated, providing valuable insights that shape how we train and support counseling professionals. The work of Clara Hill and her colleagues has been particularly influential in this arena. Hill et al. (2017) developed an evidence-based approach to helping skills training that emphasizes a sequential, structured method for developing core counseling competencies. This research has led to a shift in counselor education programs, moving away from purely theoretical instruction toward more hands-on, experiential learning opportunities.

The concept of deliberate practice, originally derived from expertise research in other fields, has found significant application in counselor development. Rousmaniere et al. (2017) have shown that engaging in focused, repetitive practice of specific skills with immediate feedback can lead to substantial improvements in counselor effectiveness. This approach challenges the notion that expertise simply comes with time, emphasizing the importance of intentional, often challenging work to refine one's craft.

Supervision models have also evolved based on empirical evidence. Bernard and Goodyear (2019) developed and refined the discrimination model of supervision, which provides a flexible framework for supervisors to address different aspects of supervisee development. This model, grounded in research on counselor development trajectories, allows supervisors to tailor their approach based on the specific needs of each supervisee, whether that is focusing on intervention skills, conceptualization abilities, or personal awareness.

The importance of multicultural competence in counseling has extended to supervision practices as well. Sue et al. (2019) emphasized the need for supervisors to address cultural issues explicitly and create a safe environment for discussing diversity-related topics. This research has led to the development of multicultural supervision models that encourage both supervisors and supervisees to explore how their own cultural backgrounds influence their work and to develop strategies for working effectively with diverse client populations.

As technology continues to play an increasing role in counseling practice, research is exploring its application in supervision and skill development. Renfro-Michel et al. (2016) investigated the effectiveness of distance supervision and the use of video-recording for skill development. These studies are helping to establish best practices for integrating technology into counselor training and supervision, particularly important in an era where telehealth and online counseling are becoming more prevalent.

Underpinning many of these developments is an emphasis on reflective practice. Building on the seminal work of Schön (1983), researchers like Neufeldt et al. (1996) showed that encouraging counselors to reflect deeply on their work can enhance self-awareness, improve clinical decision-making, and ultimately lead to better client outcomes. This research has led to the integration of reflective practices into both counselor education and supervision, helping to develop practitioners who are not just skilled, but also thoughtful and self-aware.

By grounding our approaches to training and supervision in solid empirical evidence, we guarantee that counselors are equipped not just with knowledge, but with the practical skills and reflective capacities needed to provide effective, ethical care in an ever-changing world. This integration of research into counselor development practices stands as a testament to the power of bridging the gap between research and practice in our field.

## ETHICAL CONSIDERATIONS IN APPLYING RESEARCH TO PRACTICE

As Levitt et al. (2017) emphasized, the integration of research into practice must be done thoughtfully and with full consideration of ethical implications. One key ethical consideration is the appropriate use of EBPs. While EBPs have strong empirical support, counselors must be cautious not to apply them rigidly without consideration for individual client factors. ACA's Code of Ethics (2014) stipulated that counselors should use techniques/procedures/modalities that are grounded in theory and/or have an empirical or scientific foundation, but also emphasized the importance of honoring client diversity and promoting client welfare.

Another ethical consideration is the responsible interpretation and communication of research findings to clients. Lilienfeld et al. (2013) cautioned against oversimplifying or overstating research results, emphasizing the importance of conveying both the strengths and limitations of research evidence to clients. This transparency is critical for informed consent and shared decision-making in the therapeutic process.

Looking toward the future, the field of counseling is poised for exciting developments in research-informed practice. Advances in technology and data analytics are opening new avenues for real-time integration of research into practice. For instance, Becker and Jensen-Doss (2013) described the potential of measurement-based care systems that can provide counselors with immediate feedback on client progress, allowing for data-driven adjustments to treatment plans.

The future also holds promise for more personalized, precision-based approaches to counseling. Ng and Weisz (2016) discussed the potential of modular treatment approaches that allow for flexible, personalized interventions based on client characteristics and ongoing response to treatment. This approach represents a sophisticated integration of research and practice, using empirical data to guide clinical decision-making in real time.

Moreover, there is growing recognition of the importance of practice-based evidence to complement traditional EBP. As Castonguay et al. (2013) argued, systematically collecting data from routine clinical practice can provide valuable insights that complement findings from controlled research studies. This bidirectional flow of information between research and practice holds the potential to accelerate the development of more effective, responsive counseling interventions.

Integrating research into counseling practice can significantly enhance the quality and effectiveness of the care we provide. As we move forward, it is crucial that we as counselors maintain a stance of critical reflection, continually seeking to bridge the gap between research and practice while remaining grounded in the fundamental humanistic values of our profession. By embracing a research-informed approach to practice, we position ourselves to meet the evolving needs of our clients and contribute to the ongoing advancement of the counseling field.

## LOOKING TOWARD THE FUTURE: COUNSELORS AS CONTRIBUTORS TO RESEARCH

As we look to the future of counseling, it is clear that the integration of research and practice will continue to be crucial. Counselors are not just consumers of research but can and should be active contributors to the field's knowledge base. This section explores how counselors can maintain a research mindset throughout their careers and contribute to the ever-evolving landscape of counseling research.

### CONTRIBUTING TO THE RESEARCH BASE

Counselors in clinical practice are uniquely positioned to contribute to research. Their day-to-day experiences with clients provide invaluable insights that can inform and shape future research directions. As Bager-Charleson (2014) noted, practitioner research can bridge the gap between academic knowledge and practical application.

One way counselors can contribute is through practice-based evidence. This involves systematically collecting data from their own practice to evaluate the effectiveness of interventions. Lambert (2013) emphasized that such data collection can provide insights into what works in real-world settings, complementing findings from controlled research studies.

Collaborative research partnerships between practitioners and academics are another avenue for contribution. These partnerships, as described by McLeod (2016), can lead to research that is both rigorous and relevant to clinical practice. Counselors can participate in such partnerships by offering their clinical expertise, helping to formulate research questions, and assisting in data collection and interpretation.

## MAINTAINING A RESEARCH MINDSET

Maintaining a research mindset throughout one's career is essential for EBP. This involves more than just staying current with research findings; it requires an attitude of curiosity and critical inquiry toward one's own practice.

Schön's (1983) concept of the "reflective practitioner" is particularly relevant here. By regularly reflecting on their work, counselors can identify patterns, generate hypotheses, and develop research questions based on their clinical experiences. This reflective stance can be supported by practices such as keeping a research journal or participating in research-focused peer supervision groups.

Technology can play a crucial role in maintaining a research mindset. Rousmaniere et al. (2017) discussed how digital tools for tracking client outcomes and analyzing session recordings can help counselors continuously refine their skills and contribute to practice-based research.

## FUTURE TRENDS IN COUNSELING RESEARCH

As counselors look to the future, several trends are likely to shape the research landscape:

1. Increased focus on personalized interventions: Ng and Weisz (2016) predicted a move toward more individualized treatment approaches based on client characteristics and preferences.
2. Integration of neuroscience: Beeson et al. (2019) suggested that advances in neuroscience will increasingly inform counseling interventions and our understanding of change processes.
3. Technological innovations: Fairburn and Patel (2017) foresaw a greater role for digital interventions and artificial intelligence–assisted therapy, necessitating research into their effectiveness and ethical implications.
4. Cultural adaptation of interventions: As highlighted by Sue et al. (2019), there will be an increased emphasis on adapting interventions for diverse populations and studying their effectiveness.

## LIFELONG LEARNING AND ENGAGEMENT WITH RESEARCH

To stay abreast of these developments and maintain their ability to contribute to research, counselors must commit to lifelong learning. This might involve the following:

1. Regular participation in continuing education focused on research methods and findings.
2. Engagement with professional organizations that promote research, such as the ACA's Association for Assessment and Research in Counseling.
3. Subscribing to and regularly reading key journals in the field.

4. Participating in or initiating practice-research networks, as described by Castonguay et al. (2013).

As the field of counseling continues to evolve, the role of the counselor as both a consumer and a contributor to research will become increasingly important. By maintaining a research mindset, actively contributing to the knowledge base, and staying engaged with emerging trends, counselors can assess if their practice remains cutting-edge and evidence-based. This not only enhances individual practice but also contributes to the advancement of the profession as a whole, ultimately benefiting the clients we serve.

## CONCLUSION

As we've explored throughout this chapter, the integration of research into counseling practice is a multifaceted and dynamic process that touches every aspect of our work as counselors. From developing research literacy and critically evaluating studies, to applying findings in clinical practice and assessment, to informing counselor development and supervision, research serves as a guiding light that illuminates our path toward more effective, ethical, and client-centered care.

The journey of bridging research and practice is not without its challenges. It requires us to continually update our knowledge, critically examine our assumptions, and sometimes step out of our comfort zones to embrace new approaches. However, as we've seen, the rewards of this integration are substantial. By grounding our work in empirical evidence, we enhance our ability to make informed clinical decisions, tailor our interventions to individual client needs, and ultimately improve outcomes for those we serve.

Moreover, as we've discussed, the relationship between research and practice is not unidirectional. As practitioners, we are not merely consumers of research but also potential contributors to the knowledge base of our field. Through systematic reflection on our practice, engagement in practice-based research, and collaboration with researchers, we can work toward a research agenda in counseling that remains relevant and responsive to the realities of clinical practice.

Looking to the future, the continued integration of research and practice holds exciting possibilities. Advances in technology, growing emphasis on personalized interventions, and increasing recognition of diverse methodologies all point toward a future where research and practice are more closely intertwined than ever before. As we navigate this evolving landscape, it is crucial that we remain grounded in our ethical obligations, always prioritizing client welfare and respecting the complexity of human experience.

In conclusion, the ability to bridge research and practice is not just a valuable skill, but a professional imperative for modern counselors. It allows us to honor both the science and the art of our profession, combining empirical rigor with clinical intuition and human compassion. As we continue on this journey of integration, we not only enhance our individual practice but also contribute to the advancement of the counseling profession as a whole. By embracing a research-informed approach, we position ourselves to meet the evolving needs of our clients, adapt to changing societal contexts, and ultimately fulfill our commitment to promoting mental health and well-being in the communities we serve.

# A

# Resources for Intuitive Research Methods

## BOOKS:

1. "Creative Research Methods in the Social Sciences" by Helen Kara
2. "Qualitative Research: Creative and Innovative Approaches" by Ravitch and Carl
3. "Art-Based Research" by Shaun McNiff
4. "Participatory Action Research" by Alice McIntyre
5. "Visual Methodologies" by Gillian Rose
6. "Evidence-Based Therapy Relationships" by Norcross and Wampold
7. "Principles of Therapeutic Change that Work" by Castonguay and Beutler
8. "The Making of Modern Psychiatry" by Edward Shorter
9. "Counseling and Psychotherapy Theories in Context and Practice" by Sommers-Flanagan and Sommers-Flanagan
10. "Research Methods in Psychology" by Beth Morling

## KEY ARTICLES:

1. "The Use of Creative Methodologies in Qualitative Research" by Jones and Leavy
2. "Exploring the Potential of Visual Methods in Qualitative Research" by Gillies and Bell
3. "Art as Inquiry: Creative Research Methods in Education" by Siegesmund

## ONLINE RESOURCES:

1. ResearchGate (www.researchgate.net)
2. Creative Research Methods (www.creativeresearchmethods.com)
3. Arts-Based Research Studio (www.artsbasedresearchstudio.com)
4. American Counseling Association Knowledge Center
5. PsychologyToday—Therapy and Research Blog
6. Society for Psychotherapy Research
7. Google Scholar
8. Open Science Framework (OSF)

## ORGANIZATIONS:

1. International Association of Creative Arts in Education and Therapy (IACAET)
2. Arts and Humanities Research Council (AHRC)
3. Society for Arts-Based Research (SABR)

## CONFERENCES AND WORKSHOPS:

4. International Congress of Qualitative Inquiry (ICQI)
5. Arts-Based Research Workshops (various institutions)
6. Creative Research Methods Training by Helen Kara

## ONLINE COURSES:

1. “Creative Research Methods” (Coursera)
2. “Qualitative Research Methods” (edX)
3. “Psychological First Aid” (Coursera)
4. “Improving Your Statistical Inferences” (Coursera)

## PODCASTS:

1. The Thoughtful Counselor
2. Psychology in Seattle
3. Counseling Theory and Research Podcast
4. The Upside of Down

5. Shrink Rap Radio
6. Two Psychologists Four Beers

## DOCUMENTARIES:

1. "People Say I'm Crazy"
2. "Why We Believe in Bad Science"

## ADDITIONAL RESOURCES:

1. PubMed and PsycINFO databases
2. The Professional Counselor (open-access journal)
3. Retraction Watch website
4. PsyArXiv preprint server

This streamlined version organizes the resources into clear categories, removes redundancies, and presents the information in a more concise and accessible format.

# B

# Glossary of Research Terms

A

**Action Research**: A participatory research method focused on solving practical problems through a cyclical process of planning, acting, observing, and reflecting.

**Autoethnography**: A qualitative research method combining ethnographic and autobiographical elements to explore personal experiences in a broader social and cultural context.

**ANOVA (Analysis of Variance)**: A statistical method used to compare means among three or more groups to determine whether there are statistically significant differences.

**Axial Coding**: In grounded theory, the process of relating codes (categories and properties) to each other, refining and developing the theoretical framework.

B

**Bayesian Statistics**: A statistical approach that involves updating the probability of a hypothesis as more evidence or information becomes available.

C

**Case Study**: An in-depth analysis of a single case or a small number of cases within their real-life context.

**Cluster Analysis**: A statistical technique used to classify objects (individuals, variables, or observations) into groups based on similarities.

**Cohort Study**: A longitudinal study that follows a group of people (cohort) over time to examine the development of specific outcomes.

**Content Analysis**: A systematic coding and categorizing approach used to analyze textual data for patterns, themes, or meanings.

**Convergent Parallel Design**: A mixed-methods design where qualitative and quantitative data are collected simultaneously, but analyzed separately, with results merged for comprehensive interpretation.

**Correlation**: A statistical measure that describes the extent to which two variables are related.

**Critical Discourse Analysis (CDA)**: A method for studying the ways in which language is used to construct social realities and power relations.

## D

**Dependent Variable**: The variable in an experiment that is measured and is expected to change due to manipulation of the independent variable.

**Descriptive Research**: A quantitative research method focused on systematically describing characteristics or behaviors of a population or a phenomenon.

**Discourse Analysis**: A qualitative method for analyzing written or spoken language to understand how it constructs meaning and social realities.

## E

**Embedded Design**: A mixed-methods design where one type of data (qualitative or quantitative) is embedded within a larger study using the other type to provide additional context or insight.

**Ethnography**: A qualitative research method involving in-depth study and systematic recording of cultures and social groups through immersive observation and participation.

**Explanatory Sequential Design**: A mixed-methods design that begins with quantitative data collection and analysis followed by qualitative data collection to explain or elaborate on the quantitative findings.

**Exploratory Sequential Design**: A mixed-methods design that starts with qualitative data collection and analysis to explore a phenomenon, followed by quantitative data collection to test or expand on the initial findings.

## F

**Factor Analysis**: A statistical method used to identify underlying relationships between variables by grouping them into factors based on their correlations.

**Focus Group**: A qualitative research method involving guided group discussions to gather diverse perspectives on a specific topic.

## G

**Grounded Theory**: A qualitative research method focused on generating or discovering theory through systematic data collection and analysis.

## H

**Hierarchical Linear Modeling (HLM)**: A statistical method used to analyze data that are organized at more than one level, such as students within schools or clients within therapists.

**Hypothesis**: A testable statement about the relationship between two or more variables.

## I

**Independent Variable**: The variable in an experiment that is manipulated to observe its effect on the dependent variable.

**Inferential Statistics**: Statistical methods that allow researchers to make inferences about a population based on sample data.

**Intervention Design**: A mixed-methods design that integrates qualitative and quantitative approaches to develop, test, and refine interventions.

**Interpretative Phenomenological Analysis (IPA)**: A qualitative research method focused on how individuals make sense of their personal and social worlds.

## L

**Latent Class Analysis (LCA)**: A statistical method used to identify unobserved subgroups within a population based on observed variables.

**Life History Research**: A qualitative research method involving the collection and analysis of comprehensive narratives of individuals' life experiences over time.

**Longitudinal Research**: A research method that involves studying the same participants over an extended period to observe changes and development over time.

## M

**MANOVA (Multivariate Analysis of Variance)**: A statistical method used to assess multiple dependent variables simultaneously to understand the effect of one or more independent variables.

**Meta-Analysis**: A statistical technique that combines the results of multiple studies on the same topic to derive overall conclusions.

**Mixed-Methods Research**: An approach that integrates both qualitative and quantitative research methods to provide a more comprehensive understanding of research problems.

**Multiphase Design**: A mixed-methods design involving multiple phases of data collection and analysis over time, using both qualitative and quantitative methods.

## N

**Narrative Inquiry**: A qualitative research method focused on the stories individuals tell about their lives and experiences.

**Narrative Research**: A qualitative method that examines how individuals construct and convey their life stories and identities through narrative.

**P**

**Participatory Action Research (PAR)**: A research method that involves researchers and participants working collaboratively to identify issues and develop solutions.

**Path Analysis**: A statistical technique that examines the directed dependencies among a set of variables, helping to understand the direct and indirect relationships.

**Phenomenology**: A qualitative research method that focuses on exploring and understanding the lived experiences of individuals.

**Q**

**Quasi-Experimental Research**: A research design that resembles an experimental design but lacks random assignment of participants to groups.

**Qualitative Research**: A research approach focused on exploring and understanding the depth and complexity of human experiences through non-numerical data.

**Quantitative Research**: A research approach focused on measuring and analyzing variables numerically to establish patterns, relationships, and causality.

**R**

**Randomized Controlled Trial (RCT)**: An experimental design that involves randomly assigning participants to experimental and control groups to test the effect of an intervention.

**Regression Analysis**: A statistical method that examines the relationship between a dependent variable and one or more independent variables.

**S**

**Sequential Transformative Design**: A mixed-methods design involving a two-phase approach guided by a transformative framework, with qualitative and quantitative phases conducted in sequence.

**Structural Equation Modeling (SEM)**: A statistical technique that tests complex relationships among variables, combining factor analysis and multiple regression.

**Survey Research**: A quantitative research method that collects data from a large number of respondents using questionnaires or interviews.

**Survival Analysis**: A statistical method used to analyze the expected duration of time until one or more events occur.

**T**

**Thematic Analysis**: A method for identifying, analyzing, and reporting patterns (themes) within qualitative data.

**Time-Series Analysis**: A statistical technique that analyzes data points collected at successive time intervals to identify trends and patterns over time.

**Triangulation Design**: A mixed-methods design that uses qualitative and quantitative data concurrently to validate and cross-check findings.

## V

**Visual Methods**: Qualitative research methods that incorporate visual materials (such as photographs, videos, and drawings) to gather and analyze data.

## W

**Within-Subjects Design**: An experimental design where the same participants are exposed to all conditions or treatments, allowing for comparison within the same group.

# C

# Comprehensive Research Methods Self-inventory

Instructions:
This self-inventory is designed to help you identify which research approach best fits your interests, strengths, and goals. Rate your agreement with each statement on a scale from 1 (*Strongly Disagree*) to 5 (*Strongly Agree*).

Statements:

Quantitative Research:

1. I enjoy working with numerical data and statistical analysis.
2. I am interested in identifying patterns and testing hypotheses.
3. I prefer using structured, standardized instruments for data collection.
4. I like designing experiments to determine causal relationships.
5. I am comfortable using statistical software for data analysis.

Qualitative Research:

6. I prefer exploring in-depth personal experiences and stories.
7. I value understanding the context and meaning behind behaviors.
8. I enjoy conducting interviews, focus groups, or participant observation.
9. I am comfortable with flexible, adaptive research designs.
10. I like writing detailed narrative descriptions and thematic analyses.

Mixed Methods:

11. I want to integrate both numerical data and personal experiences in my research.
12. I believe combining qualitative and quantitative data provides more comprehensive understanding.
13. I'm interested in exploring statistical relationships and deeper meanings behind data.
14. I value the depth of qualitative data and the generalizability of quantitative evidence.
15. I enjoy research designs that evolve over multiple phases.

Specific Approaches:

16. I am fascinated by understanding the essence of people's lived experiences. (Phenomenology)
17. I enjoy developing theories based on data collected from participants. (Grounded Theory)
18. I am interested in immersing myself in different cultures to understand their practices. (Ethnography)
19. I like conducting an in-depth analysis of a single case or a small number of cases. (Case Study)
20. I am drawn to exploring people's stories and how they construct their identities. (Narrative Research)
21. I value collaborative research that involves participants to bring about change. (Participatory Action Research)
22. I prefer starting with quantitative data and then using qualitative methods to explain results. (Explanatory Sequential)
23. I like starting with qualitative exploration and then testing findings quantitatively. (Exploratory Sequential)
24. I enjoy integrating qualitative and quantitative data simultaneously. (Convergent Parallel)

Scoring:
Quantitative: Add scores for Statements 1–5.
Qualitative: Add scores for Statements 6–10.
Mixed Methods: Add scores for Statements 11–15.
For specific approaches, use the highest scoring statement from 16 to 24.

Interpretation:
Your highest score indicates your preferred research approach. Consider how this aligns with your research goals and the nature of your research questions. Remember that many researchers use multiple approaches depending on their specific projects.

# References

## INTRODUCTION


American Counseling Association. (2014). ACA Code of Ethics. Author.

Amirova, A., Iskakovna, J. M., Zakaryanovna, T. G., Nurmakhanovna, Z. T., & Elmira, U. (2020). Creative and research competence as a factor of professional training of future teachers: Perspective of learning technology. *World Journal on Educational Technology: Current Issues, 12*(4), 278–289.

APA Presidential Task Force on Evidence-Based Practice. (2006). Evidence-based practice in psychology. *American Psychologist, 61*(4), 271-285.

Bager-Charleson, S. (2014). *Doing practice-based research in therapy: A reflexive approach.* SAGE.

Betan, E. J., & Binder, J. L. (2010). Clinical expertise in psychotherapy: How expert therapists use theory in generating case conceptualizations and interventions. *Journal of Contemporary Psychotherapy, 40*, 141-152.

Bezyak, J. L., Kubota, C., & Rosenthal, D. (2010). Evidence-based practice in rehabilitation counseling: Perceptions and practices. *Rehabilitation Research, Policy, and Education, 24*(1/2), 85.

Burke, L. E., Schlenk, E. A., Sereika, S. M., Cohen, S. M., Happ, M. B., & Dorman, J. S. (2005). Developing research competence to support evidence-based practice. *Journal of Professional Nursing, 21*(6), 358–363.

Burns, D. (1980). *Feeling Good: The New Mood Therapy.* Harper Collins.

Cook, S. C., Schwartz, A. C., & Kaslow, N. J. (2017). Evidence-based psychotherapy: Advantages and challenges. *Neurotherapeutics, 14*, 537-545.

Council for Accreditation of Counseling and Related Educational Programs. (2024). *2024 CACREP Standards*. Author.

Creswell, J. W., & Creswell, J. D. (2018). *Research design: Qualitative, quantitative, and mixed methods approaches* (5th ed.). Sage.

Dozois, D. J. (2013). Psychological treatments: Putting evidence into practice and practice into evidence. *Canadian Psychology/Psychologie canadienne, 54*(1), 1.

Gambrill, E. (2012). *Critical thinking in clinical practice: Improving the quality of judgments and decisions* (3rd ed.). Wiley.

Gelso, C. J. (1993). On the making of a scientist-practioner: A theory of research training in professional psychology. *Professional Psychology: Research and Practice, 24*(4), 468.

Gelso, C. J., Baumann, E. C., Chui, H. T., & Savela, A. E. (2013). The making of a scientist-psychotherapist: The research training environment and the psychotherapist. *Psychotherapy, 50*, 139–149.

Hays, D. G., & Singh, A. A. (2011). *Qualitative inquiry in clinical and educational settings.* Guilford Press.

Heppner, P. P., Wampold, B. E., Owen, J., Wang, K. T., & Thompson, M. N. (2016). *Research design in counseling* (4th ed.). Cengage Learning.

Jensen-Doss, A., Haimes, E. M. B., Smith, A. M., Lyon, A. R., Lewis, C. C., Stanick, C. F., & Hawley, K. M. (2018). Monitoring treatment progress and providing feedback is viewed favorably but rarely used in practice. *Administration and Policy in Mental Health and Mental Health Services Research, 45*, 48–61.

Kaplan, D. M., & Gladding, S. T. (2011). A vision for the future of counseling: The 20/20 principles for unifying and strengthening the profession. *Journal of Counseling & Development, 89*(3), 367-372.

Kaplan, D. M., Tarvydas, V. M., & Gladding, S. T. (2014). 20/20: A vision for the future of counseling: The new consensus definition of counseling. *Journal of Counseling & Development, 92*(3), 366–372.

Kazdin, A. E. (2008). Evidence-based treatment and practice: New opportunities to bridge clinical research and practice, enhance the knowledge base, and improve patient care. *American Psychologist, 63*(3), 146.

Kline, R. B. (2008). *Becoming a behavioral science researcher: A guide to producing research that matters.* Guilford Press.

Knowles, M. S., Holton, E. F., III, & Swanson, R. A. (2015). *The adult learner: The definitive classic in adult education and human resource development* (8th ed.). Routledge.

Lenz, S. (2020) The future of counseling outcome research and evaluation. *Counseling Outcome Research and Evaluation, 11*(1), 1-3.

Levitt, H. M., Bamberg, M., Creswell, J. W., Frost, D. M., Josselson, R., & Suárez-Orozco, C. (2018). Journal article reporting standards for qualitative primary, qualitative meta-analytic, and mixed methods research in psychology: The APA Publications and Communications Board task force report. *American Psychologist, 73*(1), 26-46.

Levitt, H. M., Morrill, Z., & Collins, K. M. (2020). Considering methodological integrity in counselling and psychotherapy research. *Counselling and Psychotherapy Research, 20*(3), 422-428.

Lilienfeld, S. O., Ritschel, L. A., Lynn, S. J., Cautin, R. L., & Latzman, R. D. (2013). Why many clinical psychologists are resistant to evidence-based practice: Root causes and constructive remedies. *Clinical Psychology Review, 33*(7), 883–900.

Martino, S. (2010). Strategies for training counselors in evidence-based treatments. *Addiction Science & Clinical Practice, 5*(2), 30.

Meltzoff, J., & Cooper, H. (2018). *Critical thinking about research: Psychology and related fields* (2nd ed.). American Psychological Association.

Mobley, K., & Wester, K. L. (2007). *Evidence-based practices: Building a bridge between researchers and practitioners.* Columbus, OH: Association for Counselor Education and Supervision.

Norcross, J. C., & Lambert, M. J. (2018). Psychotherapy relationships that work III. *Psychotherapy, 55*(4), 303-315.

Norcross, J. C., & Wampold, B. E. (2011). Evidence-based therapy relationships: Research conclusions and clinical practices. *Psychotherapy, 48*(1), 98-102.

Ray, D. C., Hull, D. M., Thacker, A. J., Pace, L. S., Carlson, S. E., & Sullivan, J. M. (2011). Research in counseling: A 10-year review to inform practice. *Journal of Counseling & Development, 89*, 349–359.

Rose, S., Bisson, J., Churchill, R., & Wessley, S. (2002). Psychological debriefing for preventing post-traumatic stress disorder (PTSD). *Cochrane Database of Systematic Reviews, 2*, 1-2.

Sackett, D. L., Rosenberg, W. M., Muir-Gray, J. A., Haynes, R. B., & Richardson, W. S. (2000). *Evidence-based medicine: How to practice and teach EBM* (2nd ed.). Edinburgh, Scotland: Churchill Livingstone.

Steele, J. M., & Rawls, G. J. (2015). Quantitative research attitudes and research training perceptions among master's-level students. *Counselor Education and Supervision, 54*(2), 134-146.

Trusty, W. T., Penix, E. A., Dimmick, A. A., & Swift, J. K. (2019). Shared decision-making in mental and behavioural health interventions. *Journal of Evaluation in Clinical Practice, 25*(6), 1210-1216. Wester, K. L., & Borders, L. D. (2014). Research competencies in counseling: A Delphi study. *Journal of Counseling & Development, 92*(4), 447–458.

Wester, K. L., Wachter Morris, C. A., & Williams, B. (2018). Research methods in counseling: Trends in the first 15 years of the *Journal of Counseling & Development*. *Journal of Counseling & Development, 96*(2), 172–183.

Wester, K. L., Mobley, A. K., & Fesperman, S. F. (2020). Counseling outcomes at CACREP-accredited programs: A pilot study. *Journal of Counseling & Development, 98*(3), 253–265.

Yates, C. (2013). Evidence-based practice: The components, history, and process. *Counseling Outcome Research and Evaluation, 4*(1), 41–54.

## CHAPTER 1

American Counseling Association. (2014). ACA Code of Ethics. Author.

American Psychological Association. (n.d.). *Psychology subfields.* https://www.apa.org/education-career/guide/subfields

Aftab, A., Nassir Ghaemi, S., & Stagno, S. (2018). A didactic course on "philosophy of psychiatry" for psychiatry residents. *Academic Psychiatry, 42*, 559–563.

Arad, H. (2017). *Integrating Relational Psychoanalysis and EMDR: Embodied Experience and Clinical Practice* (1st ed.). Routledge. https://doi.org/10.4324/9781315159775

Barton, W. E. (1998). A history of psychiatry: From the era of the asylum to the age of Prozac. *Psychiatric Services, 49*(9), 1241–1242. https://doi.org/10.1176/ps.49.9.1241

Beer, M. D. (1995). Psychosis: from mental disorder to disease concept. *History of Psychiatry, 6*(22), 177–200.

Beer, M. D. (2009). History of psychiatry and the psychiatric profession. *Current Opinion in Psychiatry, 22*(6), 594–600.

Bernard, J. M., & Goodyear, R. K. (2019). *Fundamentals of clinical supervision* (6th ed.). Pearson.

Bloom, J. W., Gerstein, L. H., Tarvydas, V. M., Conaster, J. F., Davis, E., Kater, D., Sherrard, P. A. D., & Esposito, R. (1990). Model legislation for licensed professional counselors. *Journal of Counseling & Development, 68*(5), 511–523.

Corey, G. (2017). *Theory and practice of counseling and psychotherapy* (10th ed.). Cengage Learning.

Crenshaw, K. W. (2013). Mapping the margins: Intersectionality, identity politics, and violence against women of color. In *The public nature of private violence* (pp. 93–118). Routledge.

Cutuli, J. J., Herbers, J. E., Masten, A. S., & Reed, M. G. J. (2020). Resilience in development 13. In C. R. Snyder & S. Lopez (Eds.), *The Oxford handbook of positive psychology* (p. 171). Oxford University Press.

Deacon, B. J. (2013). The biomedical model of mental disorder: A critical analysis of its validity, utility, and effects on psychotherapy research. *Clinical Psychology Review, 33*(7), 846–861.

de Shazer, S., Dolan, Y., Korman, H., Trepper, T., McCollum, E., & Berg, I. K. (2007). *More than miracles: The state of the art of solution-focused brief therapy*. Haworth Press.

Frankl, V. E. (1959). *Man's search for meaning.* Beacon Press.

Fuertes, J. N., Stracuzzi, T. I., Bennett, J., Scheinholtz, J., Mislowack, A., Hersh, M., & Cheng, D. (2006). Therapist multicultural competency: A study of therapy dyads. *Psychotherapy: Theory, Research, Practice, Training, 43*(4), 480.

Gale, A. U., & Austin, B. D. (2003). Professionalism's challenges to professional counselors' collective identity. *Journal of Counseling & Development, 81*(1), 3-10.

Georges, C. M., & Tomlinson-Clarke, S. M. (2015). Integrating positive psychology into counseling psychology doctoral education. *The Counseling Psychologist, 43*(5), 752–788.

Gibson, D. M., Dollarhide, C. T., & Moss, J. M. (2010). Professional identity development: A grounded theory of transformational tasks of new counselors. *Counselor Education and Supervision, 50*(1), 21-38.

Gladding, S. T. (2018). *Counseling: A comprehensive profession* (8th ed.). Pearson.

Gladding, S. T., & Newsome, D. W. (2018). *Clinical mental health counseling in community and agency settings* (5th ed.). Pearson.

Glosoff, H. L., Benshoff, J. M., Hosie, T. W., & Maki, D. R. (1995). The 1994 ACA model legislation for licensed professional counselors. *Journal of Counseling & Development, 74*(2), 209-220.

Goodey, C. (2021). *Development: The history of a psychological concept*. Cambridge University Press.

Hanna, F. J., & Bemak, F. (1997). The quest for identity in the counseling profession. *Counselor Education and Supervision, 36*(3), 194-206.

Hansen, J. T. (2006). Counseling theories within a postmodernist epistemology: New roles for theories in counseling practice. *Journal of Counseling & Development, 84*(3), 291–297.

Harrington, A. (2019). *Mind fixers: Psychiatry's troubled search for the biology of mental illness*. W. W. Norton.

Haslam, M. T. (2014). *Psychiatry: Made simple*. Elsevier.

Herlihy, B., Lyons, M., & Strozier, J. (2018). Professional counseling and ethical practice. In S. C. Nassar & S. G. Niles (Eds.), *Orientation to professional counseling: Past, present, and future trends.* John Wiley & Sons.

Ivey, A. E., Ivey, M. B., & Zalaquett, C. P. (2018). *Intentional interviewing and counseling: Facilitating client development in a multicultural society* (9th ed.). Cengage Learning.

Kaplan, D. M., & Gladding, S. T. (2011). A vision for the future of counseling: The 20/20 principles for unifying and strengthening the profession. *Journal of Counseling & Development, 89*(3), 367-372.

Kernes, J. L., & Kinnier, R. T. (2008). Meaning in psychologists' personal and professional lives. *Journal of Humanistic Psychology, 48*(2), 196-220.

Lin, L., Christidis, P., & Stamm, K. (2017, September). Datapoint: The mental health workforce shortage. *Monitor on Psychology*. https://www.apa.org/monitor/2017/09/datapoint

Luke, M., & Goodrich, K. M. (2010). Chi Sigma Iota chapter leadership and professional identity development in early career counselors. *Counselor Education and Supervision, 50*(1), 56-78.

Maslow, A. H. (1954). *Motivation and personality.* Harper & Row.

May, R. (1981). *Freedom and destiny.* Norton.

McAuliffe, G., & Eriksen, K. (Eds.). (2010). *Handbook of counselor preparation: Constructivist, developmental, and experiential approaches.* SAGE.

McWhirter, E. H. (1991). Empowerment in counseling. *Journal of Counseling & Development, 69*(3), 222-227.

Mellin, E. A., Hunt, B., & Nichols, L. M. (2011). Counselor professional identity: Findings and implications for counseling and interprofessional collaboration. *Journal of Counseling & Development, 89*(2), 140–147.

Miller, G. A. (2003). The cognitive revolution: A historical perspective. *Trends in Cognitive Sciences, 7*(3), 141–144.

Miller, W. R., & Rollnick, S. (2012). *Motivational interviewing: Helping people change* (3rd ed.). Guilford Press.

Moss, J. M., Gibson, D. M., & Dollarhide, C. T. (2014). Professional identity development: A grounded theory of transformational tasks of counselors. *Journal of counseling & development, 92*(1), 3-12.

Myers, J. E., & Sweeney, T. J. (2008). Wellness counseling: The evidence base for practice. *Journal of Counseling & Development, 86*(4), 482–493.

Neukrug, E. S. (2016). *The world of the counselor: An introduction to the counseling profession* (5th ed.). Cengage Learning.

Nugent, F. A., & Jones, K. D. (2009). *Introduction to the profession of counseling* (5th ed.). Pearson.

Pelusco, P. R. (2022). *Advanced principles of counseling and psychotherapy: Learning, integrating, and consolidating the nonlinear thinking of master practitioners.* Routledge.

Perls, F., Hefferline, R., & Goodman, P. (1951). *Gestalt therapy: Excitement and growth in the human personality.* Julian Press.

Pope, M. (2000). A brief history of career counseling in the United States. *The career development quarterly, 48*(3), 194-211.

Porter, R. (2003). *Madness: A brief history.* Oxford University Press.

Ratts, M. J., Singh, A. A., Nassar-McMillan, S., Butler, S. K., & McCullough, J. R. (2016). Multicultural and social justice counseling competencies: Guidelines for the counseling profession. *Journal of Multicultural Counseling and Development, 44*(1), 28–48.

Reiner, S. M., Dobmeier, R. A., & Hernández, T. J. (2013). Perceived impact of professional counselor identity: An exploratory study. *Journal of Counseling & Development, 91*(2), 174-183.

Remley, T. P., & Herlihy, B. (2020). Ethical, legal, and professional issues in counseling (6th ed.). Pearson.

Rieber, R. W., & Robinson, D. K. (Eds.). (2012). *Wilhelm Wundt in history: The making of a scientific psychology.* Springer Science & Business Media.

Rogers, C. R. (1951). *Client-centered therapy: Its current practice, implications, and theory, with chapters.* Houghton Mifflin.

Shoben, E. J., Jr. (1965). The counseling experience as personal development. *The Personnel and Guidance Journal, 44*(3), 224–230.

Shorter, E. (1997). *A history of psychiatry: From the era of the asylum to the age of Prozac.* John Wiley & Sons.

Sue, D. W., Sue, D., Neville, H. A., & Smith, L. (2019). *Counseling the culturally diverse: Theory and practice* (8th ed.). Wiley.

Woo, H., Goo, M., & Lee, M. (2016). A content analysis of research on disability: American Counseling Association journals between 2003 and 2013. *Journal of Multicultural Counseling and Development, 44*(4), 228-244.

Woo, H., Lu, J., Harris, C., & Cauley, B. (2017). Professional identity development in counseling professionals. *Counseling Outcome Research and Evaluation, 8*(1), 15-30.
Yalom, I. D. (1980). *Existential psychotherapy.* Basic Books.

## CHAPTER 2

Abu-Odah, H., Said, N. B., Nair, S. C., Allsop, M. J., Currow, D. C., Salah, M. S., Hamad, B. A., Elessi, K., Alkhatib, A., ElMokhallalati, Y., Bayuo, J., & AlKhaldi, M. (2022). Identifying barriers and facilitators of translating research evidence into clinical practice: A systematic review of reviews. *Health & Social Care in the Community, 30*, e3265–e3276. https://doi.org/10.1111/hsc.13898
American Counseling Association. (2014). ACA Code of Ethics. Author.
Bager-Charleson, S. (2014). *Doing practice-based research in therapy: A reflexive approach*. SAGE.
Barden, S. M., Sherrell, R. S., & Matthews, J. J. (2017). A national survey on multicultural competence for professional counselors: A replication study. *Journal of Counseling & Development, 95*(2), 203–212.
Beidas, R. S., Stewart, R. E., Walsh, L., Lucas, S., Downey, M. M., Jackson, K., Fernandez, T., & Mandell, D. S. (2016). Free, brief, and validated: Standardized instruments for low-resource mental health settings. *Cognitive and Behavioral Practice, 23*(4), 434–448.
Beutler, L. E., Someah, K., Kimpara, S., & Miller, K. (2016). Selecting the most appropriate treatment for each patient. *International Journal of Clinical and Health Psychology, 16*(1), 99–108.
Block, J. (1995). A contrarian view of the five-factor approach to personality description. *Psychological bulletin, 117*(2), 187.
Boisvert, C. M., & Faust, D. (2006). Practicing psychologists' knowledge of general psychotherapy research findings: Implications for science-practice relations. *Professional Psychology: Research and Practice, 37*(6), 708.
Cook, S. C., Schwartz, A. C., & Kaslow, N. J. (2017). Evidence-based psychotherapy: Advantages and challenges. *Neurotherapeutics, 14*, 537–545.
Cooper, M. (2008). *Essential research findings in counselling and psychotherapy: The facts are friendly*. SAGE.
Dickersin, K. (2005). Publication bias: Recognizing the problem, understanding its origins and scope, and preventing harm. In H. R. Rothstein, A. J. Sutton, and M. Borenstein (Eds.), *Publication bias in meta-analysis: Prevention, assessment and adjustments* (pp. 9–33). John Wiley & Sons.
Duncan, B. L., Miller, S. D., Wampold, B. E., & Hubble, M. A. (2010). *The heart and soul of change: Delivering what works in therapy* (pp. xxix–455). American Psychological Association.
Haslam, N. (2016). Concept creep: Psychology's expanding concepts of harm and pathology. *Psychological inquiry, 27*(1), 1-17.
Hensel, P. G. (2021). Reproducibility and replicability crisis: How management compares to psychology and economics—A systematic review of literature. *European Management Journal, 39*(5), 577–594. https://doi.org/10.1016/j.emj.2021.01.002
Heppner, P. P., Wampold, B. E., Owen, J., Wang, K. T., & Thompson, M. N. (2016). *Research design in counseling* (4th ed.). Cengage Learning.
Horigian, V. E., Espinal, P. S., Alonso, E., Verdeja, R. E., Duan, R., Usaga, I. M., Pérez-López, A., Marín-Navarrete, R., & Feaster, D. J. (2016). Readiness and barriers to adopt evidence-based practices for substance abuse treatment in Mexico. *Salud Mental, 39*(2), 77–84.

Huber C. R., & Kuncel, N. R. (2016). Does college teach critical thinking? A meta-analysis. *Review of Educational Research, 86*(2), 431–468.

Joober, R., Schmitz, N., Annable, L., & Boksa, P. (2012). Publication bias: What are the challenges and can they be overcome? *Journal of Psychiatry & Neuroscience: JPN, 37*(3), 149–152. https://doi.org/10.1503/jpn.120065

Jorm, A. F. (2000). Mental health literacy: Public knowledge and beliefs about mental disorders. *The British Journal of Psychiatry, 177*(5), 396–401.

Kaplan, D. M., & Gladding, S. T. (2011). A vision for the future of counseling: The 20/20 principles for unifying and strengthening the profession. *Journal of Counseling & Development, 89*(3), 367–372.

Kaplan, D. M., Tarvydas, V. M., & Gladding, S. T. (2014). 20/20: A vision for the future of counseling: The new consensus definition of counseling. *Journal of Counseling & Development, 92*(3), 366–372.

Laska K. M., Gurman, A. S., & Wampold, B. E. (2014). Expanding the lens of evidence-based practice in psychotherapy: A common factors perspective. *Psychotherapy, 51*(4), 467.

Lenz, A. S. (2015). Using single-case research designs to demonstrate evidence for counseling practices. *Journal of Counseling & Development, 93*(4), 387–393.

Levine, L. J., & Safer, M. A. (2002). Sources of bias in memory for emotions. *Current Directions in Psychological Science, 11*(5), 169-173.

Lilienfeld, S. O. (2017). Psychology's replication crisis and the grant culture: Righting the ship. *Perspectives on Psychological Science, 12*(4), 660-664.

Lilienfeld, S. O., Ritschel, L. A., Lynn, S. J., Cautin, R. L., & Latzman, R. D. (2013). Why many clinical psychologists are resistant to evidence-based practice: root causes and constructive remedies. *Clinical Psychology Review, 33*(7), 883–900. https://doi.org/10.1016/j.cpr.2012.09.008

Lilienfeld, S. O., Ritschel, L. A., Lynn, S. J., Cautin, R. L., & Latzman, R. D. (2014). Why ineffective psychotherapies appear to work: A taxonomy of causes of spurious therapeutic effectiveness. *Perspectives on Psychological Science: A Journal of the Association for Psychological Science, 9*(4), 355–387. https://doi.org/10.1177/1745691614535216

Lösel F. (2018). Evidence comes by replication, but needs differentiation: The reproducibility issue in science and its relevance for criminology. *Journal of Experimental Criminology, 14*(3), 257–278.

Marsh, H. W. (1994). Using the National Longitudinal Study of 1988 to evaluate theoretical models of self-concept: The Self-Description Questionnaire. *Journal of educational Psychology, 86*(3), 439.

Marsh, H. W., Pekrun, R., Parker, P. D., Murayama, K., Guo, J., Dicke, T., & Arens, A. K. (2019). The murky distinction between self-concept and self-efficacy: Beware of lurking jingle-jangle fallacies. *Journal of educational psychology, 111*(2), 331.

McLeod, J. (2016). *Using research in counselling and psychotherapy*. SAGE.

Mellin, E. A., Hunt, B., & Nichols, L. M. (2011). Counselor professional identity: Findings and implications for counseling and interprofessional collaboration. *Journal of Counseling & Development, 89*(2), 140–147.

Munafò, M. R., Nosek, B. A., Bishop, D. V., Button, K. S., Chambers, C. D., Percie du Sert, N., Simonsohn, U., Wagenmakers, E.-J., Ware, J. J., & Ioannidis, J. (2017). A manifesto for reproducible science. *Nature Human Behaviour, 1*(1), 1–9.

Norcross, J. C., & Lambert, M. J. (2018). Psychotherapy relationships that work III. *Psychotherapy, 55*(4), 303.

Open Science Collaboration. (2015). Estimating the reproducibility of psychological science. *Science, 349*(6251), aac4716.

Sakaluk, J. K., Williams, A. J., Kilshaw, R. E., & Rhyner, K. T. (2019). Evaluating the evidential value of empirically supported psychological treatments (ESTs): A meta-scientific review. *Journal of Abnormal Psychology, 128*(6), 500–509.

Schmidt, C., & Adkins, C. (2012). Understanding, valuing, and teaching reflection in counselor education: A phenomenological inquiry. *Reflective Practice, 13*(1), 77–96.

Tracey, T. J., Wampold, B. E., Lichtenberg, J. W., & Goodyear, R. K. (2014). Expertise in psychotherapy: An elusive goal?. *American Psychologist, 69*(3), 218.

Umstead, L. K. (2019). Exploring counselors' use of research in practice: A CQR study. *The Professional Counselor, 9*(3), 200–216.

Wampold, B. E., & Imel, Z. E. (2015). *The great psychotherapy debate: The evidence for what makes psychotherapy work* (2nd ed.). Routledge. https://doi.org/10.4324/9780203582015

Weidman, A. C., Cheng, J. T., & Tracy, J. L. (2018). The psychological structure of humility. *Journal of Personality and Social Psychology, 114*(1), 153. Wester, K. L. (2007). Teaching research integrity in the field of counseling. *Counselor Education and Supervision, 46*(3), 199-211.

Wester, K. L., & Borders, L. D. (2014). Research competencies in counseling: A Delphi study. *Journal of Counseling & Development, 92*(4), 447–458.

Wester, K. L., & Wachter Morris, C. A. (Eds.). (2018). *Making research relevant: Applied research designs for the mental health practitioner* (1st ed.). Routledge. https://doi.org/10.4324/9781315179353

Yates, C. M., DeLeon, A., & Rapp, M. C. (2017). Exploring experiential learning through an abstinence assignment within an addictions counseling course. *Professional Counselor, 7*(4), 318–329.

## CHAPTER 3

Aliyu, A. A., Bello, M. U., Kasim, R., & Martin, D. (2014). Positivist and non-positivist paradigm in social science research: Conflicting paradigms or perfect partners. *Journal of Management & Sustainability, 4*, 79.

American Counseling Association. (2014). ACA Code of Ethics. Author.

Barkham, M., Hardy, G. E., & Mellor-Clark, J. (Eds.). (2010). *Developing and delivering practice-based evidence: A guide for the psychological therapies*. John Wiley & Sons.

Beck, A. T., Steer, R. A., & Brown, G. (1996). *Beck Depression Inventory–II (BDI-II)* [Database record]. APA PsycTests. https://doi.org/10.1037/t00742-000

Bryman, A. (2006). Integrating quantitative and qualitative research: How is it done? *Qualitative Research, 6*(1), 97–113.

Carter, S. M., & Little, M. (2007). Justifying knowledge, justifying method, taking action: Epistemologies, methodologies, and methods in qualitative research. *Qualitative Health Research, 17*(10), 1316–1328.

Charmaz, K. (2014). *Constructing grounded theory* (2nd ed.). SAGE.

Creswell, J. W., & Creswell, J. D. (2018). *Research design: Qualitative, quantitative, and mixed methods approaches* (5th ed.). SAGE.

Creswell, J. W., & Plano Clark, V. L. (2018). *Designing and conducting mixed methods research* (3rd ed.). SAGE.

Creswell, J. W., & Poth, C. N. (2018). *Qualitative inquiry and research design: Choosing among five approaches* (4th ed.). SAGE.

Crotty, M. (1998). *The foundations of social research: Meaning and perspective in the research process*. SAGE.

Denzin, N. K., & Lincoln, Y. S. (Eds.). (2011). *The SAGE handbook of qualitative research* (4th ed.). SAGE.

DeVaus, D. A. (2001). *Research design in social research*. SAGE.

Feilzer, Yvonne M. (2010). Doing mixed methods research pragmatically: Implications for the rediscovery of pragmatism as a research paradigm. *Journal of Mixed Methods Research, 4*(1), 6-16.

Guba, E. G., & Lincoln, Y. S. (1994). Competing paradigms in qualitative research. In N. K. Denzin & Y. S. Lincoln (Eds.), *Handbook of qualitative research* (pp. 105–117). SAGE.

Hanson, W. E., Creswell, J. W., Clark, V. L. P., Petska, K. S., & Creswell, J. D. (2005). Mixed methods research designs in counseling psychology. *Journal of Counseling Psychology, 52*(2), 224–235.

Heppner, P. P., Wampold, B. E., Owen, J., Thompson, M. N., & Wang, K. T. (2016). *Research design in counseling* (4th ed.). Cengage Learning.

Hunsley, J., & Lee, C. M. (2007). Research-informed benchmarks for psychological treatments: Efficacy studies, effectiveness studies, and beyond. *Professional Psychology: Research and Practice, 38*(1), 21–33.

Ivankova, N. V., Creswell, J. W., & Stick, S. L. (2006). Using mixed-methods sequential explanatory design: From theory to practice. *Field Methods, 18*(1), 3–20.

Johnson, R. B., & Onwuegbuzie, A. J. (2004). Mixed methods research: A research paradigm whose time has come. *Educational Researcher, 33*(7), 14–26.

Johnson, R. B., Onwuegbuzie, A. J., & Turner, L. A. (2007). Toward a definition of mixed methods research. *Journal of Mixed Methods Research, 1*(2), 112–133.

Kemmis, S., & McTaggart, R. (2005). Participatory action research: Communicative action and the public sphere. In N. K. Denzin & Y. S. Lincoln (Eds.), *The SAGE handbook of qualitative research* (3rd ed., pp. 559–603). SAGE.

Kincheloe, J. L., & McLaren, P. (2011). Rethinking critical theory and qualitative research. In K. Hayes, S. R. Steinberg, & K. Tobin (Eds.), *Key works in critical pedagogy: Bold visions in educational research* (Vol. 32). SensePublishers. https://doi.org/10.1007/978-94-6091-397-6_23

Kleinman, A. (2004). Culture and depression. *New England Journal of Medicine, 351*(10), 951–953.

Lewin, S., Glenton, C., & Oxman, A. D. (2009). Use of qualitative methods alongside randomised controlled trials of complex healthcare interventions: Methodological study. *BMJ, 339*.

McLeod, J. (2010). *Case study research in counselling and psychotherapy*. SAGE.

McLeod, J. (2011). *Qualitative research in counselling and psychotherapy* (2nd ed.). SAGE.

Moon, K., & Blackman, D. (2014). A guide to understanding social science research for natural scientists. *Conservation Biology, 28*(5), 1167-1177.

Morgan, D. L. (2013). *Integrating qualitative and quantitative methods: A pragmatic approach*. SAGE.

Morrow, S. L. (2005). Quality and trustworthiness in qualitative research in counseling psychology. *Journal of Counseling Psychology, 52*(2), 250–260.

Patton, M. Q. (2015). *Qualitative research & evaluation methods: Integrating theory and practice* (4th ed.). SAGE.

Phillips, D. C., & Burbules, N. C. (2000). *Postpositivism and educational research*. Rowman & Littlefield.

Ponterotto, J. G. (2005). Qualitative research in counseling psychology: A primer on research paradigms and philosophy of science. *Journal of Counseling Psychology, 52*(2), 126.

Prilleltensky, I., & Nelson, G. (2002). *Doing psychology critically: Making a difference in diverse settings*. Palgrave Macmillan/Springer Nature.

Punch, K. F. (2013). *Introduction to social research: Quantitative and qualitative approaches* (3rd ed.). SAGE.

Schwandt, T. A. (1994). Constructivist, interpretivist approaches to human inquiry. In N. K. Denzin & Y. S. Lincoln (Eds.), *Handbook of qualitative research* (pp. 118–137). SAGE.

Shadish, W. R., Cook, T. D., & Campbell, D. T. (2002). *Experimental and quasi-experimental designs for generalized causal inference.* Houghton, Mifflin.

Tashakkori, A., & Teddlie, C. (2010). *SAGE handbook of mixed methods in social & behavioral research.* SAGE. https://doi.org/10.4135/9781506335193

Teddlie, C., & Tashakkori, A. (2009). *Foundations of mixed methods research: Integrating quantitative and qualitative approaches in the social and behavioral sciences.* SAGE.

Wampold, B. E., & Imel, Z. E. (2015). *The great psychotherapy debate: The evidence for what makes psychotherapy work* (2nd ed.). Routledge.

Yilmaz, K. (2013). Comparison of quantitative and qualitative research traditions: Epistemological, theoretical, and methodological differences. *European Journal of Education, 48*(2), 311–325.

## CHAPTER 4

Anthony, K. (2015). Training therapists to work effectively online and offline within digital culture. *British Journal of Guidance & Counselling, 43*(1), 36–42.

Bazeley, P. (2018). *Integrating analyses in mixed methods research.* Sage.

Braun, V., & Clarke, V. (2006). Using thematic analysis in psychology. *Qualitative Research in Psychology, 3*(2), 77–101.

Campbell, D. T., & Stanley, J. C. (1963). *Experimental and quasi-experimental designs for research.* Rand McNally.

Cartwright, N. (2007). Are RCTs the gold standard?. *BioSocieties, 2*(1), 11-20.

Charmaz, K. (2014). *Constructing grounded theory* (2nd ed.). SAGE.

Chung, R. C. Y., Bemak, F., & Grabosky, T. K. (2011). Multicultural-social justice leadership strategies: Counseling and advocacy with immigrants. *Journal for Social Action in Counseling and Psychology, 1*(1), 36–47.

Cohen, J. (1992). A power primer. *Psychological Bulletin, 112*(1), 155–159.

Concato, J., Shah, N., & Horwitz, R. I. (2000). Randomized, controlled trials, observational studies, and the hierarchy of research designs. *New England Journal of Medicine, 342*(25), 1887-1892.

Cook, T. D., & Campbell, D. T. (1979). *Quasi-experimentation: Design and analysis issues for field settings.* Houghton Mifflin.

Creswell, J. W., & Creswell, J. D. (2018). *Research design: Qualitative, quantitative, and mixed methods approaches* (5th ed.). SAGE.

Creswell, J. W., & Plano Clark, V. L. (2017). *Designing and conducting mixed methods research* (3rd ed.). Sage.

Creswell, J. W., & Plano Clark, V. L. (2018). *Designing and conducting mixed methods research* (3rd ed.). SAGE.

Creswell, J. W., & Poth, C. N. (2018). *Qualitative inquiry and research design: Choosing among five approaches* (4th ed.). SAGE.

Denzin, N. K., & Lincoln, Y. S. (Eds.). (2018). *The Sage handbook of qualitative research* (5th ed.). Sage.

Dowell, N. M., & Berman, J. S. (2013). Therapist nonverbal behavior and perceptions of empathy, alliance, and treatment credibility. *Journal of Psychotherapy Integration, 23*(2), 158–165.

Etikan, I., Musa, S. A., & Alkassim, R. S. (2016). Comparison of convenience sampling and purposive sampling. *American Journal of Theoretical and Applied Statistics, 5*(1), 1–4.

Fetters, M. D., Curry, L. A., & Creswell, J. W. (2013). Achieving integration in mixed methods designs—principles and practices. *Health Services Research, 48*(6 pt 2), 2134–2156.

Field, A. (2018). *Discovering statistics using IBM SPSS statistics* (5th ed.). SAGE.

Greene, J. C., Caracelli, V. J., & Graham, W. F. (1989). Toward a conceptual framework for mixed-method evaluation designs. *Educational Evaluation and Policy Analysis, 11*(3), 255-274.

Grimes, D. A., & Schulz, K. F. (2002). An overview of clinical research: the lay of the land. *The lancet, 359*(9300), 57-61.

Guest, G., Bunce, A., & Johnson, L. (2006). How many interviews are enough? An experiment with data saturation and variability. *Field Methods, 18*(1), 59–82.

Hofmann, S. G., Sawyer, A. T., Witt, A. A., & Oh, D. (2010). The effect of mindfulness-based therapy on anxiety and depression: A meta-analytic review. *Journal of Consulting and Clinical Psychology, 78*(2), 169–183.

Ivankova, N. V., Creswell, J. W., & Stick, S. L. (2006). Using mixed-methods sequential explanatory design: From theory to practice. *Field Methods, 18*(1), 3–20.

Jimenez-Buedo, M., & Miller, L. M. (2010). Why a trade-off? The relationship between the external and internal validity of experiments. Theoria. *Revista de Teoría, Historia y Fundamentos de la Ciencia, 25*(3), 301-321.

Johnson, R. B., & Onwuegbuzie, A. J. (2004). Mixed methods research: A research paradigm whose time has come. *Educational Researcher, 33*(7), 14–26.

Kazdin, A. E. (2020). *Single-case research designs: Methods for clinical and applied settings* (3rd ed.). Oxford University Press.

Krippendorff, K. (2018). *Content analysis: An introduction to its methodology* (4th ed.). SAGE.

Leichsenring, F. (2004). Randomized controlled versus naturalistic studies: A new research agenda. *Bulletin of the Menninger Clinic, 68*(2), 137-151.

Lincoln, Y. S., & Guba, E. G. (1985). *Naturalistic inquiry*. SAGE.

Mallinckrodt, B., Porter, M. J., & Kivlighan, D. M., Jr. (1995). Client attachment to therapist, depth of in-session exploration, and object relations in brief psychotherapy. *Psychotherapy: Theory, Research, Practice, Training, 32*(1), 85–93.

Maxwell, J. A. (2013). *Qualitative research design: An interactive approach* (3rd ed.). Sage.

Merriam, S. B., & Tisdell, E. J. (2016). *Qualitative research: A guide to design and implementation* (4th ed.). Jossey-Bass.

Morgan, D. L. (2007). Paradigms lost and pragmatism regained: Methodological implications of combining qualitative and quantitative methods. *Journal of mixed methods research, 1*(1), 48-76.

Morrow, S. L. (2005). Quality and trustworthiness in qualitative research in counseling psychology. *Journal of Counseling Psychology, 52*(2), 250–260.

Mullen, P. R., Blount, A. J., Lambie, G. W., & Chae, N. (2018). School counselors' perceived stress, burnout, and job satisfaction. *Professional School Counseling, 21*(1), 1–10.

Papathomas, A., & Lavallee, D. (2012). Narrative constructions of anorexia and abuse: An athlete's search for meaning in trauma. *Journal of Loss and Trauma, 17*(4), 293–318.

Parahoo, K. (2014). *Nursing research: Principles, process and issues* (3rd ed.). Palgrave Macmillan.

Patton, M. Q. (2015). *Qualitative research & evaluation methods: Integrating theory and practice* (4th ed.). SAGE.

Riessman, C. K. (2008). *Narrative methods for the human sciences*. SAGE.

Robson, C., & McCartan, K. (2016). *Real world research* (4th ed.). Wiley.

Rosenbaum, P. R. (2002). *Observational studies* (2nd ed.). Springer.

Rothwell, P. M. (2005). External validity of randomised controlled trials: "To whom do the results of this trial apply?" *The Lancet, 365*(9453), 82-93.

Shadish, W. R., Cook, T. D., & Campbell, D. T. (2002). *Experimental and quasi-experimental designs for generalized causal inference*. Houghton Mifflin.

Shinebourne, P., & Smith, J. A. (2011). "It is just habitual": An interpretative phenomenological analysis of the experience of long-term recovery from addiction. *International Journal of Mental Health and Addiction, 9*(3), 282–295.

Slack, M. K., & Draugalis Jr, J. R. (2001). Establishing the internal and external validity of experimental studies. *American journal of health-system pharmacy, 58*(22), 2173-2181.

Stake, R. E. (2010). *Qualitative research: Studying how things work*. Guilford Press.

Tabachnick, B. G., & Fidell, L. S. (2019). *Using multivariate statistics* (7th ed.). Pearson.

Tashakkori, A., & Teddlie, C. (2010). *Sage handbook of mixed methods in social & behavioral research* (2nd ed.). Sage.

Teddlie, C., & Tashakkori, A. (2009). *Foundations of mixed methods research: Integrating quantitative and qualitative approaches in the social and behavioral sciences*. SAGE.

Thompson, B. (2004). *Exploratory and confirmatory factor analysis: Understanding concepts and applications*. American Psychological Association.

Ungar, M., Brown, M., Liebenberg, L., Othman, R., Kwong, W. M., Armstrong, M., & Gilgun, J. (2007). Unique pathways to resilience across cultures. *Adolescence, 42*(166), 287–310.

Wind, T. R., Rijkeboer, M., Andersson, G., & Riper, H. (2020). The COVID-19 pandemic: The "black swan" for mental health care and a turning point for e-health. *Internet Interventions, 20*, 100317.

Yin, R. K. (2018). *Case study research and applications: Design and methods* (6th ed.). SAGE.

## CHAPTER 5

American Counseling Association. (2014). *ACA Code of Ethics*. Author.

American Psychological Association. (2017). *Ethical principles of psychologists and code of conduct* (2002, amended effective June 1, 2010, and January 1, 2017). https://www.apa.org/ethics/code/

Annas, G. J., & Grodin, M. A. (1992). *The Nazi doctors and the Nuremberg Code: Human rights in human experimentation*. Oxford University Press.

Appelbaum, P. S. (2007). Assessment of patients' competence to consent to treatment. *New England Journal of Medicine, 357*(18), 1834-1840.

Appelbaum, P. S., Roth, L. H., Lidz, C. W., Benson, P., & Winslade, W. (1987). False hopes and best data: consent to research and the therapeutic misconception. *The Hastings Center report, 17*(2), 20–24.

Balkin, R. S., & Kleist, D. M. (2014). *Counseling research: A practitioner-scholar approach*. American Counseling Association.

Beauchamp, T. L., & Childress, J. F. (2001). *Principles of biomedical ethics*. Oxford University Press.

Becker-Blease, K. A., & Freyd, J. J. (2006). Research participants telling the truth about their lives: the ethics of asking and not asking about abuse. *American Psychologist, 61*(3), 218.

Chamberlain, C. L. (2007). *Ethical reasons to involve demented patients in their care and why physicians fail to do so*. https://core.ac.uk/download/12208591.pdf

Corbie-Smith, G., Thomas, S. B., Williams, M. V., & Moody-Ayers, S. (1999). Attitudes and beliefs of African Americans toward participation in medical research. *Journal of General Internal Medicine, 14*, 537-546.

Dutka, P., & Astroth, K. (2022). Navigating the Institutional Review Board Process. *Nephrology Nursing Journal, 49*(1), 67–71.

Emanuel, E. J., Wendler, D., & Grady, C. (2000). What makes clinical research ethical? *JAMA, 283*(20), 2701–2711.

Fisher, C. B. (2012). *Decoding the ethics code: A practical guide for psychologists* (3rd ed.). Sage.

Fisher, C. B., Hoagwood, K., Boyce, C., Duster, T., Frank, D. A., Grisso, T., Levine, R. J., Macklin, R., Spencer, M. B., Takanishi, R., Trimble, J. E., & Zayas, L. H. (2016). Research ethics for mental health science involving ethnic minority children and youths. In A. E. Kazdin (Ed.), *Methodological issues and strategies in clinical research* (4th ed., pp. 525–543). American Psychological Association. https://psycnet.apa.org/doi/10.1037/14805-032

Forester-Miller, H., & Davis, T. (1996). *A practitioner's guide to ethical decision making.* American Counseling Association.

Hays, D. G., Wood, C., Dahl, H., & Kirk-Jenkins, A. (2016). Methodological rigor in Journal of Counseling & Development qualitative research articles: A 15-year review. *Journal of Counseling & Development, 94*(2), 172-183.

Jones, J. H. (1981). *Bad blood: The Tuskegee syphilis experiment.* Free Press.

Leong, F. T., Pickren, W. E., & Vasquez, M. J. (2011). *APA ethics code commentary and case illustrations.* American Psychological Association.

Levine, R. J., Katz, M. D., & Goldman, J. (2004). *Research ethics: A reader.* University Press of New England.

Levitt, H. M., Motulsky, S. L., Wertz, F. J., Morrow, S. L., & Ponterotto, J. G. (2017). Recommendations for designing and reviewing qualitative research in psychology: Promoting methodological integrity. *Qualitative psychology, 4*(1), 2.

Mohatt, G. V., Trimble, J., & Dickson, R. A. (2006). Psychosocial foundations of academic performance in culture-based education programs for American Indian and Alaska native youth: Reflections on a multidisciplinary perspective. *Journal of American Indian Education*, 38-59.

National Academies of Sciences, Policy, Global Affairs, & Committee on Responsible Science. (2017). *Fostering integrity in research.* National Academies Press.

National Commission for the Protection of Human Subjects of Biomedical and Behavioral Research. (1979). *The Belmont report: Ethical principles and guidelines for the protection of human subjects of research.* U.S. Department of Health and Human Services.

Ponterotto, J. G., Casas, J. M., Suzuki, L. A., & Alexander, C. M. (Eds.). (2010). *Handbook of multicultural counseling.* SAGE.

Shuster, E. (1997). Fifty years later: The significance of the Nuremberg Code. *New England Journal of Medicine, 337*(20), 1436–1440.

Sieber, J. E., & Tolich, M. B. (2013). *Planning ethically responsible research* (2nd ed.). SAGE.

Sink, C. A., & Mvududu, N. H. (2010). Statistical power, sampling, and effect sizes: Three keys to research relevancy. *Counseling Outcome Research and Evaluation, 1*(2), 1-18.

Smith, D. (2003). Five principles for research ethics. Monitor on Psychology, 34(1), 56.

Steneck, N. H. (2006). Fostering integrity in research: Definitions, current knowledge, and future directions. *Science and Engineering Ethics, 12*, 53-74.

Steneck, N. H. (2007). *ORI introduction to the responsible conduct of research.* Department of Health and Human Services, Office of the Secretary, Office of Public Health and Science, Office of Research Integrity.

Sue, D. W., Sue, D., Neville, H. A., & Smith, L. (2019). *Counseling the culturally diverse: Theory and practice* (8th ed.). Wiley.

Trickett, E. J., Beehler, S., Deutsch, C., Green, L. W., Hawe, P., McLeroy, K., ... & Trimble, J. E. (2011). Advancing the science of community-level interventions. *American Journal of Public Health, 101*(8), 1410-1419.

Wester, K. L. (2011). Publishing ethical research: A step-by-step overview. *Journal of Counseling & Development, 89*(3), 301-307.

Wester, K. L., & Borders, L. D. (2014). Research competencies in counseling: A Delphi study. *Journal of Counseling & Development, 92*(4), 447-458.

Wester, K. L., Borders, L. D., Boul, S., & Horton, E. (2013). Research quality: Critique of quantitative articles in the Journal of Counseling & Development. *Journal of Counseling & Development, 91*(3), 280-290.

Woo, H., Goo, M., & Lee, M. (2016). A content analysis of research on disability: American Counseling Association journals between 2003 and 2013. *Journal of Multicultural Counseling and Development, 44*(4), 228-244.

World Medical Association. (2013). World Medical Association Declaration of Helsinki: Ethical principles for medical research involving human subjects. *JAMA, 310*(20), 2191–2194.

## CHAPTER 6

Agee, J. (2009). Developing qualitative research questions: A reflective process. *International Journal of Qualitative Studies in Education, 22*(4), 431–447. https://doi.org/10.1080/09518390902736512

Alvesson, M., & Sandberg, J. (2013). *Constructing research questions: Doing interesting research*. SAGE.

Barkham, M., & Mellor-Clark, J. (2003). Bridging evidence-based practice and practice-based evidence: Developing a rigorous and relevant knowledge for the psychological therapies. *Clinical Psychology & Psychotherapy: An International Journal of Theory & Practice, 10*(6), 319-327.

Booth, W. C., Colomb, G. G., Williams, J. M., Bizup, J., & FitzGerald, W. T. (2016). *The craft of research* (4th ed.). University of Chicago Press.

Creswell, J. W., & Creswell, J. D. (2018). *Research design: Qualitative, quantitative, and mixed methods approaches* (5th ed.). SAGE.

Gelso, C. J. (2006). On the making of a scientist-practitioner: A theory of research training in professional psychology. *Training and Education in Professional Psychology, S*(1), 3–16. https://doi.org/10.1037/1931-3918.S.1.3

Maxwell, J. A. (2013). *Qualitative research design: An interactive approach* (3rd ed.). SAGE.

Norcross, J. C., & Wampold, B. E. (2011). Evidence-based therapy relationships: research conclusions and clinical practices. *Psychotherapy, 48*(1), 98.

Priya, M., & De Guzman, R. (2023). The Association between Problematic Smartphone Usage and Sleep Quality among Young Adults. *Indian Journal of Health and Wellbeing, 14*(2), 131–133.

Punch, K. F. (2016). *Developing effective research proposals* (3rd ed.). SAGE.

Ravitch, S. M., & Carl, N. M. (2016). *Qualitative research: Bridging the conceptual, theoretical, and methodological*. SAGE.

Schön, D. A. (1983). *The reflective practitioner: How professionals think in action*. Basic Books.

Serrat, O. (2017). The five whys technique. *In Knowledge solutions* (pp. 307–310). Springer. https://doi.org/10.1007/978-981-10-0983-9_32

Sim, Y. M., & Kaluge, D. (2023). Examining the Correlation between Macroeconomic Factors and Stock Indices: A Comparative Analysis of IHSG and Nikkei. *EkBis: Jurnal Ekonomi dan Bisnis, 7*(2), 126–139. https://core.ac.uk/download/599198299.pdf

Stoltenberg, C. D., McNeill, B. W., & Delworth, U. (2000). *IDM supervision: An integrated developmental model for supervising counselors and therapists.* Jossey-Bass.

Tracy, S. J. (2010). Qualitative quality: Eight "big-tent" criteria for excellent qualitative research. *Qualitative Inquiry, 16*(10), 837–851. https://doi.org/10.1177/1077800410383121

## CHAPTER 7

American Psychological Association. (2020). *Publication manual of the American Psychological Association* (7th ed.). Author.

Anfara, V. A., & Mertz, N. T. (2014). *Theoretical frameworks in qualitative research* (2nd ed.). SAGE.

Beck, A. T., Emery, G., & Greenberg, R. L. (1985). *Anxiety disorders and phobias: A cognitive perspective.* Basic Books.

Beutler, L. E., Someah, K., Kimpara, S., & Miller, K. (2016). Selecting the most appropriate treatment for each patient. *International Journal of Clinical and Health Psychology, 16*(1), 99–108.

Booth, A., Sutton, A., & Papaioannou, D. (2016). *Systematic approaches to a successful literature review* (2nd ed.). SAGE.

Cooper, H. (2016). *Ethical choices in research: Managing data, writing reports, and publishing results in the social sciences.* American Psychological Association.

Festinger, L. (1954). A theory of social comparison processes. *Human Relations, 7*(2), 117–140.

Fink, A. (2019). *Conducting research literature reviews: From the internet to paper* (5th ed.). SAGE.

Galvan, J. L., & Galvan, M. C. (2017). *Writing literature reviews: A guide for students of the social and behavioral sciences* (7th ed.). Routledge.

Hart, C. (2018). *Doing a literature review: Releasing the research imagination* (2nd ed.). SAGE.

Katz, E., Blumler, J. G., & Gurevitch, M. (1973). Uses and gratifications research. *The Public Opinion Quarterly, 37*(4), 509–523.

Machi, L. A., & McEvoy, B. T. (2016). *The literature review: Six steps to success* (3rd ed.). Corwin Press.

Melchert, T. P. (2015). *Biopsychosocial practice: A science-based framework for behavioral health care.* American Psychological Association.

Mertens, D. M. (2015). *Research and evaluation in education and psychology: Integrating diversity with quantitative, qualitative, and mixed methods* (4th ed.). SAGE.

Pannucci, C. J., & Wilkins, E. G. (2010). Identifying and avoiding bias in research. *Plastic and Reconstructive Surgery, 126*(2), 619–625.

Randolph, J. (2019). A guide to writing the dissertation literature review. *Practical Assessment, Research, and Evaluation, 14*(1), 13.

Ridley, D. (2012). *The literature review: A step-by-step guide for students* (2nd ed.). SAGE.

Roig, M. (2015). *Avoiding plagiarism, self-plagiarism, and other questionable writing practices: A guide to ethical writing.* Office of Research Integrity.

van Eck, N. J., & Waltman, L. (2010). Software survey: VOSviewer, a computer program for bibliometric mapping. *Scientometrics, 84*(2), 523–538.

## CHAPTER 8


Aarons, G. A., Hurlburt, M., & Horwitz, S. M. (2011). Advancing a conceptual model of evidence-based practice implementation in public service sectors. *Administration and Policy in Mental Health and Mental Health Services Research, 38*(1), 4–23.

APA Presidential Task Force on Evidence-Based Practice. (2006). Evidence-based practice in psychology. *American Psychologist, 61*(4), 271–285.

Arnett, J. J. (2008). The neglected 95%: Why American psychology needs to become less American. *American Psychologist, 63*(7), 602–614.

Banerjee, A., & Chaudhury, S. (2010). Statistics without tears: Populations and samples. *Industrial Psychiatry Journal, 19*(1), 60-65.

Barkham, M., Hardy, G. E., & Mellor-Clark, J. (Eds.). (2010). *Developing and delivering practice-based evidence: A guide for the psychological therapies.* Wiley-Blackwell.

Bickman, L. (2008). A measurement feedback system (MFS) is necessary to improve mental health outcomes. *Journal of the American Academy of Child & Adolescent Psychiatry, 47*(10), 1114–1119.

Bickman, L., Lyon, A. R., & Wolpert, M. (2016). Achieving precision mental health through effective assessment, monitoring, and feedback processes. *Administration and Policy in Mental Health and Mental Health Services Research, 43*(3), 271–276.

Boswell, J. F., Kraus, D. R., Miller, S. D., & Lambert, M. J. (2015). Implementing routine outcome monitoring in clinical practice: Benefits, challenges, and solutions. *Psychotherapy Research, 25*(1), 6–19.

Brinkmann, S., & Kvale, S. (2015). *InterViews: Learning the craft of qualitative research interviewing* (3rd ed.). SAGE.

Creswell, J. W., & Creswell, J. D. (2018). *Research design: Qualitative, quantitative, and mixed methods approaches* (5th ed.). Sage.

Creswell, J. W., & Plano Clark, V. L. (2018). *Designing and conducting mixed methods research* (3rd ed.). SAGE.

Creswell, J. W., & Poth, C. N. (2018). *Qualitative inquiry and research design: Choosing among five approaches* (4th ed.). SAGE.

De Brey, C., Snyder, T. D., Zhang, A., & Dillow, S. A. (2021). Digest of Education Statistics 2019. NCES 2021-009. *National Center for Education Statistics.*

Elfil, M., & Negida, A. (2017). Sampling methods in clinical research: An educational review. *Emergency, 5*(1), e52.

Etikan, I., Musa, S. A., & Alkassim, R. S. (2016). Comparison of convenience sampling and purposive sampling. *American Journal of Theoretical and Applied Statistics, 5*(1), 1–4.

Fisher, C. B. (2013). *Decoding the ethics code: A practical guide for psychologists* (3rd ed.). SAGE.

Fowler, F. J., Jr. (2014). *Survey research methods* (5th ed.). SAGE.

Heppner, P. P., Wampold, B. E., Owen, J., Thompson, M. N., & Wang, K. T. (2016). *Research design in counseling* (4th ed.). Cengage Learning.

Hunsley, J., & Mash, E. J. (2008). *A guide to assessments that work.* Oxford University Press.

Krueger, R. A., & Casey, M. A. (2015). *Focus groups: A practical guide for applied research* (5th ed.). SAGE.

Lambert, M. J. (2013). *Bergin and Garfield's handbook of psychotherapy and behavior change* (6th ed.). John Wiley & Sons.

Lewis, C. C., Boyd, M., Puspitasari, A., Navarro, E., Howard, J., Kassab, H., ... & Kroenke, K. (2019). Implementing measurement-based care in behavioral health: A review. *JAMA Psychiatry, 76*(3), 324–335.

Lilienfeld, S. O., Ritschel, L. A., Lynn, S. J., Cautin, R. L., & Latzman, R. D. (2013). Why many clinical psychologists are resistant to evidence-based practice: Root causes and constructive remedies. *Clinical Psychology Review, 33*(7), 883–900.

Lustgarten, S. D., Elhai, J. D., Fine, S. L., Che, T. H., & Stiles, B. (2020). Ethical and legal considerations in telemental health. In J. C. Norcross & G. R. VandenBos (Eds.), *APA handbook of clinical psychology: Applications and methods* (Vol. 3, pp. 573–588). American Psychological Association.

Martínez-Mesa, J., González-Chica, D. A., Duquia, R. P., Bonamigo, R. R., & Bastos, J. L. (2016). Sampling: How to select participants in my research study? *Anais Brasileiros de Dermatologia, 91*(3), 326–330.

Norcross, J. C., & Wampold, B. E. (2011). Evidence-based therapy relationships: Research conclusions and clinical practices. *Psychotherapy, 48*(1), 98–102.

Proctor, E. K., Landsverk, J., Aarons, G., Chambers, D., Glisson, C., & Mittman, B. (2009). Implementation research in mental health services: An emerging science with conceptual, methodological, and training challenges. *Administration and Policy in Mental Health and Mental Health Services Research, 36*(1), 24–34.

Shadish, W. R., Cook, T. D., & Campbell, D. T. (2002). *Experimental and quasi-experimental designs for generalized causal inference.* Houghton Mifflin.

Sue, D. W., Sue, D., Neville, H. A., & Smith, L. (2019). *Counseling the culturally diverse: Theory and practice* (8th ed.). John Wiley & Sons.

Torous, J., & Roberts, L. W. (2017). Needed innovation in digital health and smartphone applications for mental health: Transparency and trust. *JAMA Psychiatry, 74*(5), 437–438.

Wampold, B. E. (2015). How important are the common factors in psychotherapy? An update. *World Psychiatry, 14*(3), 270–277.

## CHAPTER 9

Altschuld, J. W., & Kumar, D. D. (2010). *Needs assessment: An overview.* SAGE.

American Psychological Association. (2006). Evidence-based practice in psychology. *American Psychologist, 61*(4), 271–285.

Baker, D. B., & Benjamin, L. T. (2000). The affirmation of the scientist-practitioner: A look back at Boulder. *American Psychologist, 55*(2), 241–247.

Barkham, M., & Mellor-Clark, J. (2003). Bridging evidence-based practice and practice-based evidence: Developing a rigorous and relevant knowledge for the psychological therapies. *Clinical Psychology & Psychotherapy, 10*(6), 319–327.

Boswell, J. F., Kraus, D. R., Miller, S. D., & Lambert, M. J. (2015). Implementing routine outcome monitoring in clinical practice: Benefits, challenges, and solutions. *Psychotherapy Research, 25*(1), 6-19.

Castonguay, L. G., Barkham, M., Lutz, W., & McAleavey, A. A. (2013). Practice-oriented research: Approaches and applications. In M. J. Lambert (Ed.), *Bergin and Garfield's handbook of psychotherapy and behavior change* (6th ed., pp. 85–133). Wiley.

Chen, H. T. (2015). *Practical program evaluation: Theory-driven evaluation and the integrated evaluation perspective.* SAGE.

Duncan, B. L., Miller, S. D., Wampold, B. E., & Hubble, M. A. (Eds.). (2010). *The heart and soul of change: Delivering what works in therapy* (2nd ed.). American Psychological Association.

Hofmann, S. G., Asnaani, A., Vonk, I. J., Sawyer, A. T., & Fang, A. (2012). The efficacy of cognitive behavioral therapy: A review of meta-analyses. *Cognitive Therapy and Research, 36*, 427-440.

Howard, K. I., Moras, K., Brill, P. L., Martinovich, Z., & Lutz, W. (1996). Evaluation of psychotherapy: Efficacy, effectiveness, and patient progress. *American Psychologist, 51*(10), 1059–1064.
Kazdin, A. E. (2011). *Single-case research designs: Methods for clinical and applied settings* (2nd ed.). Oxford University Press.
Lambert, M. J. (2010). *Prevention of treatment failure: The use of measuring, monitoring, and feedback in clinical practice.* American Psychological Association.
Levin, H. M., & McEwan, P. J. (2001). *Cost-effectiveness analysis: Methods and applications.* SAGE.
McLeod, J. (2010). *Case study research in counselling and psychotherapy.* SAGE.
McNiff, J. (2013). *Action research: Principles and practice* (3rd ed.). Routledge.
Newcomer, K. E., Hatry, H. P., & Wholey, J. S. (2015). *Handbook of practical program evaluation.* John Wiley & Sons.
Patton, M. Q. (2008). *Utilization-focused evaluation.* SAGE.
Persons, J. B. (2018). *The case formulation approach to cognitive-behavior therapy* (2nd ed.). Guilford Press.
Persons, J. B., Hong, J. J., & Anderson, P. L. (2021). *Case formulation-driven cognitive-behavioral therapy.* American Psychological Association.
Rossi, P. H., Lipsey, M. W., & Henry, G. T. (2019). *Evaluation: A systematic approach.* SAGE.
Saunders, R. P., Evans, M. H., & Joshi, P. (2005). Developing a process-evaluation plan for assessing health promotion program implementation: A how-to guide. *Health Promotion Practice, 6*(2), 134–147.
White, H. (2010). A contribution to current debates in impact evaluation. *Evaluation, 16*(2), 153–164.

## CHAPTER 10

American Psychological Association. (2020). *Publication manual of the American Psychological Association* (7th ed.). Author.
Annesley, T. M. (2011). Top 10 tips for responding to reviewer and editor comments. *Clinical Chemistry, 57*(4), 2102–2108.
Balkin, R. S., & Kleist, D. M. (2017). *Counseling research: A practitioner-scholar approach.* American Counseling Association.
Belcher, W. L. (2019). *Writing your journal article in twelve weeks: A guide to academic publishing success* (2nd ed.). University of Chicago Press.
Bem, D. J. (2003). Writing the empirical journal article. In J. M. Darley, M. P. Zanna, & H. L. Roediger, III (Eds.), *The complete academic: A career guide* (2nd ed., pp. 185–219). American Psychological Association.
Bennett, L. M., & Gadlin, H. (2012). Collaboration and team science: From theory to practice. *Journal of Investigative Medicine, 60*(5), 768–775.
Boice, R. (2000). *Advice for new faculty members: Nihil Nimus.* Allyn & Bacon.
Bourne, P. E., & Chalupa, L. M. (2006). Ten simple rules for getting grants. *PLoS Computational Biology, 2*(2), e12.
Boyer, E. L. (1990). *Scholarship reconsidered: Priorities of the professoriate.* Carnegie Foundation for the Advancement of Teaching.
Bozeman, B., & Youtie, J. (2017). *The strength in numbers: The new science of team science.* Princeton University Press.
Brewer, E., & Walkenhorst, S. (2015). *Financial management for research administrators and managers.* Academic Press.

Briney, K. (2015). *Data management for researchers: Organize, maintain and share your data for research success*. Pelagic Publishing.

Browning, B. A. (2019). *Grant writing for dummies* (6th ed.). John Wiley & Sons.

Cheruvelil, K. S., Soranno, P. A., Weathers, K. C., Hanson, P. C., Goring, S. J., Filstrup, C. T., & Read, E. K. (2014). Creating and maintaining high-performing collaborative research teams: The importance of diversity and interpersonal skills. *Frontiers in Ecology and the Environment, 12*(1), 31–38.

Coley, S. M., & Scheinberg, C. A. (2007). *Proposal writing: Effective grantsmanship* (3rd ed.). SAGE.

Committee on Publication Ethics. (2014). *What constitutes authorship?* COPE Discussion Document.

Committee on Publication Ethics. (2018). *Authorship and contributorship.* COPE Guidelines.

Côté, I. M., & Darling, E. S. (2018). Scientists on Twitter: Preaching to the choir or singing from the rooftops? *FACETS, 3*(1), 682–694.

Creswell, J. W., & Creswell, J. D. (2018). *Research design: Qualitative, quantitative, and mixed methods approaches* (5th ed.). SAGE.

Creswell, J. W., & Poth, C. N. (2018). *Qualitative inquiry and research design: Choosing among five approaches* (4th ed.). SAGE.

Duarte, N. (2008). *Slide:ology: The art and science of creating great presentations.* O'Reilly Media.

Fine, M. A., & Kurdek, L. A. (1993). Reflections on determining authorship credit and authorship order on faculty–student collaborations. *American Psychologist, 48*(11), 1141–1147.

Frassl, M. A., Hamilton, D. P., Denfeld, B. A., de Eyto, E., Hampton, S. E., Keller, P. S., Sharma, S., Lewis, A. S., Weyhenmeyer, G. A., O'Reilly, C. M., Lofton, M. E., & Catalán, N. (2018). Ten simple rules for collaboratively writing a multi-authored paper. *PLoS Computational Biology, 14*(11), e1006508.

Friedland, A. J., & Folt, C. L. (2016). *Writing successful science proposals* (3rd ed.). Yale University Press.

Galvan, J. L., & Galvan, M. C. (2017). *Writing literature reviews: A guide for students of the social and behavioral sciences* (7th ed.). Routledge.

Goodson, P. (2017). *Becoming an academic writer: 50 exercises for paced, productive, and powerful writing* (2nd ed.). SAGE.

Gump, S. E. (2004). Writing successful covering letters for unsolicited submissions to academic journals. *Journal of Scholarly Publishing, 35*(2), 92–102.

Huff, A. S. (1999). *Writing for scholarly publication.* SAGE.

Hyland, K., & Jiang, F. (2020). *Academic discourse and global publishing: Disciplinary persuasion in changing times.* Routledge.

International Committee of Medical Journal Editors. (2019). *Recommendations for the conduct, reporting, editing, and publication of scholarly work in medical journals.* Author.

Kazdin, A. E. (2003). Publishing your research. In M. J. Prinstein & M. D. Patterson (Eds.), *The portable mentor: Expert guide to a successful career in psychology* (pp. 85–99). Springer.

Kiene, A., & Kiene, H. (2012). From reductionism to holism: Systems-oriented approaches in cancer research. *Global Advances in Health and Medicine, 1*(5), 68–77.

Kosslyn, S. M. (2007). *Clear and to the point: 8 psychological principles for compelling PowerPoint presentations.* Oxford University Press.

Lo, B., & Field, M. J. (Eds.). (2009). *Conflict of interest in medical research, education, and practice.* National Academies Press.

Locke, L. F., Spirduso, W. W., & Silverman, S. J. (2014). *Proposals that work: A guide for planning dissertations and grant proposals* (6th ed.). SAGE.

Lovejoy, T. I., Revenson, T. A., & France, C. R. (2011). Reviewing manuscripts for peer-review journals: A primer for novice and seasoned reviewers. *Annals of Behavioral Medicine, 42*(1), 1–13.

Machi, L. A., & McEvoy, B. T. (2016). *The literature review: Six steps to success* (3rd ed.). Corwin Press.

Newport, C. (2016). *Deep work: Rules for focused success in a distracted world.* Grand Central Publishing.

Nosek, B. A., Alter, G., Banks, G. C., Borsboom, D., Bowman, S. D., Breckler, S. J., Buck, S., Chambers, C. D., Chin, G., Christensen, G., Contestabile, M., Dafoe, A., Eich, E., Freese, J., Glennerster, R., Goroff, D., Green, D. P., Hesse, B., Humphreys, M., ... Yarkoni, T. (2015). Promoting an open research culture. *Science, 348*(6242), 1422–1425.

Oster, S., & Cordo, P. (2015). *Successful grant writing for health and human service professionals* (4th ed.). Springer Publishing Company.

Pearlman, B., & Camarena, L. (2018). Developing and presenting professional presentations. In C. J. Robey & M. S. Schuler (Eds.), *Handbook of research methods in clinical psychology* (pp. 205–220). Wiley-Blackwell.

Porter, R. (2007). Why academics have a hard time writing good grant proposals. *Journal of Research Administration, 38*(2), 37–43.

Pyrczak, F., & Tcherni-Buzzeo, M. (2019). *Evaluating research in academic journals: A practical guide to realistic evaluation* (7th ed.). Routledge.

Reynolds, G. (2011). *Presentation Zen: Simple ideas on presentation design and delivery* (2nd ed.). New Riders.

Roig, M. (2015). *Avoiding plagiarism, self-plagiarism, and other questionable writing practices: A guide to ethical writing.* Office of Research Integrity.

Schwartz, M. A. (2018). The importance of stupidity in scientific research. *Journal of Cell Science, 131*(1), jcs189991.

Seglen, P. O. (1997). Why the impact factor of journals should not be used for evaluating research. *BMJ, 314*(7079), 498–502.

Shamoo, A. E., & Resnik, D. B. (2015). *Responsible conduct of research* (3rd ed.). Oxford University Press.

Sieber, J. E., & Tolich, M. B. (2013). *Planning ethically responsible research* (2nd ed.). SAGE.

Silvia, P. J. (2019). *How to write a lot: A practical guide to productive academic writing* (2nd ed.). American Psychological Association.

Smith, E., & Master, Z. (2017). Best practice to order authors in multi/interdisciplinary health sciences research publications. *Accountability in Research, 24*(4), 243–267.

Solomon, D. J. (2014). A survey of authors publishing in four megajournals. *PeerJ, 2*, e365.

Steneck, N. H. (2006). Fostering integrity in research: Definitions, current knowledge, and future directions. *Science and Engineering Ethics, 12*(1), 53–74.

Sword, H. (2012). *Stylish academic writing.* Harvard University Press.

Wager, E. (2009). Recognition, reward and responsibility: Why the authorship of scientific papers matters. *Maturitas, 62*(2), 109–112.

Walterbusch, M., Gräuler, M., & Teuteberg, F. (2017). *How trust is defined: A qualitative and quantitative analysis of scientific literature.* In Proceedings of the 50th Hawaii International Conference on System Sciences.

Winston, R. B., Jr. (1985). A suggested procedure for determining order of authorship in research publications. *Journal of Counseling & Development, 63*(8), 515–518.

## CHAPTER 11

American Counseling Association. (2014). ACA Code of Ethics. Author.

American Psychological Association. (2006). Evidence-based practice in psychology. *American Psychologist, 61*(4), 271–285.

Bager-Charleson, S. (2014). *Doing practice-based research in therapy: A reflexive approach.* Sage.

Becker, K. D., & Jensen-Doss, A. (2013). Computer-assisted therapies: Examination of therapist-level barriers to their use. *Behavior Therapy, 44*(4), 614–624.

Bernard, J. M., & Goodyear, R. K. (2019). *Fundamentals of clinical supervision* (6th ed.). Pearson.

Bordin, E. S. (1979). The generalizability of the psychoanalytic concept of the working alliance. *Psychotherapy: Theory, Research & Practice, 16*(3), 252–260.

Bornstein, R. F. (2017). Evidence-based psychological assessment. *Journal of Personality Assessment, 99*(4), 435–445.

Boswell, J. F., Kraus, D. R., Miller, S. D., & Lambert, M. J. (2015). Implementing routine outcome monitoring in clinical practice: Benefits, challenges, and solutions. *Psychotherapy Research, 25*(1), 6–19.

Castonguay, L. G., Barkham, M., Lutz, W., & McAleavey, A. A. (2013). Practice-oriented research: Approaches and applications. In M. J. Lambert (Ed.), *Bergin and Garfield's handbook of psychotherapy and behavior change* (6th ed., pp. 85–133). Wiley.

Creswell, J. W., & Creswell, J. D. (2018). *Research design: Qualitative, quantitative, and mixed methods approaches* (5th ed.). SAGE.

Eubanks, C. F., Muran, J. C., & Safran, J. D. (2018). Alliance rupture repair: A meta-analysis. *Psychotherapy, 55*(4), 508–519.

Fairburn, C. G., & Patel, V. (2017). The impact of digital technology on psychological treatments and their dissemination. *Behaviour Research and Therapy, 88*, 19-25.

Finn, S. E., & Tonsager, M. E. (1997). Information-gathering and therapeutic models of assessment: Complementary paradigms. *Psychological Assessment, 9*(4), 374–385.

Gelso, C. J. (2006). On the making of a scientist-practitioner: A theory of research training in professional psychology. *Training and Education in Professional Psychology, S*(1), 3–16.

Greenhalgh, T. (2014). *How to read a paper: The basics of evidence-based medicine* (5th ed.). Wiley-Blackwell.

Heppner, P. P., Wampold, B. E., Owen, J., Thompson, M. N., & Wang, K. T. (2016). *Research design in counseling* (4th ed.). Cengage Learning.

Hill, C. E., Baumann, E., Shafran, N., Gupta, S., Morrison, A., Rojas, A. E., & Gelso, C. J. (2017). Is training effective? A study of counseling psychology doctoral trainees in a psychodynamic/interpersonal training clinic. *Journal of Counseling Psychology, 64*(4), 440–453.

Jacobson, N. S., & Truax, P. (1991). Clinical significance: A statistical approach to defining meaningful change in psychotherapy research. *Journal of Consulting and Clinical Psychology, 59*(1), 12–19.

Kazantzis, N., Whittington, C., & Dattilio, F. (2016). Meta-analysis of homework effects in cognitive and behavioral therapy: A replication and extension. *Clinical Psychology: Science and Practice, 23*(1), 99–115.

Kazdin, A. E. (2019). Annual research review: Expanding mental health services through novel models of intervention delivery. *Journal of Child Psychology and Psychiatry, 60*(4), 455–472.

Lambert, M. J. (Ed.). (2013). *Bergin and Garfield's handbook of psychotherapy and behavior change* (6th ed.). Wiley.

Lambert, M. J. (2017). Implementing routine outcome monitoring (ROM) in clinical practice. *Journal of Health Service Psychology, 43*, 55–59.

Lambert, M. J., Morton, J. J., Hatfield, D., Harmon, C., Hamilton, S., Reid, R. C., Shimokawa, K., Christopherson, C., & Burlingame, G. M. (2004). *Administration and scoring manual for the Outcome Questionnaire-45*. OQ Measures.

Levitt, H. M., Bamberg, M., Creswell, J. W., Frost, D. M., Josselson, R., & Suárez-Orozco, C. (2017). Journal article reporting standards for qualitative primary, qualitative meta-analytic, and mixed methods research in psychology: The APA Publications and Communications Board task force report. *American Psychologist, 73*(1), 26–46.

Lilienfeld, S. O., Ritschel, L. A., Lynn, S. J., Cautin, R. L., & Latzman, R. D. (2013). Why many clinical psychologists are resistant to evidence-based practice: Root causes and constructive remedies. *Clinical Psychology Review, 33*(7), 883–900.

Luborsky, L., Crits-Christoph, P., Mintz, J., & Auerbach, A. (1980). The Penn Psychotherapy Project: A general intro. In L. Luborsky & P. Crits-Christoph (Eds.), *Understanding transference: The core conflictual relationship theme method* (pp. 5–20). Basic Books.

McLeod, J. (2016). *Using research in counselling and psychotherapy.* Sage.

Meltzoff, J., & Cooper, H. (2018). *Critical thinking about research: Psychology and related fields* (2nd ed.). American Psychological Association.

Neufeldt, S. A., Karno, M. P., & Nelson, M. L. (1996). A qualitative study of experts' conceptualization of supervisee reflectivity. *Journal of Counseling Psychology, 43*(1), 3–9.

Ng, M. Y., & Weisz, J. R. (2016). Annual research review: Building a science of personalized intervention for youth mental health. *Journal of Child Psychology and Psychiatry, 57*(3), 216–236.

Norcross, J. C., & Lambert, M. J. (2018). Psychotherapy relationships that work III. *Psychotherapy, 55*(4), 303–315.

Norcross, J. C., & Lambert, M. J. (2019). *Psychotherapy relationships that work: Volume 1: Evidence-based therapist contributions* (3rd ed.). Oxford University Press.

Peterson, C., & Seligman, M. E. P. (2004). *Character strengths and virtues: A handbook and classification.* Oxford University Press.

Reason, P., & Bradbury, H. (Eds.). (2008). *The SAGE handbook of action research: Participative inquiry and practice* (2nd ed.). SAGE.

Renfro-Michel, E. L., O'Halloran, K. C., & Delaney, M. E. (2016). Using technology to enhance adult learning in the counselor education classroom. *Adultspan Journal, 15*(2), 109–119.

Rousmaniere, T., Goodyear, R. K., Miller, S. D., & Wampold, B. E. (Eds.). (2017). *The cycle of excellence: Using deliberate practice to improve supervision and training.* John Wiley & Sons.

Scheel, M. J., Davis, C. K., & Henderson, J. D. (2012). Therapist use of client strengths: A qualitative study of positive processes. *The Counseling Psychologist, 40*(4), 468–496.

Schön, D. A. (1983). *The reflective practitioner: How professionals think in action.* Basic Books.

Seligman, M. E., Rashid, T., & Parks, A. C. (2006). Positive psychotherapy. *American Psychologist, 61*(8), 774–788.

Shiffman, S., Stone, A. A., & Hufford, M. R. (2008). Ecological momentary assessment. *Annual Review of Clinical Psychology, 4*, 1–32.

Sue, D. W., Sue, D., Neville, H. A., & Smith, L. (2019). *Counseling the culturally diverse: Theory and practice* (8th ed.). John Wiley & Sons.

Sullivan, G. M., & Feinn, R. (2012). Using effect size—or why the p value is not enough. *Journal of Graduate Medical Education, 4*(3), 279–282.

Swift, J. K., Callahan, J. L., & Vollmer, B. M. (2015). Preferences. In J. C. Norcross (Ed.), *Psychotherapy relationships that work: Evidence-based responsiveness* (2nd ed., pp. 301–315). Oxford University Press.

Wampold, B. E. (2015). How important are the common factors in psychotherapy? An update. *World Psychiatry, 14*(3), 270–277.

Wampold, B. E., & Imel, Z. E. (2015). *The great psychotherapy debate: The evidence for what makes psychotherapy work* (2nd ed.). Routledge.

Watkins, L. E., Sprang, K. R., & Rothbaum, B. O. (2018). Treating PTSD: A review of evidence-based psychotherapy interventions. *Frontiers in Behavioral Neuroscience, 12*, 258.

Wojtalik, J. A., Eack, S. M., Smith, M. J., & Keshavan, M. S. (2018). Using cognitive neuroscience to improve mental health treatment: A comprehensive review. *Journal of the Society for Social Work and Research, 9*(2), 223-260.

www.ingramcontent.com/pod-product-compliance
Lightning Source LLC
LaVergne TN
LVHW060448061126
851857LV00016B/1765